BASIS FOR BUSINESS

C1

ANNE HODGSON
CAROLE EILERTSON

ADVISERS
ANDREAS GRUNDTVIG, HAMBURG
GABRIELLA HIRTHE, WEISSACH IM TAL
MARION KARG, SCHWÄBISCH GMÜND
MINDY EHRHART KRULL, DRESDEN
KAREN RICHARDSON, GÖPPINGEN
DR. MIRIAM ZEH-GLÖCKLER, LEIPZIG

Basis for Business C1

Kursbuch mit MP3-CD

Im Auftrag des Verlages erarbeitet von

Anne Hodgson

Carole Eilertson *(Extra Practice, Skills files)*

mit Unterstützung von Louise Kennedy *(Skills files)*

Beratende Mitarbeit

Andreas Grundtvig, Hamburg; Gabriella Hirthe, Weissach im Tal; Marion Karg, Schwäbisch Gmünd; Mindy Ehrhart Krull, Dresden; Karen Richardson, Göppingen; Dr. Miriam Zeh-Glöckler, Leipzig

Redaktion

Janan Barksdale, Berlin; Anna Batrla (Projektkoordination)

Bildredaktion

Uta Hübner, Nicole-Simone Abt, Sophie Wilhelm

Projektleitung

Murdo MacPhail, Andreas Goebel

Umschlaggestaltung

hawemannundmosch, konzeption und gestaltung, Berlin

Layout und technische Umsetzung

finedesign, Berlin

Illustration

Andreas Terglane, Kassel

zum vorliegenden Kursbuch sind auch erhältlich
Workbook   ISBN 978-3-06-521021-8
Teaching Guide (online)   ISBN 978-3-06-520474-3

www.cornelsen.de

1. Auflage, 4. Druck 2021

Druck: AZ Druck und Datentechnik GmbH, Kempten

ISBN 978-3-06-521020-1

PEFC zertifiziert
Dieses Produkt stammt aus nachhaltig bewirtschafteten Wäldern und kontrollierten Quellen.
www.pefc.de

PEFC/04-31-2260

Welcome to Basis for Business C1

Das neu entwickelte **Basis for Business C1** hilft Ihnen, sich auch in anspruchsvolleren Arbeitssituationen im Englischen sicher zu fühlen. **Basis for Business C1** wurde speziell für deutschsprachige Lernende konzipiert.

Die *Welcome-Unit* ermöglicht Ihnen einen leichten Einstieg in das Lehrwerk. Hier können Sie Ihre Lernziele festlegen und sich mit anderen Kursteilnehmern darüber austauschen.

Alle *Units* sind klar strukturiert und bieten Ihnen ein Thema aus dem Geschäftsleben mit aktuellem Praxisbezug. Am Anfang jeder *Unit* geben die Lernziele einen kurzen Überblick über den Inhalt. Eine kommunikative *Warm-up*-Übung stimmt Sie auf das Thema des Abschnitts ein.

Die acht *Units* sind in vier Abschnitte untergliedert. Darin finden Sie unter anderem:

➔ *Part A & B,* in denen die Grundlagen für die neuen Strukturen und Sprachmittel gelegt werden. *Did you know?*-Kästen (1) vermitteln interessante Hintergrundinformationen; Redemittel werden in blauen *Phrase boxes* (2) präsentiert.

➔ Die *Food for thought*-Kästen (3) laden mit einer Frage zum Meinungsaustausch ein.

➔ *Part C*: Hier begegnen Sie authentischen Firmen und Personen und erfahren etwas über deren Arbeitsweise oder Fachgebiet.

➔ Informationen zur Grammatik (4) in grünen Kästen. Eine Erläuterung zusammen mit vertiefenden Übungen folgt im Bereich *Extra practice*.

➔ Die *Extra practice,* in der Sie das Gelernte anwenden und vertiefen können. Die Kategorie *Typical mistakes* (5) weist Sie hier auf mögliche Transferfehler vom Deutschen ins Englische hin. Jede *Unit* schließt mit dem *Outside view* (6) – hier erhalten Sie Tipps zum Umgang mit interkulturellen Herausforderungen.

In den vier *Business files* können Sie die Schwerpunkte der vorherigen Units wiederholen und Aspekte der geschäftlichen Kommunikation in einem Rollenspiel oder einer Simulation üben.

Die *Skills files* im Anhang helfen Ihnen, essentielle kommunikative Fähigkeiten zu erarbeiten (z. B. ,framing a proposal').

Zusätzlich können Sie sich unter www.cornelsen/business-english.de die Wortlisten zum Buch herunterladen. Hier können Sie neue Wörter nachschlagen und finden in den *Useful phrases*-Kästen Beispiele für idiomatische Wendungen.

Das separat erhältliche *Pocket Workbook* bietet Ihnen viele zusätzliche Übungen, um das Erlernte zu vertiefen. Die Hörtexte zum Kursbuch und zum *Workbook* finden Sie auf der dem Kursbuch beiliegenden MP3-CD.

Viel Spaß und Erfolg mit *Basis for Business C1* wünschen Ihnen Autorenteam und Redaktion!

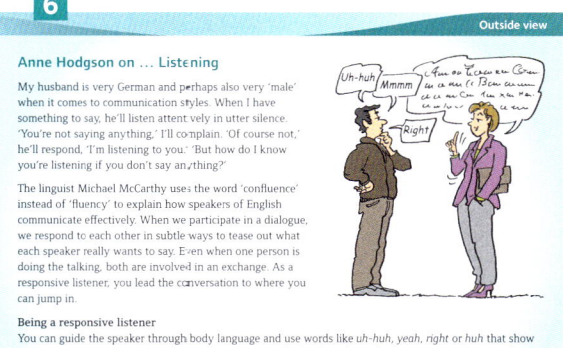

1
■ Did you know?
'Kaizen' is Japanese for 'change for the better'. First implemented after World War II, kaizen aims to eliminate waste by continuously improving standardized processes.

2
Making informal recommendations
She suggests finding another supplier.
I'd recommend not scheduling staff leave at those times.
I generally advise starting as early as possible.

3
Food for thought
One of the partners in your company shares your values. The other doesn't, but is a genius.
Whom do you trust more?

4
Being less direct
We **were** just **wondering** if we could …
I **was thinking** … Why don't we …?
I **was hoping** to find out more.

5
Typical mistakes
1 He has expert **knowledge** on this topic.
   NOT … expert *knowledges*
2 We need some **proof** of the efficacy of this ingredient.
   NOT … need some *proof of the efficacy* …
3 They are **testing** a new software system.
   NOT … are *proving a new* …
4 Please fill in this **form**.
   NOT … *fill in this formula*.
5 *Branche ≠ branch*
   What **sector / industry / field** do you work in? (*Branche*)
   Which **branch** do you work in? (*Zweigstelle / Niederlassung*)
6 an **analysis**, two **analyses**
   How many analyses [ə'næləsi:z] have you done?
   NOT … *How many analysis* …?

6
Outside view
Anne Hodgson on … Listening
My husband is very German and perhaps also very 'male' when it comes to communication styles. When I have something to say, he'll listen attentively in utter silence. 'You're not saying anything.' I'll complain. 'Of course not,' he'll respond, 'I'm listening to you.' 'But how do I know you're listening if you don't say anything?'

The linguist Michael McCarthy uses the word 'confluence' instead of 'fluency' to explain how speakers of English communicate effectively. When we participate in a dialogue, we respond to each other in subtle ways to tease out what each speaker really wants to say. Even when one person is doing the talking, both are involved in an exchange. As a responsive listener, you lead the conversation to where you can jump in.

Being a responsive listener
You can guide the speaker through body language and use words like *uh-huh, yeah, right* or *huh* that show you are paying attention. Say *I know what you mean, absolutely* and *exactly* if you agree, and *yes,* and … to begin a turn of your own. To change directions, say *yes, but …* or *well, actually.* Ask for greater clarity from the speaker with *So, are you saying that …?,* or play for time as you prepare to speak by saying *Oh, I don't know …* .

Since we native English speakers are so used to confluence, speaking to less responsive people can feel to us like talking to a brick wall. Choose your words wisely, and this wall will come tumbling down.

in utter silence	ganz still
confluence	Zusammenfluss
to tease out	herauskitzeln
to play for time	Zeit gewinnen

Table of contents

Welcome!

① 🔊2-4 **Listen to three people talk about specific situations in which they communicate in English at work. Take notes about each situation and the challenges the speakers mention.**

Jörg Sprung, packaging engineer

Peter Glück, former entrepreneur, now manager

Carla Lopez, team leader

Communicating in English at work

Name	When (context)	With whom	To do what	Challenges
Jörg	online meetings (teleconferences) \n\n phone calls	international partners, mostly in Asia	to take notes for technical reports	understanding Asian accents, speakers who talk fast and are not clear
Peter				
Carla				

② 👥 **List two typical situations where you need English at work and complete the table. Compare your situations with a partner's.**

Communicating in English at work

When (context)	With whom	To do what	Challenges to work on

3 Explore your cultural learning style. Decide in each case whether you agree more with a or b and tick the correct box. Then check what your answers mean in the key.

1 a ☐ We should decide together on the objectives and the content of the English course.
  b ☐ The trainer should define the course objectives and strictly follow a syllabus.

2 a ☐ It is more important to me to be able to express myself clearly than to use standard phrases.
  b ☐ I want to become more familiar with the standard phrases that native speakers use.

3 a ☐ I learn best when my trainer and my group support my performance.
  b ☐ I learn best when I am challenged by my trainer and group to perform and compete.

4 a ☐ I want a single trusted and accepted source of information.
  b ☐ I prefer having several sources of information, even if they contradict each other.

5 a ☐ Grammar explanations are incomplete unless they give detailed analysis of how and when a form is used.
  b ☐ Practical examples of grammar in context are more helpful than rules.

6 a ☐ I want to know the structure of the course in advance and cover the areas we agree on.
  b ☐ Each lesson should be flexible depending on the areas that appear to require more practice.

7 a ☐ I want to see the immediate relevance of what I am learning.
  b ☐ I will discover the relevance of what I am learning in time.

Key

Depending on what you ticked, your cultural learning style may be:

1 a more equality oriented (focused on peers)
  b more authority oriented (focused on leaders)

2 a more individualistic (focused on your self-expression)
  b more collectivist (focused on your expression as a member of a community)

3 a more nurturing (giving and expecting support)
  b more challenging (enjoying and expecting competition)

4 a more stability seeking (wanting to know what to expect)
  b more uncertainty accepting (comfortable with not knowing what is coming)

5 a more analytical (seeking to understand structure)
  b more holistic (seeking to understand the context)

6 a more focused on the clock (relying on schedules)
  b more focused on the event (relying on adaptation)

7 a more linear in your idea of time (controlling the process)
  b more cyclical in your idea of time (trusting the overall process)

👥 With a partner, discuss in what ways you are similar and in what ways your learning styles differ?

> About point 6: I have to get work done by a certain time, so I need to plan, otherwise I won't have a workable solution by a given deadline. I need to plan my learning the same way.

> I'd prefer to plan in advance too, but I don't think learning works that way. I prefer to change direction when necessary. In fact, it's similar at work. I have to react to changes a lot.

4 Write about your personal language goals. What do you want to be able to do better at the end of this course?

I want to improve:

5 The people you will meet in this book have different jobs and are of different nationalities, but they all do business in English.

Look at the map and pictures of some of the characters from the book. Use the clues in a–h to write the correct name next to each picture.

.... **1**
I'm having a lot of trouble with someone in Atlanta. Maybe the tone of my emails is not quite right. Luckily, I can ask my American colleague, Bob, to help me.

Unit 4

.... **2**
I've just completed a very complicated delivery and am writing a report to ensure that the whole process goes more smoothly next time.

Unit 2

.... **8**
My clients and I have to discuss complex issues in simple terms. There are many technical and legal issues, as well as different values and mentalities to deal with.

Unit 8

.... **7**
Today I am pitching our services to potential customers from Cape Town. Before I tell them about our product, I'm going to find out what they want.

Unit 5

a Daniel Fox sells green financial services. More and more of his customers are foreign companies setting up their offices in Germany.

b Doris Jelinek is responsible for HR at a large engineering company based in the Ruhr area.

c Anna Hattig, a 26-year-old, is heading up the launch of a new line of cosmetics for the Asian market.

d Udo Baier works for a provider of environmental testing services and is responsible for purchasing tools and instruments.

e Manu Khullar is an IT consultant who works with international firms to improve compliance.

f Ivo Schenk hardly makes mistakes in English, but doesn't understand the finer points of communicating internationally.

g Nina Ziegler is an engineer working at a German company that supplies assembled units to a European aerospace programme.

h Ellen Wagner works as a project manager for an international automotive supplier based in Germany.

Today I'm asking for a proposal from a consultant in Bristol related to a major energy project I'm coordinating. I want him to understand exactly what we require. [3]

Unit 3

I'm having lunch today with a sales rep from the UK who is very interested in how B2B purchasing works here in Germany. I'm looking forward to 'talking shop' with him. [4]

Unit 7

Our team includes a marketing expert from Hong Kong, so our kickoff meeting today is going to be in English. Leading a team at my age is an exciting challenge. [5]

Unit 1

I oversee performance reviews and today will be reviewing the latest addition to our department, a young man from Australia. Naturally the review will be in English. [6]

Unit 6

6 Meet some of the industry professionals we interviewed. What do you think their industries and areas of expertise are?

1	Jens Kröger (Endress + Hauser) → *Unit 1, page 15*	**a**	Railway Cargo / Improving Efficiency
2	Jens-Erik Galdiks (SBB Cargo) → *Unit 2, page 24*	**b**	English Language / Intercultural Communication
3	Gabriele Vollmar (Wissen + Kommunizieren) → *Unit 3, page 37*	**c**	Process Automation Engineering / Human Resources
4	Dr Gill Woodman (LMU Munich) → *Unit 4, page 47*	**d**	Biopharmaceuticals / Business Development
5	Dr Simon Moroney (MorphoSys) → *Unit 5, page 59*	**e**	Executive Search / Career Development
6	Franz-Josef Nuß (STEIN12 MANAGER SICHTEN) → *Unit 6, page 68*	**f**	Consulting / Knowledge Management

Working together

- talk about jobs and industries
- write your profile
- respond to different communication styles
- discuss on-the-job training

Part A Exchange information

▶ **Discuss with a partner.**

- What industries have you worked in and what positions have you held?
- How would you explain your current work responsibilities and your professional background to a foreign business partner?
- What expert knowledge and special skills have you developed over the course of your career?
- How have the skills needed in your industry changed since you began your career?

❶ Match verbs and nouns to describe some of the things you do at work. Which of the activities that you do are specific to the department or industry you work in? Which are common to all businesses?

> I attend meetings nearly every day.

> Now and then I draft contracts but I hardly ever have to …

attend   arrange   schedule
coordinate
participate in
liaise with   draft
submit   negotiate (with)
audit   file   present
design   research
process
conduct   facilitate

proposals   contracts
tenders   budgets
accounts   tours
processes   negotiations
results
presentations
emails   meetings
trials   research   data
staff
stakeholders   suppliers
customers

❷ Ben Yong and Azra Winter work for Wilde AG, a cosmetics company. They will soon be on a project team together and are meeting for the first time. Look at the activities Ben mentions. What department does he work in?

So, what do you do exactly?
And what brought you here, if you don't mind me asking?
Are you originally from China, then?
But do you ever …?
Well, you know, actually …
And so, last month I …
Really? That's great!
I see.

conduct market research

run focus groups

research claims and trademark issues

analyse packaging and displays

collect raw data

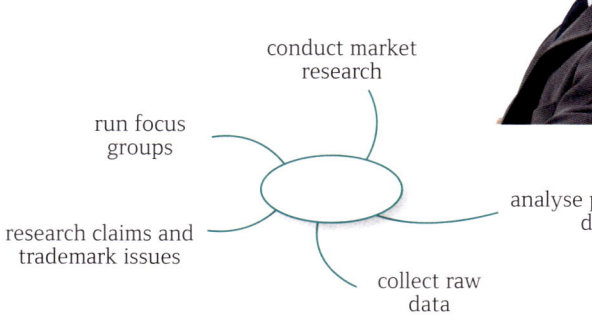

🔊 05 **Now listen to see if you were right.**

3 Listen again and correct the false information in Ben's online profile.

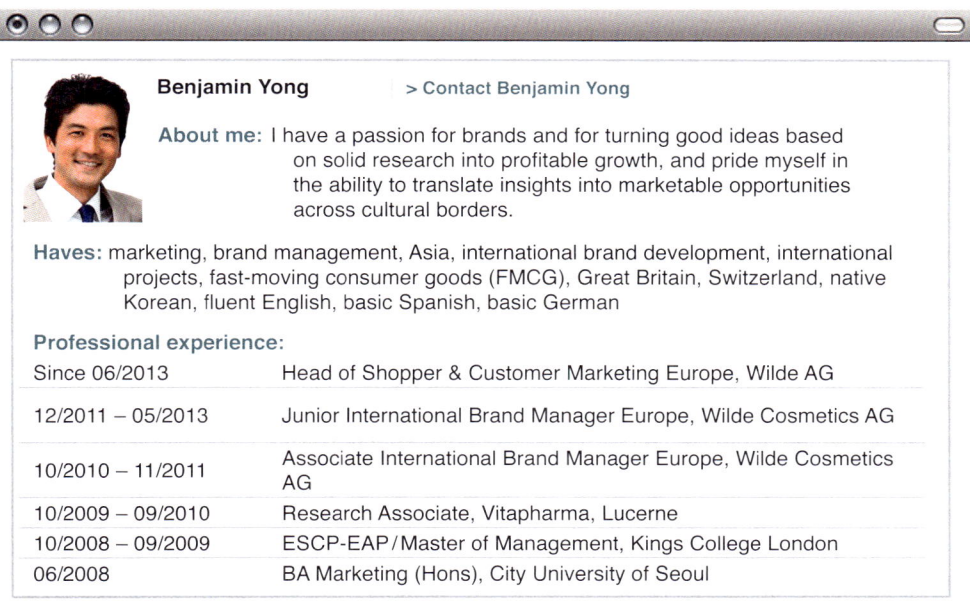

Benjamin Yong | > Contact Benjamin Yong

About me: I have a passion for brands and for turning good ideas based on solid research into profitable growth, and pride myself in the ability to translate insights into marketable opportunities across cultural borders.

Haves: marketing, brand management, Asia, international brand development, international projects, fast-moving consumer goods (FMCG), Great Britain, Switzerland, native Korean, fluent English, basic Spanish, basic German

Professional experience:

Since 06/2013	Head of Shopper & Customer Marketing Europe, Wilde AG
12/2011 – 05/2013	Junior International Brand Manager Europe, Wilde Cosmetics AG
10/2010 – 11/2011	Associate International Brand Manager Europe, Wilde Cosmetics AG
10/2009 – 09/2010	Research Associate, Vitapharma, Lucerne
10/2008 – 09/2009	ESCP-EAP/Master of Management, Kings College London
06/2008	BA Marketing (Hons), City University of Seoul

4 🔊 06 **Azra tells Ben about her career. Listen and correct the false statements below.**

1 Azra has been working for Wilde AG since 2000.
2 She changed departments before she went on parental leave.
3 She went back to work after her first child.
4 She has started working full-time again.
5 She has recently become head of efficacy trials.

5 Summarize Azra's career from these notes.

> Born in Sarajevo; moved with family to Hamburg when young
> Chemistry 2000 – 2004 (work-study programme)
> Wilde AG 2000 – today
> 9/2004 – 3/2007 Scientist/chemist in Skin Research Laboratory
> 4/2007 – 5/2011 maternity leave (3 children)
> from 5/2011: part-time work in Skin Research
> 1/2012: transfer to Final Skin Products
> from 1/2013: full-time & Head of Efficacy Trials

6 👥 **Use the template below to present yourself to your partner. Leave out any phrases that are not relevant and answer any questions your partner may have.**

I have a background in … and have been working in … for the past … years. From … to …, I … After that, I went on to … My main area of expertise is … Over the years, I have … My current responsibilities include …

On a personal note, I'm originally from … but have lived in … for … I'm single / married / in a relationship and have … children. When I'm not working, I enjoy / like to …

7 Write up your profile for a networking site or a company website. Add a succinct personal statement that reflects your main strengths and / or vision.

■ **Did you know?**

The 'mommy track' describes the diminishing opportunities of women in the workforce after they become mothers. The term originated in the USA in 1989.

Talking about experience

I **went** on maternity leave in 2007.
I**'ve** only recently **started** working full-time again.
I **haven**'t **dealt** with compliance issues yet.
I**'ve been working** for this company since 2000.

Self-introduction

When meeting new colleagues or business partners, fine-tune your own introduction by first finding out more about the other person.

→ *Skills file, page 120*

Part B Build relationships

▶ Having 'good communication skills' is one of the basic requirements of most jobs these days. What are the characteristics of a good communicator? How can the language you use help you build rapport or influence co-workers?

① 🔊07 Ralf Mehring is a senior manager at Wilde AG. Today he is introducing the new project manager, Anna Hattig, to her team. Who is Anna? How does she try to build rapport with the team? How does each individual respond?

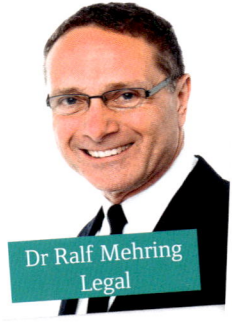

Dr Ralf Mehring
Legal

Anna Hattig
Project manager

Azra Winter
R&D

Ben Yong
Marketing

Jörg Sprung
Packaging

② Listen again and complete these extracts from the meeting. What techniques do the speakers use to actively build rapport?

Ben: That sounds really exciting.

Azra: ....[1] quite a challenge to move from one industry to another.

Anna: ....[2], in many ways they're similar, but ....[3], many of the variables change from business to business …

Ben: ....[4], and from product to product. …

Azra: ....[5].

Anna: ....[6], so I'll need your support.

Anna: So, Jörg, ...[7] you're the creative head of packaging.

Jörg: I'm not sure what you mean by 'creative'. I'm a packaging engineer.

Anna: Yes, but ....[8] proud of your many patents.

Jörg: Oh, ...[9]. Yes, the folding box …

Being less direct

We **were** just **wondering** if we could …
I **was thinking** … Why don't we …?
I **was hoping** to find out more.

③ Look at these sentences from the dialogue. Which sentence is used to formulate a polite request, and which is used to make a suggestion? Why do you think the speakers use this type of language?

1 I was thinking that it might help if you … shadowed us.
2 Ben and I were just wondering if we could use first names.

Now reformulate these sentences using the past continuous.

1 Please can you let me have your pen?   *I was wondering if …*
2 We need to ask for more support.
3 Can I get his contact details?

4 👥 Study the Merrill-Reid diagram on communication styles below. What style do you think Ralf, Anna, Azra, Ben and Jörg have? Are they analytical, driver, amiable or expressive types? What about you? Where do you fit on the diagram?

I think Ralf is the 'driver' type. He is assertive and focuses on the task at hand.

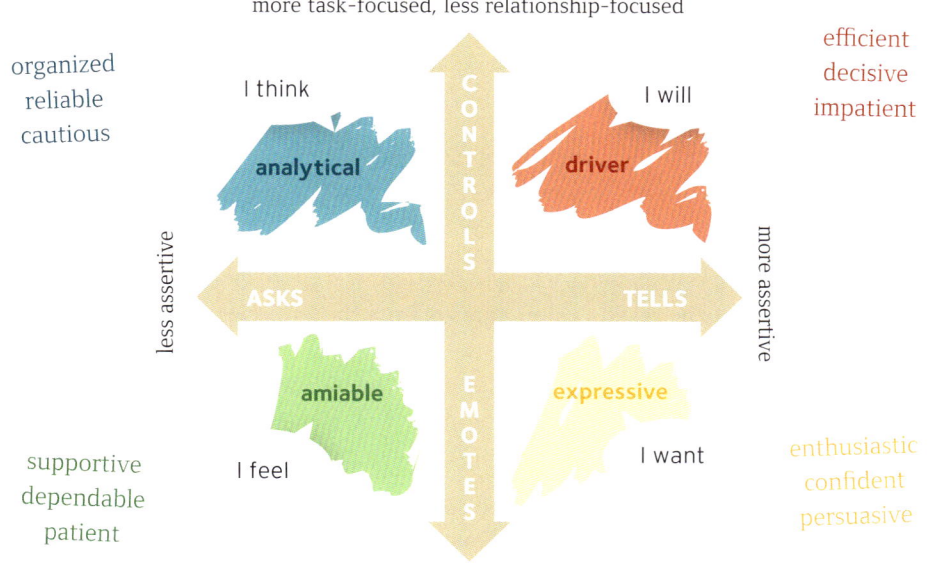

Did you know?
Psychologists David Merrill and Roger Reid define four basic personal styles of social communication based on how assertive and how relationship or task-focused you are. Recognizing your communication style can help you understand and adapt to that of others, and bridge personal and cultural differences.

5 Put yourself in Anna's shoes. It's your first day. How would you react to these responses to your statement?

Analytical: So what exactly does the job involve? Are you responsible for ...?

Driver: OK, just let me know what we can work on together.

You: This is my first job as a project manager.

Amiable: You must be slightly overwhelmed. Can I help with anything?

Expressive: How exciting. It'll be great, you'll see.

Which speakers focus more on the relationship? Which ones focus more on the task? What is the effect?

6 👥 Try out the communication styles in a role-play. Choose roles and use the information on your role cards to have a discussion.

→ Partner A: file 1, page 98   → Partner C: file 14, page 103
→ Partner B: file 29, page 110   → Partner D: file 18, page 105

Debrief: How did you react when somebody was too amiable or too direct? What problems arose when people didn't adapt to each other's style?

7 👥 Work with a partner, preferably somebody you don't know very well. Ask about each other's work background or a challenging situation that you had to deal with.

Food for thought

When you listen closely, you see things from a new perspective.
Do you ask yourself:
"How would I feel if that happened to me?" or
"How is that person feeling about what happened?"

Part C Skill up

▶ **What workplace skills would you like to develop? How does your company support you?**

❶ **Conduct a survey: How many people in your class …**

· did an apprenticeship?
· went to a vocational college?
· completed a work-study programme?
· obtained an advanced degree?
· have taken part in advanced training courses?
· have been sent on secondment to a subsidiary?
· are currently completing on-the-job training?
· think self-driven studies are more effective than taking courses?

Summarize and present the results using phrases from the list below.

everyone · all of those who · almost all of us · the majority · a minority ·
half of the group · some of us · three out of eight · just a few · no one

❷ **Meet Endress+Hauser, a Swiss family-owned company founded in 1953. What does it produce, and what values does its profile communicate?**

▾ Corporate   ▾ Our Global Offering   ▾ Worldwide

Welcome to the world of Endress+Hauser

Wherever you are, you'll find something that involves Endress+Hauser. Drink a glass of water, eat a sandwich, open the newspaper or take a pain reliever, whether a bold concrete bridge spans overhead or whether your plane takes off after being refuelled – process automation is always in the background. Customers throughout the world trust us to make their processes reliable, safe, efficient and environmentally friendly.

Since 1953 we have continued to serve our customers with innovative and cutting edge measurement instrumentation, automation solutions and services.

http://www.endress.com/

**Europe
America
Asia
Africa
Pacific Region**

❸ **Read the interview on page 15 and answer these questions.**

1 How do they decide who needs what training at Endress+Hauser?
2 How are auditing and customer expectations connected to training plans?
3 How do training needs differ for those on the shop floor, in marketing and in R&D? What kinds of language skills do the different kinds of staff need?
4 How does the company deliver technical training to staff at remote production centres?
5 What does Jens Kröger mean by 'the European way', 'long noses' and 'hungrier'? What does he imply but not say explicitly?

Talking about training and career development

I trained as a …
I completed my studies in …
I am currently enrolled in a course on …
I was sent on secondment (BE) to Italy. [sɪˈkɒndmənt]
I went on temporary assignment (AE) to our plant in Texas.

■ **Did you know?**

In the US, a college degree is becoming the new high school diploma, the new minimum requirement for even lowest-level jobs. Many jobs that didn't require a high school diploma in the past – positions like dental hygienists, cargo agents, clerks and claims adjusters – now require a college degree. Europe on the other hand is looking to Germany's industry-subsidized dual system of education and training to solve youth unemployment.

Successful Business: In conversation with Jens Kröger, Endress+Hauser

What kinds of skills does the rank-and-file worker or employee need in the 21st century?

Endress+Hauser, based in Reinbach near Basle, Switzerland, has production centres in 12 countries, with over 100 sales centres and representations, and 10,000 employees worldwide. We spoke to Jens Kröger, Head of HR Development at the Maulburg plant, about the training and development his department provides across functions, plants and cultural borders.

Successful Business: What kind of on-the-job training do you provide to employees?

Jens Kröger: When employees come on board, we work with them and their line managers to set up a customized development curriculum based on a framework. They're briefed on their job requirements and the company credo and culture, including kaizen. We are ISO certified and audited, as required by our customers, so we have to ensure that every department can provide appropriate staff development for each employee.

SB: How do you work with employees in your plants oversees?

JK: We have separate training streams for production, marketing and R&D, each with different requirements.

Manufacturing processes are the same in all of our plants, and we provide technical and language training for them here. As you can imagine, when foreign workers are here, everyone uses English, yet nobody speaks it perfectly. Learning cultural aspects of communication is key, such as admitting you don't know or understand something, and finding a workaround, like drawing a picture to explain things.

Marketing employees need language skills to give presentations and explain concepts, while engineers in R&D have to be able to conduct video conferences to coordinate projects from China to the USA.

SB: Do you send people abroad or have business partners from abroad work at your factory?

JK: Well, 10 or 15 years ago it was more common to send people to China, Japan or India to improve processes 'the European way', so to speak. That has changed quite dramatically. Today you can find enough skilled people locally, so we send our staff out on short secondments only. Why should we send Europeans over to China? The Chinese don't really want to see the 'long noses', especially not in a core industry. But we do send students abroad for internships, to learn intercultural skills. There they see that people over there are not only just as good as we are, they're also more aggressive, more growth oriented. They're 'hungrier', so they spend more time studying than our young people do!　　　▶ SB

---

④ 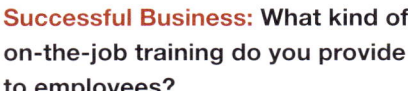 **Discuss the following in small groups.**

1 How is training organized at your company? What, if any, are the similarities to the training programmes at Endress+Hauser?
2 What skills have you acquired over the years, and how did you acquire them?
3 What type of training have you most recently completed?
4 How important is training to the success of a company?

⑤ 👥 **Look at these scenarios and decide what skills these employees need to keep up to date. What additional training do they need to handle the special assignment?**

1 An engineer is going to China to explain a new instrument used in production.
2 A team assistant has to set up a new international team.
3 A junior manager is to be sent to South America to help establish a new sales centre.
4 A foreman has to give a tour of the factory to a foreign delegation.
5 A staff member in purchasing has to negotiate with a new supplier in Ukraine.

■ **Did you know?**
'Kaizen' is Japanese for 'change for the better'. First implemented after World War II, kaizen aims to eliminate waste by continuously improving standardized processes.

❶ Test yourself. Look at the following statements. Each person A–D has worked with or for a company called LGR Ltd. Who still has a connection to the company? Tick the appropriate box(es).

- ☐ **A:** I've been with the company in various functions since 2010.
- ☐ **B:** I didn't much enjoy working for LGR.
- ☐ **C:** I've completed several projects for LGR.
- ☐ **D:** I've been working for LGR for a few months.

Talking about experience: simple past vs present perfect (continuous)

1 I **attended** a seminar last week.
She**'s worked** on two projects this year.

2 **Have** you **written** to the suppliers?
– Yes, I**'ve written** to them but I **haven't received** a response yet.
– Yes, I **wrote** to them yesterday.

3 First I **worked** for Vitapharma, then I **moved** on to a company based in Madrid.
She**'s drafted** the report. It's on her desk.
They**'ve** just **come**. Let's go and pick them up.

4 He **worked** in the company for several years. (*He no longer works there.*)
She**'s worked** there for several years.
(*She still works there.*)

5 They **have been testing** the products for months now. The trials are almost finished.
He**'s been talking** to the team for over an hour.
I**'ve been living** here since 2011.
(Not: I ~~am living~~ here since 2011.)

Note that Americans tend to use the present perfect less than British speakers.

🇺🇸 I just called him.
Did you send the email?

🇬🇧 I've just called him.
Have you sent the email?

The **simple past** and **present perfect** are both used to talk about experience and past events, but there are several differences. We use the **simple past** when the time period referred to is over (*yesterday, a year ago*) and the **present perfect** when it is not (*today, this week*) (**1**).

We use the **simple past** when the time given is specified or understood, and the **present perfect** (with e.g. *ever, already, not … yet*) when it is unspecified (**2**).

We use the **simple past** to talk about a sequence of events in the past with no connection to now, and we use the **present perfect** to talk about recent past events and to highlight their connection to now (**3**).

Whereas the **simple past** is always used to talk about finished actions or states, the **present perfect simple** can be used with *for* or *since* to talk about situations or states that are still happening now or on a regular basis (**4**).

We can also use the **present perfect continuous** instead of the simple form to talk about ongoing actions or states, especially if we want to emphasize the duration (**5**).

❷ Complete the sentences using the simple past or present perfect (simple or continuous). Fill in *for*, *since* and *ago* where appropriate.

1 We .... (just submit) our final proposal.

2 **A:** How long .... (live) in Germany now?

   B: Me? .... about five years.

3 They .... (research) that particular market .... January.

4 **A:** When .... you first .... (design) these trials?

   B: Well, we .... (conduct) the first ones about three years

   ....

5   A: What kind of terms .... he .... (negotiate)?

    B: Nobody knows yet, but they .... (discuss) the issue

       .... hours now.

6   A: .... Paul .... (draft) that report?

    B: I'm not sure. I .... (not speak) to him yet this morning, but

       with a bit of luck he .... (finish) it yesterday.

7   She has an MBA. She .... (complete) it four years ....

    and .... (work) here ever ....

8   How long .... (he audit) the accounts? It

    seems like he .... (do) it .... ages.

> Whether you use 'a' or 'an' with an
> acronym depends on how the first
> letter is pronounced.
>
> <u>an MBA</u>   [ˌem biː ˈeɪ]
> but <u>a BA</u>
>   [ˌbiː ˈeɪ]

③ Fill in the missing verbs in this dialogue between a boss and a new member of the team. Make sure the verbs are in the correct tense: simple past or present perfect (simple or continuous).

   draft · become · design · make · run · take part

Ian: So, ... you ....[1] much progress over the last few months?

Kim: Yes, the department ....[2] much more customer-oriented. We're getting good

       feedback. Last month my team and I ....[3] a new catalogue that we will be sending

       out soon, and I ....[4] a report on how we can make our call centre more efficient. It

       will be on your desk tomorrow.

Ian: Excellent. You ....[5] in workshops on best practice in your previous position, didn't you?

Kim: Yes, I did. While I was at Turner's, I even ....[6] several workshops myself.

Ian: Well, I hope you have one in the pipeline for here!

④ Which words or phrases do not collocate? Cross out one or two words per line.

   1 to conduct   trials · ~~tenders~~ · meetings · ~~contracts~~

   2 to negotiate   accounts · contracts · with suppliers · tenders

   3 to submit   proposals · customers · tenders · research

   4 to audit   accounts · processes · negotiations · suppliers

   5 to facilitate   budgets · emails · meetings · research

   6 to submit · to draft · to attend · to coordinate   documentation

   7 to arrange · to liaise with · to email · to process   stakeholders

   8 to schedule · to conduct · to process · to attend   tours

   9 to conduct · to file · to research · to submit   claims

   10 to process · to participate in · to present · to conduct   data

⑤ What is happening in sentences 1–6? Match them to the descriptions a–f.

1 Is everybody happy with that suggestion?

2 I was wondering if I could just make a phone call.

3 I'm not sure this will work without doing more research.

4 Come on, let's get started.

5 Can we lay this out together step by step?

6 That must be quite a lot of work. I'll be happy to help.

The speaker …

a expresses caution before proceeding.

b gets people motivated to begin something.

c encourages an analytical approach.

d builds rapport by offering support.

e makes a polite request.

f tests the atmosphere in the room.

Now match these responses to the sentences above.

A Thanks. I'd really appreciate some help.

B Of course, go ahead. We'll wait.

C Definitely. Let's try to be quite methodical here.

D Well, I think we should wait for Ben. He should be here any minute now.

E So, are you saying you need a little more time?

F Actually, I have a slightly different proposal.

Being less direct: past continuous

1 While I **was working** there, I also researched claims and trademark issues.
Azra and Ben **were sitting** in the conference room when Anna entered.

2 I **was** just **wondering** if you could help me.
We **were hoping** that we could finish early.
I **was thinking** …. What if we scheduled a new meeting?

You are most likely already familiar with how the past continuous is used to talk about actions that were in progress at a specific time in the past (**1**).

The past continuous can also be used with verbs like *wonder*, *hope* and *think* to make requests and suggestions sound less direct and thus more polite (**2**).

⑥ Which expressions a–f can be used to make these sentencess less direct?

1 <u>We think</u> we should try out a new supplier.
2 <u>I have a great idea</u>. What if we ran a new trial?
3 <u>I'll</u> make some coffee. Anybody want some?
4 <u>We need</u> your boss's agreement first.
5 <u>I want to</u> make a quick phone call.
6 <u>We would like them to</u> meet us tomorrow.

a I was just thinking I would
b We were hoping they could
c I was wondering if I could
d We were wondering if
e I was thinking …
f I was actually hoping we might be able to get

⑦ Find a polite way for these people to express their thoughts in a team meeting. Use the past continuous.

1 This meeting is so boring. We need to take a break … now!

*Excuse me.
I was …*

2 This is a waste of my time. I hope we can just have a video conference next time, and I know John agrees with me.

3 I need a lift to the airport after the meeting. Maybe someone can help?

8 Translate into English.

1 Unser neues Teammitglied verfügt über hervorragende Kenntnisse im Bereich der Verbrauchsgüter.
2 Schauen Sie, hier ist der Nachweis, dass das Produkt erfolgreich ist.
3 Wir haben den Inhaltsstoff noch nicht im Labor geprüft, aber wir sind zuversichtlich, dass er eine Wirkung zeigen wird.
4 Die Kunden mussten als Teil der Umfrage mehrere Formulare ausfüllen.
5 In welcher Branche arbeiten Sie?
6 Er arbeitet schon seit einigen Monaten in dieser Filiale, wird aber bald in unsere Hauptniederlassung nach Wien umziehen.
7 Wir verwenden die Kundenumfragen um unterschiedliche Analysen durchzuführen.

Typical mistakes

1 He has expert **knowledge** on this topic.
NOT   … expert ~~knowledges~~ …
2 We need some **proof** of the efficacy of this ingredient.
NOT   … need some ~~prove~~ of the efficacy …
3 They are **testing** a new software system.
NOT   … are ~~proving~~ a new …
4 Please fill in this **form**.
NOT   … fill in this ~~formule~~.
5 *Branche* ≠ branch
What **sector** / **industry** / **field** do you work in? (*Branche*)
Which **branch** do you work in? (*Zweigstelle/Niederlassung*)
6 an **analysis**, two **analyses**
How many analyses [əˈnæləsiːz] have you done?
NOT   How many ~~analysis~~ …?

Outside view

Anne Hodgson on … Listening

My husband is very German and perhaps also very 'male' when it comes to communication styles. When I have something to say, he'll listen attentively in utter silence. 'You're not saying anything,' I'll complain. 'Of course not,' he'll respond, 'I'm listening to you.' 'But how do I know you're listening if you don't say anything?'

The linguist Michael McCarthy uses the word 'confluence' instead of 'fluency' to explain how speakers of English communicate effectively. When we participate in a dialogue, we respond to each other in subtle ways to tease out what each speaker really wants to say. Even when one person is doing the talking, both are involved in an exchange. As a responsive listener, you lead the conversation to where you can jump in.

Being a responsive listener
You can guide the speaker through body language and use words like *uh-huh*, *yeah*, *right* or *huh* that show you are paying attention. Say *I know what you mean*, *absolutely* and *exactly* if you agree, and *yes, and …* to begin a turn of your own. To change directions, say *yes, but …* or *well, actually*. Ask for greater clarity from the speaker with *So, are you saying that …?*, or play for time as you prepare to speak by saying *Oh, I don't know …* .

Since we native English speakers are so used to confluence, speaking to less responsive people can feel to us like talking to a brick wall. Choose your words wisely, and this wall will come tumbling down.

in utter silence	ganz still
confluence	Zusammenfluss
to tease out	herauskitzeln
to play for time	Zeit gewinnen

2 Business processes

Part A Describe and analyse processes

In this unit you will …

- describe processes and core operations
- review and solve problems with processes
- write a report
- read recommendations from business practice

▶ **Discuss with a partner.**

- What are the core operations at your company and in your industry? Which ones are you involved in?
- What mechanisms are in place to ensure that processes change with the times in terms of cost, dependability, speed and flexibility?

1 **This flow chart summarizes the order process at Computrade, an online marketplace for digital devices. When is the order cancelled?**

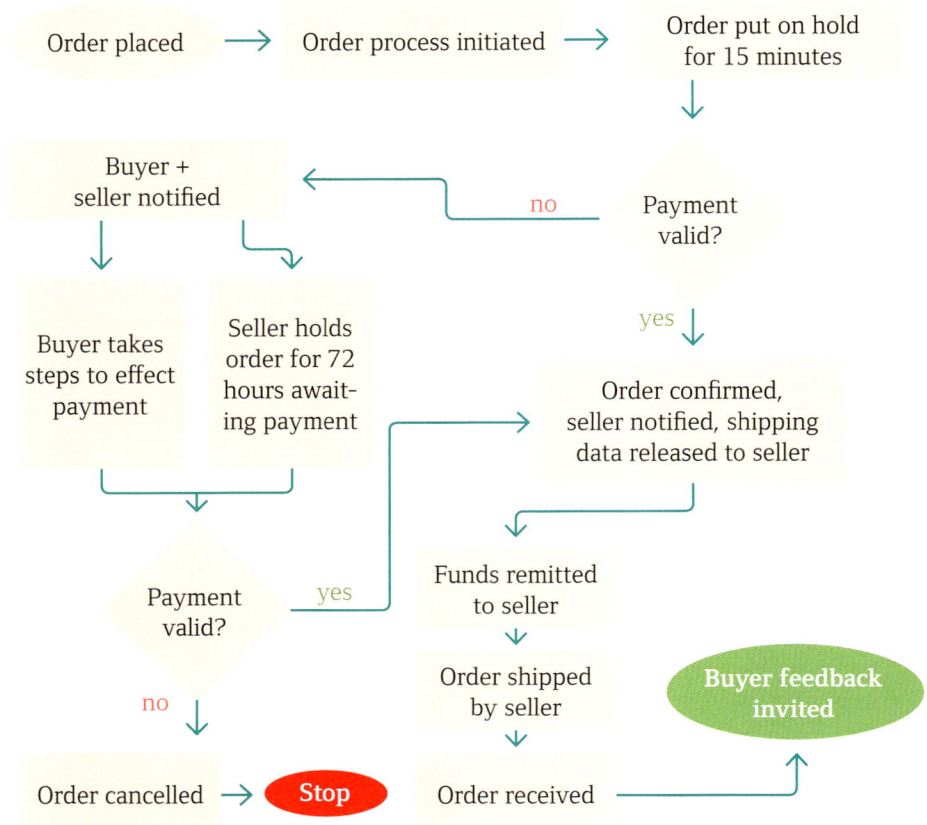

Focusing on the process

The order process **is initiated** in the system.
Buyers **are invited** to give feedback.
The process **has** just **been reviewed**.

Describing processes

If the order is confirmed, then …
Unless the payment is valid, the order won't be shipped.
Before the seller is notified …
While the order is being processed, …
The seller is not sent a notification until …
As soon as the buyer pays, …
Once / After the buyer has paid, …

Now complete these sentences about the process in your own words.

1 After the order has been placed, *the order process is initiated in the system.*
2 If validation is unsuccessful, …
3 The seller is not notified of the pending order until …
4 The order is automatically cancelled unless …
5 As soon as payment has been remitted, …
6 Finally, the buyers are invited to …

2 👥 **With a partner, take it in turns to describe the entire process. What happens in each step? What are the consequences? Which contractual party is responsible at each stage?**

3 👥 Think of a process that you are involved in at work and create a flow chart. Use the phrases below to present your flow chart to your partner.

If you look at this flow chart, you'll see …
Over / Up here on the left you can see …
This part over / down here on the right shows …

Look again at the process you have described. Are there any 'problem areas'? Has the process ever been changed? If so, why and how? Tell a partner.

to increase speed   to improve flexibility   to meet new standards

to cut costs   to reduce waste   to raise quality

4 👂08 👥 Listen to Martin, an IT expert at Computrade, present a problem to Maria, the quality manager there. What was the problem and what are the causes? What is going to happen next? Present the case to your partner using phrases from the box.

5 Listen again to complete these phrases with the missing verbs.

1 *improve* the user experience

2 .... response time

3 .... the specific issues that were causing trouble

4 .... the efficiency of our operations

5 .... a sustainable solution

Now complete Maria's brief report using the phrases above.

First of all, they noticed …
Then they decided to …
The result was that …
This meant (that) …
They discussed three possible causes: firstly …; secondly …; finally …
In the end, they decided …
The next steps will be to …

IT has decided to broaden the range of our services and to serve multiple platforms after recent incidents have shown this to be a key area for development.

Initially, an update was introduced to ....¹ and ....². **However**, this triggered a sudden increase in trouble tickets. Diagnostic tests were **then** able to ....³. **Although** the update was aborted, **in the end** the incident demonstrated the importance of finding new technical solutions. **As a result**, IT is now planning to ....⁴ for several platforms in order to ....⁵.

6 Study the linking words in bold in the report above. Which ones make a logical connection? Which make a chronological one? Can you add more words of your own?

Logical: *however, …*
Chronological: *initially, …*

Introducing new information

Introduce key information at the end of a sentence.
· An update was introduced. (*focus on the process*)
· The update was introduced to simplify the order process. (*focus on the purpose*)
· In order to simplify the process, we introduced an update. (*focus on the solution*)

Part B Make recommendations

▶ **Do you agree or disagree? Discuss with a partner.**

'The perfect supply chain is not a chain at all. Instead, it's an intricate network of suppliers, distributors and customers who share carefully managed information about demand, decisions and performance, and who recognize that success for one part of the supply chain means success for all. The problem, of course, is that companies do not always want to share.'

– Hau L. Lee, Stanford University

1 👥 **Nina Ziegler is an engineer working for a first-tier (direct) supplier of cabin interiors to Airbus. Take it in turns to define in your own words some key phrases she uses regularly at work. If you are not sure what the words mean, look them up.**

Lead time is the delay between the beginning and completion of a process, so long lead items are probably ...

to clear construction plans	to build to specifications
long lead items	at short notice · original equipment
reviewing phase	manufacturer (OEM) supplier
to meet / miss a deadline	on / ahead of / behind schedule
preliminary / critical design review (PDR / CDR)	within / under / over budget

Making informal recommendations

She suggests finding another supplier.
I'd recommend not scheduling staff leave at those times.
I generally advise starting as early as possible.

2 🔊 09 **You are sitting next to Nina on the train and hear only her side of a telephone conversation. Who do you think she is talking to? What problems has she been facing and what solutions has she found?**

Listen again and complete these sentences.

1 In order not to fall behind schedule, Nina advises ...
2 To avoid being short-staffed in the critical phases, she recommends ...
3 Since there is a shortage of suppliers, she suggests ...
4 To be ready for unexpected changes, she advises ...

3 Nina has written this short formal report. Fill the gaps with linking words from the box.

although · as a result · because · however · initially · overall · therefore

Introduction

This report summarizes adjustments made in production order no. A380–Frz786 and makes recommendations to improve operations.

Description

The following adjustments were made:
- The 3D simulation of long lead items was initialized after PDR rather than after CDR. This change to the process enabled us to cope with the number of long lead items.
- A change order from Airbus concerning the lamp system required redesign after CDR. This could normally have been handled by our team within the given time frame.

...................¹, a shortfall of staff due to scheduled leave forced us to outsource a part of the additional production to an OEM supplier. ....², a key unit was not ready in time for regular transport and had to be delivered by special delivery and installed on site.

Conclusions

...................³, beginning simulation earlier again proved effective but required additional flexibility to cope with change orders. Poor staff planning did not reflect this need for flexibility and required us to find external solutions.

Recommendations

For future projects we ....³ strongly recommend that staff leave be avoided at key times. We also advise that work schedules be closely coordinated with external partners along the supply chain.

4 Brainstorm best practice for working with external partners at your company. Then use phrases like those in the first part of the grammar box to make formal recommendations in writing.

5 🔊 10 Marion works in controlling for a logistics supplier to Airbus. She gets a call from Carole, the manager of one of the company's materials storage centres. What exactly is the problem? Take notes and report.

What do you think the speakers meant by the following? Explain to a partner.

1 We're concerned that they may have been passing proprietary information on to a competitor.
2 We've always relied on Zetcom to jump in at short notice.
3 They were counting on repeat orders.
4 For all we know, these claims could be unsubstantiated.
5 The other supplier we were using has gone belly up.

6 Listen again to complete the gaps. What do these sentences have in common?

1 What if you .... the IT service suppliers at the Hamburg warehouse?
2 I frankly .... cost at this point.

How do they differ from the formal written recommendations you made in exercise 4?

7 Write Marion's very short formal report. Use this outline and appropriate linking words.

Introduction ➜ Description ➜ Conclusions ➜ Recommendations

➜ *Effective report writing: skills file, page 121.*

Making suggestions and recommendations

Formal
We recommend that he **review** the process.
We suggest that anyone involved **get** in touch asap.
We advise that the schedules **be** closely **coordinated.**

Informal
You**'d** get top quality if you **used** them.
If it **weren't** for the strike, we**'d** be OK!

Part C Improve systems

▶ Do systems simplify your life at the workplace or make it more difficult? Brainstorm examples for both.

1 Look at this definition and the example below. Then add another example to the table and describe RAMS in context.

> **RAMS** stands for *reliability*, *availability*, *maintainability* and *safety*. It represents a set of requirements imposed on a system to ensure that it **1** will successfully perform its assigned or designed (intended) functions, **2** will be ready for use when required, **3** can be maintained in its operational state over its specified useful life and **4** will run safely and ensure the safety of its users.

context	reliability	availability	maintain-ability	safety
computer	doesn't crash	at work & on the road	up-to-date model	service contract, no viruses, firewall

2 Jens-Erik Galdiks, the Head of Rolling Stock Technology at SBB Cargo AG, a subsidiary of Swiss Federal Railways, explains to his team how they are improving their railway fleet operations, and introduces a major new initiative.

Jens-Erik Galdiks

"As you know, it's my job to look closely at processes to see how we can improve our operations. The need to do this is triggered by new legislation on the one hand and market pressure on the other, both as a consequence of railway deregulation. Specifically, we ensure ongoing compliance with the ever-changing
5 regulations regarding RAMS. Any kind of change means investment. And to get a real return on that investment, instead of simply fulfilling the letter of the law, we take a holistic approach to operations, get the big picture, and do our best to invest in ways that really make a difference for the business.

So overall, we have been seeking out the ways in which we can save resources
10 and improve the quality of our services. Sometimes the solution can be surprisingly simple. For example, recently we looked closely at how often we inspect certain parts in our locomotive fleet, and found we were able to cut the number of inspections by
15 half without affecting our services negatively. Other ways we've improved our operations have been to reduce excess inventory, optimize our car type portfolio and increase the mileage per car. These measures have
20 allowed us to raise the efficiency of our rolling stock by almost 25 %.

Reducing the number of cars increased the efficiency of rolling stock by 23% over 5 years

Rolling stock

■ Rentals
■ Owned

100 % 96 % 88 % 82 % 77 %
2007 2008 2009 2010 2011

Transports per car

%
110
100
90
2007 2008 2009 2010 2011
+9 %

Main drivers of increased efficiency

→ Reduced excess inventory   → Optimised planning & control
→ Eliminated inefficient car types   → Reshaped transport portfolio

■ **Did you know?**
Enterprise resource planning
(ERP) is a system used to manage
and coordinate all the resources,
information and functions of a
business.

One of the key tools for making these improvements is our ERP system. What
we are currently looking at is how to create and implement a new inventory
module to coordinate rolling stock maintenance. This will let us track the
25 expensive, long-life spare parts used in our rolling stock as they are replaced
in workshops across Europe. The challenges that we will need to meet
together will be to develop ways to direct the work of these very diverse and
far-flung workshops through portal solutions. We'll really need to do our
homework here to make sure that the mechanics are familiar with the system
30 and actually use it. We'll also need to ensure that the information they require
is available at each location in one of the local languages."

Answer these questions.

1 What were the original reasons for change processes at SBB Cargo?
2 What key changes have been carried out, and what have they achieved? Use the
visuals to give your answer.
3 What new initiative does Jens present? Where does he anticipate challenges?

❸ **Match verbs and noun phrases to make collocations used in the talk.**

1	get	a	the letter of the law
2	affect	b	a holistic approach
3	do	c	the big picture
4	take	d	our services negatively
5	meet	e	a challenge
6	fulfil	f	our homework

❹ **Look at this extract from the talk. How does the underlined word in the second
sentence relate to the underlined phrase in the first?**

**Referring to previous
information**

To communicate clearly in
writing, link back to information
introduced in the previous
sentence.

It's my job to look closely at processes to see how we can improve our operations. The
need to do this is triggered by new legislation … (lines 1–2)

Now look back at the text and say what the underlined words below refer to.

1 These measures have allowed us to raise the efficiency of our rolling stock … (line 19)
2 This will let us track the expensive, long-life spare parts … (line 24)

❺ **Rewrite Jens-Erik Galdiks' presentation as a brief formal report summarizing the years
2007–2011, and giving an outlook on the new project. Make sure you link sentences
effectively and try to use at least two collocations from exercise 3.**

Food for thought

Digitalization has changed
many work processes… for
the better or for the worse?

❻ **Discuss in small groups.**

1 What kinds of systematic improvement processes have been implemented at your
workplace recently?
2 Do you or your colleagues use an ERP system at work? If so, how has your place
of work changed as a result?
3 What are the advantages and disadvantages of using ERP? How could the experience
be improved? Share oral and written recommendations with another group.

① **Test yourself. A customer has asked a supplier for some important paperwork. In which of the following statements does the supplier make it clear that she herself has sent the paperwork to the customer? Tick the appropriate box(es).**

☐ **A:** I have instructed the dispatch department to send you the paperwork.

☐ **B:** You have been sent the necessary paperwork.

☐ **C:** I sent you the paperwork last week.

☐ **D:** The necessary paperwork has already been forwarded to you.

Focusing on the process: passive voice

1 The engineers **ran** some diagnostic tests.
Some diagnostic tests **were run** by the engineers.

2 The order **was dispatched** after the payment **had been validated**.
Buyers **are invited** to give feedback.
All our orders **are dispatched** promptly.
Unfortunately, some mistakes **have been** made.

3 These steps **were taken** to simplify the process.
This **is done** to ensure quality.

4 We **have sent** the buyer an order.
The buyer **has been sent** an order.
An order **has been sent** to the buyer.
(Not: An order has been sent ~~the buyer~~.)

Active sentences focus on *who* or *what* does an action (i.e. the agent). **Passive sentences** focus on the process itself. You can use the preposition *by* to add the agent to a passive sentence (**1**).

We tend to use the **passive**
• when the agent is unimportant, unknown or understood.
• to avoid having to mention the agent, e.g. when something has gone wrong and we don't want to state who or what is responsible (**2**).

Note how infinitive clauses are used to focus on the purpose of an action (**3**).

Some verbs can take two objects (e.g. *send, give, lend, offer*). Either object can be the subject of a passive sentence. If the indirect object comes second, a preposition must be used (**4**).

② **Look at this diagram of a company's invoice payment procedure. Complete the description by using the simple present passive form of the verbs below.**

meet · place · receive · remit · return · review

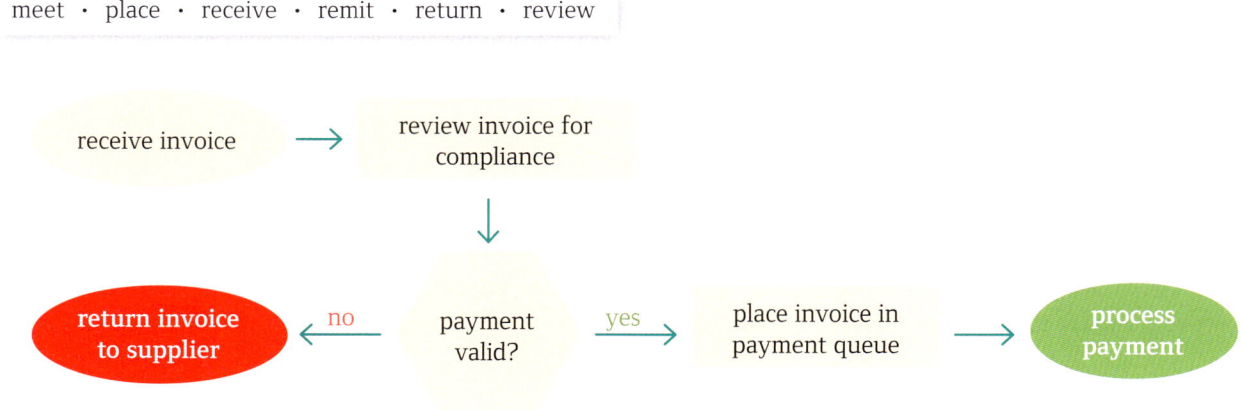

As soon as an invoice ....¹, it ....² for compliance. If the basic requirements (such as the inclusion of the purchase order number and sales tax) ....³, the invoice ....⁴ in a payment queue and subsequently funds ....⁵ to the supplier. Unless the aforementioned details are included, the invoice ....⁶ to the sender.

3 Put the correct form of the verbs (active or passive) in this excerpt from a description of a factory tour. Modify the tense of the verbs as necessary.

Last month ....¹ (we take) on a tour of a factory that ....

...........................² (make) components for aircraft entertainment systems. At the factory ....

...........................³ (we greet) by a cheerful receptionist who ....⁴ (inform)

Dave Johnson, the QA Manager, that ....⁵ (we arrive). After

....⁶ (he hand) us some safety goggles, Dave ....⁷ (tell)

us that approximately 700 people ....⁸ (employ) in that location. One thing

....⁹ (not mention) during the tour though: Soon, about a third of the

workforce ....¹⁰ (downsize), as a new plant ....¹¹
(currently build) overseas in order to produce these components more cheaply.

4 The following sentences use the active voice and focus on solutions. Match up the beginnings and endings. Then change the sentences around so that the speaker uses the passive voice and concentrates on purpose.

Example: le A cheaper supplier was chosen to cut costs.

1	To cut costs	a	we are organizing a series of workshops.
2	In order to simplify the system	b	we are not scheduling any staff leave at key times.
3	To avoid being short-staffed,	c	we will launch a marketing campaign.
4	To prevent further complaints,	d	they have streamlined the interface.
5	In order to win more clients,	e	we chose a cheaper supplier.
6	In order to train our staff,	f	they will offer clients immediate refunds.

5 Look at this extract from a report on the difficulties experienced by customers trying to access an online subscription, and complete the gaps with the correct form of the verbs below.

access · allow · enter · instruct · lead · log on · notify · pinpoint

A customer attempted to ....¹ to her account in order to read the journal TRADE-X. *At first* she

tried to ....² the system from a mobile application on her smartphone, *but* this

...................................³ to a systems crash. When she tried again from her desktop computer, the system

...................................⁴ her to ....⁵ her password and log on, but *then* blocked her access to the

journal. *In the end* she gave up, and our company ....⁶ of the problem. *Because of* this and

similar reports, I ....⁷ to ....⁸ the specific issues that caused
the problem, *though* in the absence of a completely new platform, I believe only minor improvements will be possible.

Which of the following linking words can be used to replace the *less formal ones* in the text?

a	as a result of	c	however	e	finally ....
b	subsequently	d	whereby	f	initially ....

Making suggestions and recommendations: second conditional and subjunctive

1   If I **were** you, I **would wait** a while before making a final decision.
    What if we **jumped** in at short notice?

2   I suggest (that) he **seek** further solutions.
    (Not: I suggest (that) he ~~seeks~~ further solutions.)
    The writer of the report recommended that new factory facilities **be found**.
    My boss insists that the factory **try** that.
    They requested that Jan **not be promoted**.

Note that in British English <u>should</u> is often used instead of the subjunctive.
- I suggest that he should seek further solutions.
- She recommended that new facilities should be found.

The **second conditional** can be used to make informal suggestions and recommendations. The verb after *if* is always in the past subjunctive mood which has the same form as the simple past, except for the verb *to be* where *were* is used for all persons (**1**).

Certain verbs such as *suggest*, *propose*, *demand*, *recommend*, *insist*, *ask*, *request* and *urge* can be used to make more explicit or formal suggestions or recommendations. These verbs are followed by a verb in the **subjunctive mood** which is used to stress urgency or importance, or to express indirect commands. The present subjunctive in English has the same form as the simple verb (**2**).

6 Complete the suggestions and recommendations by matching the sentence halves.

1   He suggested that costs
2   If I were you,
3   Jane recommended that he
4   I wouldn't attempt it
5   He advised us that that the proposed changes
6   What if we simply

a   I'd refuse the offer.
b   decided not to go ahead?
c   be cut dramatically.
d   not be made.
e   complete the report by Thursday.
f   if I were you.

Which of the recommendations above are very formal?

7 Complete this extract from an oral report on improving operations with the words and phrases below.

actually · finally · first of all, we noticed · secondly · resulting in ·
so overall this meant that · the next steps · so we decided to

....[1] that productivity was low in the factory, ...[2] investigate. First, we asked the workers about the working conditions, ...[3] we consulted the managers and ....[4] we did a detailed survey of the competition. The research ....[5] turned out to be a bit of a challenge ....[6] the project took a bit longer than expected, ...[7] a delay before we could hand in our findings, but here they are now. In our opinion, ...[8] will be critical. We have quite a few suggestions …

8 Reformulate the oral suggestions into more formal recommendations using the prompts provided. Use the subjunctive mood and the passive voice wherever possible.

1   "Why don't we buy new machines?"

    I suggest ....

2   "If I were the manager, I would hire highly skilled staff."

    We propose that the manager ....

3 "What if we cut costs radically?"

I suggest ....

....

4 "We should give the workers better training courses."

I propose that ....

....

9 Translate into English.

1 Die schlechte wirtschaftliche Lage wird uns wahrscheinlich nicht betreffen.

2 Sobald die Zahlung erfolgt ist, wird die Ware ausgeliefert.

3 Wir müssen mit den Auswirkungen der Veränderungen leben.

4 Ich notiere mir immer die Namen von neuen Kollegen.

5 Er hat sich vorher einige Notizen gemacht.

6 Sie hat mir geraten, das System zu überprüfen.

7 Er kann sehr gute Ratschläge geben.

8 Wie kann man gewährleisten, dass die Prozesse sich verbessern werden?

Typical mistakes

1 to affect ≠ (to) effect
The update **affected** nearly all our systems. (*betreffen*)
Payment **was effected** by means of a bank transfer. (*erfolgen*)
The **effect** of the changes was widespread. (*Resultat*)

2 Can you please **make a note of** that?
NOT   *Can you please ~~notice~~ that?*

3 He consulted his **notes**.
NOT   *He consulted his ~~notices~~.*

4 to advise = *raten*
He **advised** us to choose a new supplier.
advice = *Ratschlag / Ratschläge*
The **advice** she gave me was quite helpful.
NOT   *The ~~advices~~ she gave me …*

5 to assure sb = *jmdn einer Sache versichern*
He **assured** them that nobody would be downsized.
to ensure sth = *etw gewährleisten*
These measures will **ensure** safety and efficiency.

Outside view

Anne Hodgson on … Time

The other day my friend Khushi told me about the time a deer died in her garden. There it lay, a big, heavy load, so she jumped into action to dispose of it. She asked the neighbours. She called the authorities. She even tried lifting it herself. There was no solution in sight. When she awoke the next morning, the deer was gone. Nature had taken over.

Our focus on getting results means that we plan ahead. But in fact, there are different ways of looking at time. One way is to recognize cycles, such as the seasons or Shakespeare's seven ages of man. Another way, typical at the workplace, is to be geared to the future, planning what we wish to achieve. A third way is to look to the past, following what has been laid down as law. These different perspectives tend to clash in international projects.

Agreeing on times
A reminder to stick to the original plan will invariably run into trouble with people more in tune with cycles and more willing to adapt to changes at any moment. Therefore, it makes sense to touch base occasionally, asking *How are things going?* or *How are you getting on with the project?* to make sure that everyone still knows what is expected and needed. Those of us who feel the need to micromanage can learn from Khushi's experience and realize that we are part of a larger system; if we trust in the overall process, we might find that, given time, problems will take care of themselves.

to dispose of sth	etw entsorgen
geared to sth	auf etw ausgerichtet
invariably	immer, ausnahmslos
in tune with	im Einklang mit
to touch base	(wieder) Kontakt aufnehmen

In this business file you will ...

- discuss the causes of a problem
- give a short talk and discuss possible solutions
- write a report with your recommendations

📁 A team meeting

1 Read this extract from a team leader's quarterly report, and answer the questions.

1 What problems has the team encountered?
2 Have you met with similar problems at work?
3 What do you think could help avoid problems like this?

In the first quarter, AG retired and GW left the company. As a result, issues arose soon after for those taking over their responsibilities, namely:
- AG had not reported that a key second-tier supplier was in trouble. The business has since failed, causing unexpected problems.
- GW had informal contacts with a first-tier supplier that enabled short-term deliveries. These were not documented, making it difficult for GW's successor to negotiate comparable terms.

Both cases involved knowledge not shared with the rest of the team.

2 🔊 11 Now listen to the team leader announce the forthcoming meeting at which four possible solutions to the problems will be presented. What do the team members need to do next?

A

Hold regular 10-minute video conferences

B

Specify roles in the team more clearly

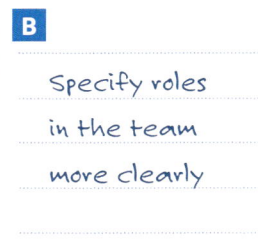

C

Share information in a project wiki

D

Build better relationships in the team

❸ Do a role-play or a simulation of a problem-solving meeting.

1 In groups of four, choose **Option 1** (a role-play based on the scenario in excercises 1 and 2) or **Option 2** (a simulation using your own work situation or ideas).

Option 1

Choose a proposal (A–D) and use the information in your file and the phrases in the left column of the language box to prepare for the role-play.

➔ *Proposal A: file 2, page 98*
➔ *Proposal B: file 33, page 111*
➔ *Proposal C: file 10, page 102*
➔ *Proposal D: file 34, page 112*

Option 2

Think of a realistic situation where you and the members of your team have to solve a problem and can share ideas by reporting individually on alternative solutions. Make notes:

What's the situation? ➔ Who's involved? ➔ What vocabulary / phrases do you need?

Agree on the problem, then think of a solution you would like to present, and prepare arguments for and against.

Are you meeting with colleagues from your group or department, or with visiting colleagues?

Use the phrases in the left column of the language box to help you prepare.

2 Now hold the meeting.
· First, review the problem presented at the last meeting (**Option 1**) or decided on above (**Option 2**).
· Then take it in turns to give your talks. Keep them short (2–4 minutes) and answer any questions from the rest of the team in a brief Q&A session.
  ➔ *Short talks: skills file, page 122*
· As a team, discuss the proposals and agree on which action to take.

❹ Write a report briefly describing the problem and recommending the solution your team has agreed on. Use phrases from Unit 2 and the language box below, and refer to the skills file on page 121.

Participating in a meeting	Writing a report
Reporting and clarifying	**Introducing the report**
One of the key issues is …	This report summarizes the suggestions made by … to …
Specifically, …	The purpose of this report is to (present / recommend) …
When you say …, are you referring to …?	The team met on … to discuss ideas submitted by …
Could you clarify what you mean by …?	The team agreed to …
Disagreeing in a team	**Describing and analysing**
I'm (not really) convinced that …	In the past week / month / quarter …
I would be very surprised if …	Due to …, the team has had …
Frankly, … / To put it bluntly, …	As a result, … has proved to be . .
Agreeing on actions	**Recommending formally in writing**
We might want to consider having …	We therefore propose that the team (hold / share) …
I was wondering if we could try changing …	We suggest / request / recommend that …
Wouldn't it make more sense if we introduced …?	Should this not produce results within …, … will …

- discuss schedules and clarify next steps
- request and examine a Proposal for Services
- read about Scrum and knowledge management

Part A Discuss projects

▶ How can project managers get everyone on board to ensure success?

① 👥 Ellen Wagner at Schulze, a car parts manufacturer, is coordinating a project to save energy costs. She has emailed the heads of department at Schulze and receives this reply from IT. Read the email and Ellen's notes, then discuss the questions below.

1 What is Ellen pleased about?
2 What does she need to follow up on, and why?
3 What questions might she ask regarding the MDM project?

To: ellen.wagner@schulze.com
From: yves.barbe@schulze.com
Date: 15 December 20..
Re: 'Energy Project' kickoff 25 Jan 20..

Bill and I would be very ==happy to partner in this timely project==. We ==can both make the kick-off meeting== on 25 January. Here are our answers to your queries:

❘ What projects in your department aim to reduce energy costs? What is their status?

We're currently implementing a portfolio of 'Green IT' projects to reduce the amount of energy + maintenance required by our networks and storage devices.
1 Just completed: moving servers to a data centre (significantly reduces air conditioning)
2 Being piloted: updating cloud computing systems
3 ==Behind schedule==: mobile device management (==MDM==) *(off-track – why?)*
4 In the pipeline: various programming projects
You'll find our Project Portfolio and Project Status Reports attached.

(what's the problem?)

❘ How could the cross-departmental Energy Project contribute to your goals?

(not in budget! intern?)

==MDM== is a time-consuming project, and may be ==unpopular with stakeholders==. We've laid the groundwork, but ==additional corporate communications== and ==staff== would help.

❘ What resources (expertise, plans in the pipeline, unused staff potential) could you contribute to the Energy Project? *(define/limit scope)*

Bill could schedule a workload of 20 hours in Jan. to report on our projects and on how we expect them to save energy. ==Would you like a presentation?== *(great)*

I'm leaving town over Christmas, but will be back on 29 Dec. If I don't see you before then, happy holidays!
Yves

PROJECT STATUS REPORT

Project 3: MDM	Status
Cost / Resources	🟢
Scope / Work	🟢
Quality / Specifications	🟢
Time / Schedule	🟡
Overall	🟡

PROJECT PORTFOLIO

Individual projects	Milestones	Status
1 Server relocation	10 Dec 20..	✔
2 Cloud computing: pilot	30 Mar 20..	🟢
Cloud computing: evaluation	30 Jun 20..	🟢
Cloud computing: implementation	31 Jul 20..	🟢
3 MDM: guidelines	30 Nov 20..	✔
MDM: implementation	31 Jan 20..	🟡
4 Programming	pipeline	🟡

🟦 **Did you know?**
Stoplight indicators in a project schedule show the status of each task.
- 🔴 immediate action needed
- 🟡 non-critical tasks are late
- 🟢 projects on track

2 🎧12 **Ellen calls Yves to follow up on her queries. What answers does she get? What solution does she suggest?**

3 **Match words from the two lists to make phrases used in the dialogue. Then explain what the phrases mean.**

costs · to flesh out ·
to hammer out · to oversee ·
the scope · to train staff

communications ·
the details · in compliance ·
of the workload ·
the procedures · skyrocketed

4 **Study these sentences from the dialogue about plans:**

1 I'm meeting with HR to hammer out the details tomorrow.
2 You'll be hearing from me shortly.
3 The Energy Project would be overseeing everything.

In which sentence is the speaker …

a referring to already scheduled plans?
b imagining a hypothetical scenario going on now or in the future?
c forecasting an event expected to proceed according to plan?

Swap the tenses in sentences 1–3. How does the meaning change?

5 👥 **Tell a partner about your concrete and tentative plans.**

> I'm going to our Athens office next week. While I'm there, I'll be checking in on Adam's project. If I had more time, I'd be meeting with Maria too. Maybe next time.

6 👥 **Follow the steps below to discuss projects and schedules.**

1 Form two equal groups (A and B). In your group, decide whether to report on one of your own projects or to answer Ellen's email to 'your' department at Schulze. Make sure groups A and B have different scenarios.
2 As a group, discuss the information in your file (see below) and visualize the status of your chosen project.
   → *Own project: file 3, page 99*
   → *Facility Management at Schulze: file 13, page 103*
   → *Technical Services at Schulze: file 15, page 104*
3 Working individually, write an email to the project coodinator.
   → *Effective emails: skills file, page 124*
4 Choose a partner in the other group and exchange emails. Study the email you have received and note details that need clarifying or confirming.
5 Now conduct two telephone role-plays. Take turns acting as the project coordinator to call your partner and clarify and confirm details in the email.

Talking about concrete and tentative plans

We're getting a student trainee starting in January.
I'll be sending you the job description after Christmas.
She'd still be reporting to me.

Clarifying and confirming details

Before we go any further, let me make sure I've understood.
If I understand you correctly, …
I hear what you're saying, but …
Can you spell it out for me?
Could you explain this step by step?
Just thinking aloud for a moment, …

Part B Request a proposal

▶ Does your company offer services to, or hire services from, other companies? When does it make good business sense to hire an independent contractor?

1 Match the expressions with the same meaning.

1	ballpark figure	**a**	rough estimate
2	benchmark	**b**	to be short of money
3	the bottom line	**c**	money spent on something
4	expenses	**d**	net profit or loss
5	to feel the pinch	**e**	standard of excellence
6	to be on the same page	**f**	to think in a similar way

2 🔊 13 Ellen Wagner from Schulze calls a consultant to ask whether he can provide services for the Energy Project. Listen and take notes. What exactly does she expect, and what can he provide? What will the services cost?

Energy Consulting Ltd

Tom Stiller
Energy Consulting Ltd
Bristol
+44 117 933 2555
stiller@ec.co.uk

3 👥 With a partner, summarize Ellen's requirements and the consultant's specifications from your notes.

Ellen: What we require / need / want / don't want (to do) is …
Consultant: What we can do / offer / provide is …
Ellen: We're (not) supposed to …
Consultant: That should(n't) … if we…

Now summarize your requirements orally for a project of your own.

4 👥 Role-play a call from a new client to a contractor in which you negotiate terms and conditions. Choose one of the options below.

Option 1: your own workplace scenario. First define the type of services required, then choose roles and turn to your partner file:
➜ *Partner A (client): file 19, page 106*
➜ *Partner B (consultant): file 6, page 100*

Option 2: intercultural workshops for your department or company.
➜ *Partner A (client): file 32, page 111*
➜ *Partner B (consultant): file 8, page 101*

5 Read Ellen's request for proposal. Which details had she not mentioned on the phone?

Dear Mr Stiller

Thank you for talking with me this morning and for your offer to provide us with a proposal for your services. As agreed, here are our requirements.

Schulze Automotive Holding GmbH & Co. KG is a leading supplier of metal structures to the automotive industry. We are currently seeking to identify means to reduce energy costs sustainably within two to five years. The Energy Project has therefore been set up to identify new projects and integrate existing projects into a portfolio. This pilot project involving the staff of five departments (IT, Purchasing, Facility Management, Technical Service and Logistics) will be completed by the end of the year.

We request your detailed proposal for a set of three facilitation workshops, with an initial and a final report, as outlined in your verbal offer of this morning. Work should begin on agreement of the contract and be completed within six months. Please ensure that the details of your proposal comply with the attached service agreement.

Thank you for submitting this proposal within 48 hours.

In what order are the following points mentioned in the email?

company profile   specification of requirements
submission guidelines   formal request
restatement of timeline or urgency   reference to previous contact

6 Use the structure you have identified above to write an RFP for the services you discussed 'over the phone' in Exercise 4.

7 Tom Stiller from Energy Consulting has submitted a Proposal for Services. Match the excerpts from the document (a–g) to the section headings and descriptions (1–7).

1 Formal letter opening   c   5 Fees
2 The Contractor   6 Warranty and Confidentiality
3 Procedure   7 Formal letter closing
4 Timing and Fulfilment

a   … Realization of the project on schedule depends on the timely provision of
    information … within the agreed period. … I shall personally oversee the project …
b   … We use our own proprietary assessment tool, EnergyControl© and other proven
    methods to facilitate the development of …
c   … I appreciate your confidence in Energy Consulting Ltd, and am happy to provide you
    with a proposal, the details of which are set out below. …
d   Any information given to us shall remain confidential. Access to or by third parties is
    strictly prohibited. …
e   … We propose, in Stage 1, to compile a Preliminary Report analysing … In Stage 2, the
    Contractor shall provide … The Final Report will summarize …
f   … We shall make every effort to support you with this important project. If you have
    any questions, please do not hesitate to contact me. …
g   … In addition, up to 20% of the overall fee (including VAT) will be billed for any
    out-of-pocket expenses …

Look back at the proposal excerpts to find examples of …
1 key standard phrases to show business-like courtesy.
2 highly formal language.
3 the use of *will* and *shall* to express duty and contractual obligation.

Did you know?

A 'Request for Proposal' (RFP) specifies customer requirements and invites suppliers to submit offers, often as part of a bidding (or tender) process.

A 'Proposal for Services' is a written offer from an independent contractor specifying the service and prices, as a basis for contract negotiations.

Part C Share knowledge

▶ **Do you agree or disagree? Discuss with a partner.**

> 'The only irreplaceable capital an organization possesses is the knowledge and ability of its people. The productivity of that capital depends on how effectively people share their competence with those who can use it.'
>
> *– Andrew Carnegie*

Explaining terminology

A meeting at a regular time is called a 'jour fixe'.
A 'topless meeting' is one without laptops.
The 'daily stand-up (meeting)' is a short status meeting held every day.
'Scrum' means …
'Critical path' is the term for …

1 **Do a class survey: How effective are the following for sharing knowledge in a team?**

regular jours fixes
topless meetings
daily stand-up meetings
meetings on Monday morning

2 **Describe the pictures below. How can they be used to illustrate two contrasting approaches to teamwork?**

Relay race: passing the baton

Rugby: going the distance together

■ Did you know?

Scrum is a way to restart play in rugby in which team members mass together and, with their heads down, try to gain possession of the ball. Scrum project management is based on a cross-functional team that 'tries to go the distance as a unit, passing the ball back and forth'.

3 👥 **Work with a partner to discuss the two approaches above. First study the information in your file and present it to your partner, explaining new terms as necessary, for example:**

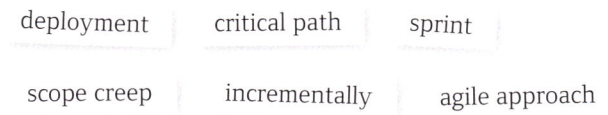

| deployment | critical path | sprint |
| scope creep | incrementally | agile approach |

Then discuss the advantages and disadvantages of each approach.

➜ *Partner A – Waterfall development: file 7, page 100*
➜ *Partner B – Scrum development: file 22, page 107*

4 **Read the interview on the next page and answer these questions.**

1 What kind of knowledge does Gabriele Vollmar say is especially difficult to pass on?
2 How does she say traditional project management reduces knowledge sharing?
3 What techniques in Scrum does she recommend or use herself? What for?
4 Where does she say people share the best quality of knowledge, and why?

Successful Business: In conversation with Gabriele Vollmar

Cultivating knowledge sharing with Scrum

Gabriele Vollmar, consultant and author of *Knowledge Gardening*, speaks about her role in improving knowledge management using Scrum project management methods.

Gabriele Vollmar   www.wissen-kommunizieren.de

Successful Business: You facilitate knowledge management projects across departments and workplace generations. Please explain: What is knowledge management?

Gabriele Vollmar: Knowledge management is the art of making what people know about their work available to others in the organization they work for. It is much easier for people to state the bare facts connected to the job than to explain how they get the job done. But the key to cultivating a learning organization is to make those methods explicit so that others can learn them.

SB: And is there any connection between knowledge and project management?

GV: Definitely. Knowledge is shared in projects, from drafting specifications down to project reports. The problem is that in the traditional waterfall method, sharing knowledge is artificially constrained by the way it is concentrated at the beginning, in the planning phase. After that, most communication focuses on proced-ures rather than on the actual goal of

the project. There is very little communication with the stakeholders, so at the end they are confronted with a product designed by someone else.

But knowledge is not between file folders and not on hard drives; knowledge is in the minds of people. And we know, the best way to share knowledge is to meet over by the water cooler or espresso machine and talk things over. Telling and listening to stories keeps things complex and based on experience. Scrum has that type of communication built into the project culture in many ways — through co-location, constant user accessibility and the daily stand-up.

SB: In your projects, what kind of Scrum methods do you use?

GV: One very useful element is the sprint retrospective meeting, where team members reflect on the past sprint and discuss what went well and what should be improved. We turn that into a lessons learned workshop. With facilitation cards, we ask the participants to respond in writing to specific questions, and then sort and pin their cards on a pinboard to

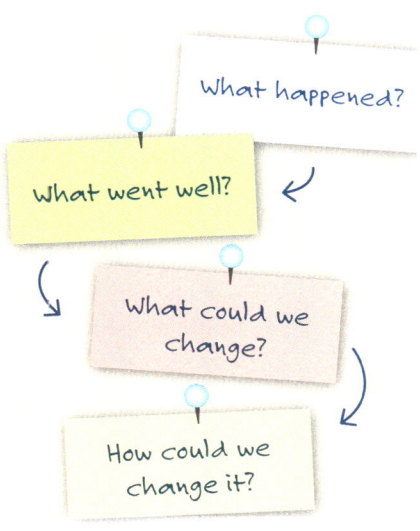

A lessons learned workshop

compile feedback. This separates individuals from their personal opinions, and allows us to assess the overall picture more objectively.

We summarize what the participants say on a flipchart, and come up with a concrete action plan. That might be, for example, to modify a process or a template, or invest in qualification measures. The outcomes can then be presented in team meetings or in the organization wiki. That way, projects become an indispensable part of organizational learning. ▶ **SB**

---

5 👥 **Discuss in small groups.**

1 What project management tools are used to manage progress in projects you have worked on? How effective are they?
2 Would the Scrum methods mentioned above help, or cause additional problems?

Food for thought

Managing progress: The map says one thing, the sign on the road says something else. Which one do you believe?

1 Test yourself. You are asking your colleague about her future business trip to Thailand. Which question could also be seen as an offer? Tick the appropriate box.

- ☐ **A:** Would you be meeting with Jane Smith, by any chance?
- ☐ **B:** Will you be needing a company laptop?
- ☐ **C:** Are you doing a tour of the factory there?
- ☐ **D:** Will you be staying in the same hotel for the whole of the trip?

Talking about concrete and tentative plans: present continuous, future continuous and conditional continuous

1 What **are** you **doing** over Christmas?
I'm **leaving** town.
2 This time next year we **will be using** tablet computers throughout the company.
Next week at this time he **will be telling** people news they won't want to hear.
3 She **would be reporting** to me (if we hired her). What project **would** she **be working** on?
Would you **be meeting up** with Tim later, by any chance? If so, can ask him to call me?
4 **Will** you **be needing** / **Would** you **be needing** any extra equipment with that project? I can get you the guidelines if you like.

The **present continuous** (*be doing*) can be used to talk about future appointments and concrete arrangements (**1**).

The **future continuous** (*will be doing*) is used to indicate concrete actions that will be in progress at a specific time in the future (**2**).

The **conditional continuous** (*would be doing*) is used to talk about actions that might be happening at some time in the future. It is often used to tentatively discuss or ask about future plans (**3**).

Both the **future continuous** and the **conditional continuous** can be used to offer assistance in a polite and tactful manner (**4**).

2 Complete the questions and statements by matching the sentence halves, then put them into a logical order.

2e, ...

1 That's why I'm sure they won't be
2 This afternoon our group is
3 However, I'm pretty sure they wouldn't
4 I'm not sure what they'll be discussing either
5 I won't be going, though, because I
6 The reason I say that is because, as far as I know,

a because I haven't seen the agenda.
b going into that matter in any depth.
c am flying to Switzerland in a couple of hours.
d be talking about Project Excellence.
e holding a meeting.
f that particular project won't be starting until next year.

3 Which continuous form or forms can be used in the discussion below? Cross out any forms that do not fit.

Dirk: OK, that was very informative. So we   are / will be / would be   ¹ laying the groundwork for the system over a period of several weeks then.

Kate: Starting from June 1st. Yes, that sounds doable.

Boris: I agree. If we moved more quickly, we   are / will be / would be   ² running the risk of having the system crash.

Kate: Speaking of software problems, Dirk, you know I have an appointment with Jake tomorrow afternoon, right?

Dirk: Oh, I had forgotten about that. What time   are you / will you be / would you be   ³ meeting him exactly?

Kate: Let me see … at 3 pm.   Are you / Will you be / Would you be   ⁴ joining us? You are more than welcome.

Dirk: Well, what exactly   are you / will you be / would you be   ⁵ discussing?

Kate: Technical stuff mostly, like that recent systems crash.

Dirk: Mmm, maybe not then. It's not really that relevant for me.

Boris: Kate, just wondering but by any chance   are you / will you be / would you be   ⁶ going over the timeline at the meeting? If so, I would love to join you!

Highlighting information using *that* and *what*

1   We're famous for great customer service.
Great customer service – **that's what** we're famous for.
That's essentially **what works** best for most companies.
I agree. **That's** probably **what** we need to do.
2   **What** annoyed us most **was** the fact that our supplier didn't inform us earlier.
What we don't want to do **is** outsource the project.
Not: ~~That what~~ we don't want to do is outsource the project.

Changing the word order in a sentence can help highlight or emphasize important information.

To add a sentence giving further details about a topic *already* mentioned, use the structure *that's what*. An adverb can be added between *that's* and *what* to add or soften emphasis (**1**).

To draw attention to a topic when it is *first* mentioned, use the structure *What* … + *to be* to start the sentence (**2**).

4 Rewrite the sentences using the words in brackets.

1   They need to see the results now. (What)

    .What they need to see now are the results.......................................   ....

2   We are supposed to ask head office first. (What / probably)

    ....

3   This company is well known for its high-quality products. (… that's what …)

    ....

4   We don't know the scope of the project yet. (What)

    ....

5   We are hoping for a firm commitment from your side. (… that's what …)

    ....

6   We will agree not to disclose any confidential material. (What / definitely)

    ....

7   We appreciate your confidence in us. (What / really)

    ....

5 Complete the extract from a telephone conversation with the words and phrases below.

> assuming · before we go any further · if I have understood you correctly ·
> just thinking aloud for a moment · step by step · would you be willing

Anu: Do you have time to discuss things now or are you tied up?

Neil: No, let's talk now. The ballpark figure you just gave me sounds rather high and, let's face it, we are all feeling

the pinch. ....[1], I'd like to ask a question. ....[2] we pay

the price you are asking, ...[3] to add a little extra value to the deal?

Anu: OK, the thing is I'm not quite sure what you're suggesting. Can you explain it ....[4]?

Neil: Sure, well, ...[5], we are on the same page as far as the quality is

concerned. But what about the payment terms? ....[6], but if you
were to extend better terms, we might have a deal.

Clarifying compliance: *should, be supposed to* and *shall*

1 Any information **should** remain confidential.
The permit **should not** be granted.
2 He **was supposed to** send the contract by
Tuesday, but he didn't.
3 Any information given to us **shall** remain
confidential.
This clause **shall not** apply to international
franchisees.
4 I **shall** personally oversee this project.

> Be careful: 'Shall' can also mean 'may' or 'can':
> • Shall I help you with that?

The modal verb *should* can be used to signify obligation or compliance. In this usage it has the meaning of *must* (**1**).

Be supposed to refers to a requirement that is not necessarily legally binding (**2**).

Shall can indicate a level of formality or seriousness. The emphatic use of *shall* (and *will*) is still common today in formal documents (especially contracts) in reference to compliance and legally binding contractual obligations (**3**) or to imply a command or promise (**4**).

6 Complete the sentences (1–5) with the words below, then match them to the descriptions (a–e).

> accordingly · exclusively · never · otherwise · presumably · thus

1 You shall not in whole or part resell, supply or ....make available the BTS system to third parties.

2 You should not rely ....on the information provided on this site. The data is still experimental

and ....we cannot accept responsibility for any damages you may incur.

3 ....we are supposed to do the paperwork first.

4 You will ....discuss sensitive matters or proprietary information in public places.

5 So you want to extend the contract? Shall we amend it ....?

a an extract from an employment contract
b a clause in a sales contract
c a strong recommendation by an online provider
d a comment about a preferred or required sequence
e a suggestion to change an agreement

7 Translate into English.

1 Die Firma hat die neuen Maßnahmen schnell und konsequent implementiert.
2 Sie haben den Vertrag gestern nicht unterschrieben. Deshalb müssen wir nun alles neu durchdenken.
3 Er hat bis jetzt den gesamten Prozess überwacht, aber ein wichtiges Detail hat er übersehen.
4 Das war ein Versehen. Es wird nicht wieder vorkommen.
5 Wir müssen effiziente Kontrollmaßnahmen entwickeln, sonst bekommen wir den Vertrag nicht.
6 Momentan habe ich leider nur wenig Freizeit.
7 Wir brauchen die Ersatzteile dringend.
8 Mit dem neuen Energieplan haben wir viel Geld gespart.

Typical mistakes

1 *konsequent* ≠ consequently
The framework is not applied **consistently**. (*konsequent*)
Sales dropped and **consequently** staff were laid off. (*deshalb*, *infolgedessen*)
2 *übersehen* ≠ to oversee
Sorry, I must have **overlooked** that clause. (*übersehen*)
He **oversaw** the negotiations. (*überwachen*)
3 oversight = *Aufsicht* and *Versehen*!
Who has **oversight** of the process?
That was a serious **oversight**. I hope he never makes that mistake again.
4 *sparen* ≠ spare
How much can we **save** by changing suppliers? (*sparen*)
What does she do in her **spare** time? (*Frei-*)
Can I get the **spare** parts from you too? (*Ersatz-*)

Outside view

Anne Hodgson on … Writing

In a project, the best form of communicating key information may be with a smile over coffee. But if your colleague is in São Paulo or Mumbai, you might need to send an email instead. So, how will they know the message is important and that you're smiling?

Focus their attention
First, acknowledge their need to understand the facts by trimming unnecessary fat. Use a concise reference line, like *March status report* or *Teleconference 27 April*. Then start with a sentence that says why you are writing: *This is to confirm …* or *I'm writing to follow up on our phone call of this morning*. Make your language specific and concrete and avoid unecessary repetition.

Build a relationship
Then, about that smile … Stop and think about what you smile at your colleagues for. Is it to get them on board? Can it hide embarrassment when things go wrong? Does it make you feel happier about yourself and your work? You can smile in writing, too, by adding a short, friendly sentence: *I know that's a lot to take in at once* or *I hope that was clear. If not, just drop me a line*. Or you might want to add a thank you, such as *Thanks for all the work you put into the presentation*, or a greeting like *Hope things are going well for you* to show your colleagues that you appreciate them.

Combine these two aspects, and you're doing much better than you would with a smiley.

International teams

- communicate about operations and logistics
- practise teleconferencing language
- practise dealing with conflict
- examine cultural differences

Part A Collaborate across distances

▶ **What factors would you consider when choosing a method of transport for your products? Has your company or have any of your suppliers ever used an unusual shipping method?**

❶ 👥 **Customer demands create interesting logistical challenges. With a partner, discuss the demands (1–6) and match them to the featured company profiles (a–f). Then use the highlighted words to describe any solutions your company uses.**

1   provide everyone with fresh groceries
2   sell the latest fashion at low cost in branded city outlets
3   schedule deliveries to the exact needs of production
4   secure a long-term supply of spare parts
5   provide overnight delivery and returns
6   ensure health and safety at the warehouse

a
The clothing retailer delivers ==pre-sorted== hanging garments, ==tagged== and ==ready for sale==, to shops, saving ==storage space==.

b
==Cross docking== and flexible ==multimodal== transport (rail, road, waterways) simplify ==just-in-time delivery== to processing plants.

c
Bananas are placed in ==interim storage== to ripen on ==pallets== in ==temperature controlled== containers before delivery to ==points of sale==.

d
An integrated automotive spare parts ==supply chain== provides a ==collaborative logistics network== open to all participating brands.

e
This mail order company has an ==automated pallet warehouse== with ==radio frequency controlled forklifts== and ==picking vehicles==.

f
Wi-fi-based RFID (radio frequency identification) provides ==item-level and box-level tagging==, for real-time ==tracking and tracing==.

❷ **Read how a steel multinational and a freight forwarder work together. How does this help them save resources? Does your company have similar partnerships?**

Operating in 50 countries, United Steel is one of the leading suppliers of quality steel products. In response to continued pressure to keep prices low, the company is developing international logistic chains with DB Schenker Rail. United Steel now uses rail rather than road or water routes from its works in Sosnowiec, Poland to processing plants in Western Europe to reduce delivery times. Its steelworks in Eisenhüttenstadt are piloting DB's capacity-management cargo booking system for state-of-the art planning and scheduling.

3 🔊14 United Steel account manager Tim Henry needs to reschedule deliveries from Eisenhüttenstadt and Sosnowiec to Lyons. He has asked Anke Kern to facilitate a conference call with the two mills. Look at the agenda, then listen to the first part of the call. How does Anke check that everyone is there and can hear?

Anke Kern, Logistics
Clara Kopf, Trainee
Eisenhüttenstadt

Tim Henry,
Account Manager
HQ, Luxembourg

Alisa Petrova, Production
Logistics, on assignment in
Sosnowiec

Piotr Novak,
Operations
Sosnowiec

Agenda

Conference Call   27.05.20.. / 8:00 -   **Call-in number:**   +49 3364 62788

Objective: To reschedule June 12th and June 19th deliveries of steel coils (standard and non-standard) from Sosnowiec and Eisenhüttenstadt

4 🔊15 Now listen to the second part of the teleconference and answer the questions.

1 Why is Tim Henry rescheduling two deliveries? What knock-on effects will this have?
2 What issues arise? What solutions does the team come up with?
3 Who will do what next? Formulate action items for the minutes.

Action items
Alisa Petrova to get quote for …

5 How does Anke solve communication problems during the teleconference? What phrases does she use to do the following? What else could she have said in each case?

1 tell someone they're too quiet
2 ask everyone to say their names
3 delegate a turn to someone
4 instruct people to let someone finish
5 keep a participant on track
6 warn someone about a bad line

6 👥 Get into teams of 3–4. You are planning a trip abroad for a large group of people and their equipment / instruments / gear with logistical support on site. First select a card below and think of the challenges you will have to meet. Write a quick agenda, then allocate the roles below and hold the teleconference.

a trade-fair road show
a scientific excursion
a 120-person orchestra
your own idea

→ *Partner A – Planning team, telecon facilitator: file 23, page 107*
→ *Partner B – Planning team: file 11, page 102*
→ *Partner C – Support on site: file 24, page 108*
→ *Partner D – Support on site: file 36, page 112*

Giving polite instructions
Can you just repeat that last part?
Try speaking directly into the microphone.
Go ahead and print out a copy, while you're at it.
If you'd just …
You might want to …

Being polite: It's not what you say, it's how you say it.

Taking part in teleconferences

Facilitator
Can everybody hear me OK?
(Name), did you want to comment on this?
We haven't heard what (name) has to say about this.
So, I think what you're saying, (name), is …
In other words, … / To recap, …
→ *Skills file, page 126*

Participants
(Name) here / speaking.
Sorry, was that (name) just now?
Excuse me, could you just …?
Sorry to butt in, but could I …?
I just need to get something – be back in a second.

43

Part B Deal with conflict

▶ **Discuss with a partner.**

· Have you ever worked in a virtual team, i.e. where the team members operate in different locations, time zones or languages? What are the pros and cons?
· How might differences in culture affect 'virtual' teamwork? What tips do you have for dealing with potential conflicts?

■ Did you know?

There is a certain traditional cultural preference for 'straight talk' in many parts of the US. For cultures with a more indirect style, this can seem brash. However, Americans generally avoid being direct when offering criticism and giving orders, which they consider potentially damaging to business relationships. This is where conflicts with the more 'direct' Germans tend to arise.

Food for thought

You want to apologize and make sure that your good relationship has not been damaged. Do you make a phone call or write an email?

1 **Ivo works for a multinational in Paderborn. He is having trouble with Doug, a fellow team member based at the US subsidiary in Atlanta, about a purchase order to a supplier called Wico. Read Doug's email and Ivo's reply, and tick the correct statements.**

1 ☐ Doug has sent a purchase order directly to the supplier with Ivo in cc.
2 ☐ Doug has told Ivo that the order has been taken care of and he shouldn't worry.
3 ☐ Doug has asked Ivo to place the order with the supplier and arrange payment.
4 ☐ Ivo tells Doug that the order has been taken care of and the payment made.
5 ☐ Ivo was told by the supplier that the order had been placed by somebody in the US.
6 ☐ Ivo tells Doug that the order will be sent to the supplier's US subsidiary and that accounting will be dealt with later.

Ivo Schenk <ivo.schenk@TRK.com>
To Doug Manning
23 May 09:12 (20 minutes ago)

Hi Doug

Wico Germany will send these 200 pcs this Friday to Wico USA without any PO. According to Wico Germany, this was all agreed with someone in the US. In this exceptional case, financial issues will be settled later, as the people involved are out of the office.
In the future I will not accept these kinds of emails from your side blaming Rose and me for not fully understanding your poor communication with both Wico US and Wico Germany.
Best wishes
Ivo

On Fri, May 20 at 23:07 Doug Manning wrote:

> Ivo,
>
> Wico Germany is confused and has informed you incorrectly. We are not able to, and have not issued, a PO to them. They have seen a copy of our PO to Paderborn only, which is the PO they are referencing (see attached). With this PO, Paderborn should open the budget and make the PO directly to Wico Germany.
> It seems we have had several instances now where poor communication or confusion has caused some trouble for us with you. In the future it will be helpful if you can please call me directly to discuss these issues before drawing conclusions without fully understanding the situation.
>
> Thanks,
> Doug

What is the tone of the emails? How do Ivo and Doug interpret the situation and what changes do they suggest for future dealings with each other?

2 🔊 16 **Now listen as Ivo asks Bob, a close colleague who is originally from the US, for advice about what to do next. What does Bob recommend?**

3 👥 **Look at some of the idioms Bob used when giving advice. In small groups, discuss what they mean, then decide whether or not Bob recommended the actions.**

1   talk it over
2   give someone a piece of your mind
3   put it in writing
4   tell someone off

5   make a big thing out of something
6   put someone on the spot
7   ease off a little
8   play it cool

4 **Look at Ivo's complaint about Doug. How did Bob recommend that Ivo raise the issue with Doug, by saying a or b?**

> **Ivo:** Doug's always doing things and not telling me. He never copies me into his emails.

a   You are always forgetting to copy me into your emails. And then you complain that I don't know what's happening.

b   I noticed that you didn't copy me into your email. So, next time, could you copy me in to let me know what's going on?

👥 **Tell a partner about someone's irritating behaviour. Decide how to ask the person in question to change it. Use these examples or your own.**

coughs into phone during conference calls

sends update at the last minute

forgets to notify the team

blames everyone else

uses difficult jargon

5 🔊 17 **Ivo finds a message from Doug in his voicemail. Does Doug admit to making any mistakes? If you were Ivo, what would you think of the message?**

What exactly did Doug say? Use words from the box to rephrase the sentences below, then listen again to check.

> I guess · I suppose · kind of · may have · probably · sort of

1   I misinterpreted the situation.
2   We got off on the wrong foot.
3   I was surprised, after that last email.

6 **Ivo calls Doug back, but gets *his* voicemail. Formulate his message for Doug, admitting some misunderstandings in the past and suggesting changes. End by thanking Doug for his message and attempt to reach you.**

7 **Think back to a conflict you had with somebody, and formulate a voice message admitting a misunderstanding and suggesting a change in behaviour. Include a 'thank you'.**

Asking others to change their behaviour

I noticed that you didn't copy me into your email.
NOT: ~~You're always forgetting to copy me into emails!~~
Next time, could you send me the update a few days earlier?
Can you (try and) … ?
It would help if you sent …
I'd appreciate it if you would …
It would be (really) great if we could …

Note how 'please' is not used in the requests above.

Admitting misunderstandings

I guess I sort of …
I probably …
We may have …
I suppose we kind of …

Food for thought

After you help someone, do you prefer a personal thank-you for your efforts, or an apology for the trouble it may have caused you?

Part C Balance clarity and tact

▶ **Discuss with a partner.**

'I often find that the Germans speak English very well, but have more difficulty in understanding the language.'
— *British BMW employee*

1 👥 **Study the chart below and discuss these questions.**

1 When do you feel the need to be clear? When do you prefer to be tactful? Where would you see yourself on a line between the two extremes?
2 What style and language do you think is more typically British or German?
3 What problems can personal preferences regarding clarity and tact cause?

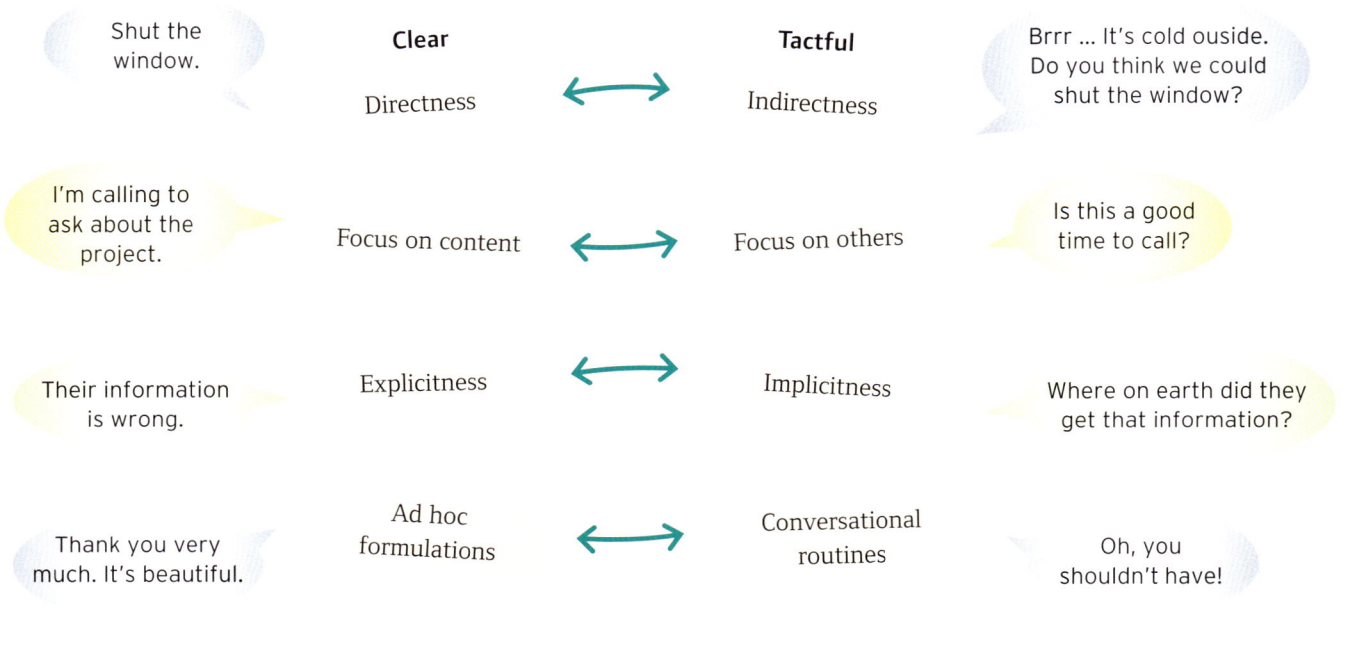

	Clear		**Tactful**	
Shut the window.	Directness	←→	Indirectness	Brrr ... It's cold ouside. Do you think we could shut the window?
I'm calling to ask about the project.	Focus on content	←→	Focus on others	Is this a good time to call?
Their information is wrong.	Explicitness	←→	Implicitness	Where on earth did they get that information?
Thank you very much. It's beautiful.	Ad hoc formulations	←→	Conversational routines	Oh, you shouldn't have!

2 **Read the article on page 47, then discuss these questions.**

1 Why does Gill Woodman say that Germans often reject indirect request formulations? Do you agree or disagree?
2 What exactly irritated the woman on the bus? What would you have felt in that situation?
3 How do the British use irony? Why do you think they do it? What is your reaction to someone who is being ironic?

3 **Find words or phrases in the article which mean the following:**

1 most important
2 to expect sth unreasonable or inconvenient from sb
3 suddenly, without planning
4 to accept sth for what it appears to be (rather than look for hidden meaning)
5 to criticize sb
6 to make use of sth, especially sth bad, when there is no other solution

Intercultural differences in conversation

Linguist Dr Gill Woodman of the Ludwig Maximilian University Munich is an expert in German–British communication and has done research and conducted interviews at BMW. Here she summarizes a few of her findings.

It's really quite risky to generalize, but the overriding difference appears to be that Germans lay more importance on clarity, while the British have a preference for tact. For example, in cross-cultural communication, Germans sometimes feel uncomfortable when using standard English request formulations ('Would you mind writing me a report?') which seem too 'soft'. They often don't believe that anybody would feel any need to carry out a request if it was formulated so indirectly. The British use these formulations when they feel a request would impose on the other person.

Germans add more explicit detail, as illustrated by an anecdote reported by a British woman. She was standing in a crowded bus, when the driver asked her (in German) 'Can you move up a bit? Other people want to get on the bus, too.' This final phrase telling her what people wanted really annoyed her. She found it unnecessarily explicit, which to her made it sound rather unfriendly and aggressive.

Germans also tend to use ad hoc formulations, i.e. they say something spontaneously on the spur of the moment, whereas the British seem to have a larger range of 'pre-packed' conversational routines. Many German learners of English will initially take this kind of talk at face value and commonly consider the English

Dr Gill Woodman

way of communicating superficial. In situations where one person wishes to reproach another for some unacceptable behaviour, Germans will tend to be quite explicit ('I can't accept this kind of behaviour'), whereas the British will often resort to irony ('Why don't you go drown yourself in coffee!').

---

4 Differences in preferred styles also affect written communication. Look at the emails and discuss the questions below.

1 Which email was written with a focus on clarity, which with a focus on tact? Which one do you prefer, and why?
2 How do you think someone with a preference for a different style would feel on receiving the emails below?

A

We have major scheduling problems and have to get everyone back on track. Let's have a teleconference to adjust the schedule.

Are you free on Thursday, 9–9.30? Please send out an invitation to the team.

Also, please call Ralf and tell him we have to postpone the delivery again by a week. I can't specify the exact date, but I'll give you the information asap.

B

As you know, we've been having some major scheduling problems. I think we should have a teleconference about this fairly soon so we can get everyone back on track.

Would you be able to manage Thursday am? If so, could you send out an invitation to the team?

Also, sorry, but would you mind calling Ralf to tell him we'll need to postpone the delivery by a week? I'm afraid I can't specify the exact date yet, but I'll let you know as soon as I have it.

Thanks for your help.

5 Write an email balancing tact and clarity to suit the recipient. Use these prompts or your own ideas.

we need to solve problem with X by Friday ➜ can't change schedule ➜ meet on Wed or Thur ➜ needs to review attached report / give feedback and confirm asap

■ **Did you know?**
Native speakers use the word 'sorry' far more frequently in situations where nobody has done any harm (e.g. when passing too closely or asking a favour) than in important matters.

1 Choose appropriate words or phrases to complete the text. You will not need every word or phrase.

> incoming goods · outgoing goods · point of sale · RFID technology · shipped ·
> storage · supply chain · tagged · temperature-controlled · track and trace

Hyalun Logistics

About Us

Some like it cold! We transport goods direct from the producer to the ....[1]. Your

....[2] are ....[3] with Wi-fi-based

....[4], then placed in our advanced ....[5]

containers and ....[6] to the desired destination. You will be able to ....[7] all of your

....[8] in real time thanks to our patented GoodsTracer® software system.

2 Complete the questions and statements from a teleconference by matching the sentence halves.

1 Was there anything	a off-track, so can we get back to the main point please?
2 If we could just	b introduce yourselves please.
3 You might just want to go ahead and	c you wanted to add there?
4 Just to be sure I've	d Thomas finish his point?
5 Can you just let	e slow down there.
6 Very interesting but I think we might be getting a bit	f got that, did you mean that …?

Now match the sentences to a description.

A telling participants not to speak as fast
B stopping an interruption
C encouraging a speaker to make a point
D getting back to the main topic
E paraphrasing to clarify understanding
F instructing people to say their names

3 Choose the correct words to complete the idiomatic expressions.

1 I'm afraid I'm in trouble with my boss. She told me   up / off / over   for forgetting to phone a client.

2 Don't make a big thing   out of / over / by   the mistake. Apologize and move on.

3 They   put / held / took   me on the spot at the meeting with all their questions.

4 They can't act like that! I'm going to give them a   spot / piece / part   of my mind!

5 Why don't you talk it   up / by / over   with him and solve the problem?

6 I think he should ease   off / on / over   a little. He's being too aggressive.

④ Find polite but firm alternatives for the complaints 1–6 by matching the sentence halves below.

1 You never provide overnight deliveries and returns.

2 You are always using extremely idiomatic language during our teleconferences. Please stop.

Always + -ing is mostly used to complain! Try to avoid it when addressing someone directly.
- *She's always forgetting to do things.*
- ~~You're always correcting me in meetings.~~

3 Stop talking so loudly, Ken.

6 Mr Norton, this time remember to use the surname first when you are in Hungary.

4 You are always forgetting to fill in the right form.

5 You never return my phone calls.

a You might want to	you sometimes don't fill in the right form.
b One thing that puzzles me	as simple as possible please, because …
c Keep things	to provide overnight deliveries.
d I've noticed that you don't seem	keep your voice down.
e If you could just	is that you hardly ever get back to me.
f I have the impression that	use the surname first …

⑤ What should you say? Choose the best response in each situation.

1 You get a present from a business acquaintance.
   a 'You shouldn't have!'
   b 'I wouldn't mind one!'

2 You are tired and you want to leave a reception.
   a 'It's been great but I'd like to leave now.'
   b 'It's been great but I must be going now.'

3 You offer someone another cup of coffee, and she says: 'I wouldn't mind one.'
   a 'Here you are!'
   b 'OK, maybe later then.'

4 Somebody needs a lift home. You offer to help.
   a 'I don't mind taking you.'
   b 'I won't mind.'

5 An important business partner has misinterpreted your point.
   a 'I'm afraid you don't understand.'
   b 'There may have been a misunderstanding.'

6 Your business partner says he needs a document which you know is unnecessary.
   a 'Sorry, but that's a bit irritating.'
   b 'Uhm, I'm slightly puzzled.'

6 **Rearrange the following sentences to make more tactful versions of the thoughts below.**

You never understand me!

1 be misunderstanding / we might / I suppose / one another / just

....

....

2 in the future / if we could / more often / I'd appreciate it / communicate

....

....

You are always avoiding me and deliberately not answering my phone calls.

Give me more time to prepare!

3 had / it would help / more time to prepare / if I / next time

....

....

4 got off / we might have / it seems / on the wrong foot

....

....

Last time we met it was a disaster.

I need it today!

5 try and / at the latest / can you / by the end of the day / send it to me ?

....

....

6 a bit / that / has taken me / certainly / by surprise

....

....

That's a shock.

7 **Make this very direct email more tactful by replacing the underlined phrases with a–j below.**

a actually not the ones we agreed on
b am not sure I
c at the earliest possible opportunity
d it might not be a bad time to
e looking forward to seeing

f seem to be occurring rather too frequently
g should
h unfortunately we received
i wanted
j and having the chance

Dear Jane,

I hope you are doing well.

The samples you sent were <u>wrong</u> [1]. We <u>want</u> [2] the latest model and <u>you sent</u> [3] last season's items. Problems like this <u>are always happening</u> [4] and I <u>don't</u> [5] understand why. We <u>must</u> [6] clarify this <u>asap</u> [7].

By the way, I've heard you are coming to the meeting next month. Let's meet up and discuss the issue. <u>We must</u> [8] clarify this.

<u>Hopefully I will see</u> [9] you there <u>as I really want</u> [10] to clear things up.

Sally

8 **Translate into English.**

1 Es war nicht korrekt, die vertraulichen Informationen per E-Mail weiterzuleiten.
2 Die Logistik ist ziemlich kompliziert, aber ich bin überzeugt davon, dass wir bald eine gute Lösung finden werden.
3 Dafür kannst du ihm nicht die Schuld geben; er hatte einfach nicht alle Informationen.
4 Sie hat beim Abendessen mit dem Geschäftspartner ihr Weinglas umgeschüttet und sich ziemlich blamiert.
5 Mit der Präsentation des neuen Produktes hat sich unsere Konkurrenz ganz schön blamiert.
6 Nach der Telefonkonferenz waren wir alle etwas irritiert. Wer ist jetzt für die Lieferung verantwortlich?
7 Es ärgert mich, wenn jemand seine E-Mails nicht zügig beantwortet.

Typical mistakes

1 It is not **right / proper** to treat her like that.
   NOT   *It is not* ~~correct~~ ...
2 **Logistics are** an important part of our strategy.
   NOT   ~~Logistic is~~ *an important part* ...
3 *blamieren* ≠ blame
   The company **failed miserably** in their strategy. / They **made a fool of themselves**. (*sich blamieren*)
   He **blamed** the delay on his assistant. (*jmdm die Schuld geben*)
4 *irritieren* ≠ irritate
   I'm **confused**. What's the procedure again? (*irritieren*)
   Her behaviour **irritates** me; I find it so annoying. (*ärgern; nerven*)

Outside view

Anne Hodgson on ... Politeness

My students find it aggravating, but directness and results-orientation don't always get the job done. Take the case of Sarah. Wanting to check a colleague's report for calculation errors, she wrote: *Please send me the report so I can run through the numbers*. Did adding *please* make the request polite, the way it would in German? Not really. In fact, her email came across as pushy, with unpleasant repercussions for Sarah. So what could she have written? She could, for example, have offered an explanation: *Could you send me the report? I just wanted to double-check some of the figures, which may have changed.*

Politeness strategies

Overall, politeness means acting in a manner that allows others the freedom to say no, or to suggest an alternative solution without losing face. All cultures, languages and dialects have ways of allowing that. So, contrary to popular belief, English is not more polite than, say, German; we just employ different strategies.

'Positive politeness' aims to make others feel good about themselves. It's a strategy often used in the US, and includes a great deal of thanks and praise that might make some British or German people squirm: *You've done a really excellent job on this proposal! Just send me a copy and I'll update the figures.* At the other end of the extreme, many British and Asian people are more comfortable with 'negative politeness', which aims to avoid imposing on others, and tends to include apologies: *Sorry to trouble you, but would you mind sending me your report? I just wanted to check something.* Too much of that tends to make Germans and Americans a bit uncomfortable.

So you see, understanding politeness in its many forms and facets is rather a job in itself. But once you know some of the basics, you hold the key to getting your job done.

aggravating	ärgerlich
pushy	aufdringlich, penetrant
repercussions	negative Auswirkungen
to squirm	sich winden

Business file 2

In this business file you will ...

- hold a teleconference
- plan how to handle a logistics supplier
- take the minutes of a meeting
- draft an email or an invitation to tender

A teleconference

① **Read the short article. What responsibilities has Medtec outsourced to Loglab? What issues could arise in operations?**

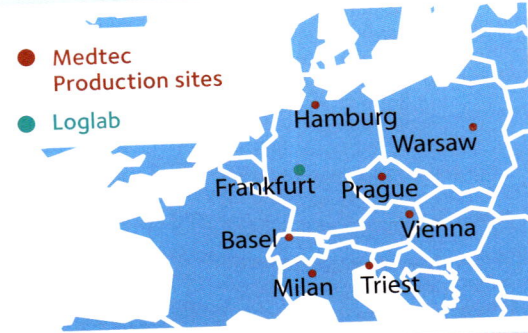

● Medtec Production sites

● Loglab

Medtec, a leading provider of medical technology with production sites around the world, has contracted out warehousing and value added services (packaging, labelling, import / export) to **Loglab**, a provider of third-party logistics (3PL). Using Loglab's automated multi-user warehouse outside Frankfurt/Main as their European hub, Medtec now supplies its customers in Europe and Africa directly from one central location. Every day, between 100 and 150 orders are communicated and processed via an interface linking Medtec's SAP and Loglab's warehouse management system (WMS). Orders received before 2 pm are dispatched the same day.

Did you know?

A party is 'in breach of contract' if they fail to perform any term of a contract, written or oral, without a legitimate legal excuse.

② 🔊 18-22 **Valerie, account administrator at Medtec Warsaw, has saved five voicemail messages to document an incident. The first one is from Ian, an account manager at Medtec Hamburg. Read the questions below, then listen to the messages and take notes.**

1. What went wrong and who was involved?
2. What should be done to prevent the problem from happening again?
3. What does Ian mean by 'get hold of', 'rubbish', 'get this sorted', 'knackered' and 'pack it in'? Judging from his language, how well does he know Valerie?
4. What are Ian and Valerie going to do next to set things straight?

③ **Do a role-play or a simulation of a problem-solving teleconference.**

1. In groups of four, choose **Option 1** (a role-play based on the scenario above) or **Option 2** (a simulation using your own work situation or ideas).

Option 1

Choose a role (A–D) and read the agenda in your file. Then use the information there and the phrases in the left column of the language box to prepare for the telecon.

→ *Partner A (Ian): file 4, page 99*
→ *Partner B (Valerie): file 20, page 106*
→ *Partner C (Johanna): file 26, page 108*
→ *Partner D (Jan): file 16, page 104*

Option 2

Think of a realistic situation where you and the members of your virtual team have to solve a problem in a teleconference. Make notes.

What's the situation? → Who's involved? → What vocabulary / phrases do you need?

In your team, decide what the problem is. Then, on your own, think of a way to solve it.

Which members of the virtual team do you know and who are you talking to for the first time?

Use the phrases in the left column of the language box to help you prepare.

2 Now hold the teleconference.
- Begin by introducing yourselves briefly and reviewing the agenda.
- Clarify the problem that you are meeting to solve.
- Discuss the options and agree on what action to take.

4 **Write the minutes. Then, depending on the outcome of your meeting, follow up with a piece of writing. If you chose Option 1, you could do one of the following:**

- Write a formal email to Loglab telling them that you are dissatisfied and specifying your expectations.
- Write an internal email to a decision-maker at Medtec explaining the situation and asking to schedule a meeting.
- Draft an invitation to tender so you can find an alternative logistics supplier.

> **Did you know?**
>
> An 'invitation to tender' (ITT), or 'tender' for short, is a special procedure for generating competing offers from different bidders. A company may also approach specific contractors and request them to submit a proposal (RFP).

Participating in a teleconference	Writing emails, tenders and minutes
Doing sound checks	**Clarifying conditions in a formal email**
Can everyone hear me OK?	It has come to our attention that there have been …
What's the sound like at your end?	Unfortunately, Loglab has been unable to meet …
There seems to be some static or background noise.	As you will see from the attached report, …
I lost you there for a moment.	Our terms and conditions will need to be followed more
I'm not getting all of this.	closely.
Do you want to try hanging up and dialing in again?	Unless …, we will be forced to …
Checking in and clarifying the situation	**Explaining the situation in an informal email**
How are you doing?	We have recently been having …
So, I hear you've been having …	This has caused quite a bit of …
I'm sorry to hear that things have been a bit …	Would it be possible to meet to discuss …?
I understand that you've encountered …	This would allow us to formulate …
Exchanging ideas and planning next steps	**Writing a tender**
Are you saying that …?	Medtec is a leading manufacturer of …
In that case, why don't we …?	… inviting suppliers to tender for the provision of …
Shall we / I ask … to …?	Logistics and warehousing is required from (date) …
So, if you could contact …, I'll …	Your tender must be supplied in compliance with …
Would you be free on (date) at (time)?	Tenders shall be addressed to …
I don't think I can manage (date).	Tenders received after this date shall not be considered,
Could you make it on / at …?	but shall be opened, recorded, marked 'late' and returned
	to sender.
Signing off	**Writing minutes**
Well, I think we've covered just about everything.	It has been agreed to / that …
I think we can sign off / hang up then.	We / We've decided to …
Thanks, everyone, for coming.	(Name) is to meet / contact / write …
OK, speak again soon. Have a good day / week.	The next conference is to take place on … at …

Sustainable business

In this unit you will …

- explore sustainability
- review financial performance
- pitch financial services
- practise business storytelling and reporting

Part A Discuss performance

▶ 'Sustainable' has two meanings. In which way are the companies mentioned in the hyperlinks sustainable (or not)? What about the company where you work?

sustainable: *adj.* **1** involving the use of natural products and energy in a way that does not harm the environment **2** that can continue or be continued for a long time

Energy sector

- Nuclear plant shuts down after malfunction
- Wind turbine producer goes bankrupt
- Utility company rebounds after crisis
- Boom in offshore wind power market

Relating past events

They **wanted** to reduce costs. At the time, subsidies **were causing** margins to decline. They **had launched** a programme in 2007.

---

1 👥 A major utility company has published its annual report for 2012 on the internet. Read these extracts and relate what happened in your own words. How well do you think the company was doing at the end of the year?

1 The European energy sector is undergoing fundamental changes. Political intervention is making our business challenging. In addition, the subsidized expansion of renewables in Germany is causing the margins and utilization of conventional power stations to decline. To cope with the challenges, we have implemented comprehensive measures to reduce costs and increase earnings.

2 A basic principle of sustainable business practice is that, in the long run, you can only spend as much as you earn. In 2007, we launched the biggest investment programme in our history, and have since spent about 28 billion euros, much more than we could finance from our operations. We now aim to reduce the resulting debt to improve our financial flexibility and expect to bring our investments and dividends fully in line with our cash flow from operations over the next three years.

Describing performance results

Production rose / fell by just over / under x %.
Prices were up / down by around / roughly x %.
Earnings amounted / came to …
They reported an increase / a decrease of x % in net income over the previous year.

6.406 bn = 'six point four oh six billion'

6,406 m = 'six billion, four hundred and six million'

---

2 Find words or phrases in the extracts that mean the following:

Extract 1
1 growth enabled by public funding
2 reducing profits from and the use of non-renewable energy
3 to resolve the problems
4 a connected set of actions

Extract 2
5 not immediately but at some time in the future
6 lowering the amount of money owed
7 money coming in and paid out, and its availability

3 🔊 23 Listen to a newscast presenting gains and losses for the utility giant, and answer these questions.

1 How did the company perform in 2012? Correct the three errors in the notes.
2 Why was 2011 such a disaster? Had the company fully recovered by 2012?

2012 compared to 2011:
- Electricity production: +10.4%
- Operating result: EUR 6,406 m, −10%
- Net income: EUR 1,306 bn, −27.7%
- Earnings per share: EUR 23, −36.4%

4 Find an annual report online and present the results for a selected year.

5 You will hear Peter Glück tell the story of how he built up his wind turbine business. Before you listen, match the phrases below (1–5 with a–e, and 6–10 with f–j) to reconstruct some of the business moves he describes. Which ones do you think contributed to growth?

1	raise	**a**	in the trainee programme
2	license	**b**	equity capital
3	take advantage	**c**	out production
4	invest	**d**	the company's reputation
5	damage	**e**	of government subsidies
6	cut the	**f**	risky long-term liabilities
7	sell one's	**g**	stake in the company
8	default	**h**	on payments
9	bail	**i**	payroll in half
10	develop	**j**	the company out

🔊 24 Now listen to Peter relate the story of the rise and fall of Windcraft AG.
Take notes on key figures and use the phrases above to answer the questions.

1 What were the highlights during the expansion of the company?
2 What problems did Windcraft encounter, and how did the company try to solve them?
3 How well do you think the founder realized his aim of running a sustainable business?

6 Use the phrases in the box and some of the verbs below to retell the story of Windcraft.

… allowed / permitted / enabled Windcraft to …
… encouraged / motivated / convinced the company to …
… forced / caused the founder to …

7 Look at these sentences. What decisions were made and how did they affect the present?

If we **hadn't opted** for aggressive growth, we **might have survived**.
If we **had kept** our focus, we **might** still **be** in business today.

8 👥 Work with a partner to formulate business problems and their negative effects. What opportunities did the companies below miss? What should or could each company have done for a more positive outcome?

Example: cash-flow problems ➡ couldn't buy the equipment.

> If the company hadn't had cash-flow problems, they could have bought the equipment.

> They should have bought the equipment on credit.

> What if they hadn't been able to get credit?

> They could have leased the equipment.

1 credit rating was low ➡ no credit, couldn't grow
2 debtors defaulted on payments ➡ cash-flow problems
3 failed to refinance a loan ➡ continued to pay high interest
4 lacked qualified staff ➡ failed the audit
5 price war brought down margin ➡ lost money on product

Food for thought

What would inspire you to play by the rules: a well-written rule book, or the story of a guy who broke the rules … and learned his lesson?

Telling a (business) story

When …
That meant that …
So, essentially, …
In other words, …
So there we / they were, …
In the end, …
To cut a long story short, …
Looking back, …

Discussing past decisions with hindsight

If I **hadn't focused** on young people, they **would not have had** opportunities.
We **wouldn't have experienced** those problems if we **had fixed** the technology.
We really **should have focused** on the technical problems.
Maybe we **could have solved** them.

Part B Pitch a proposal

▶ Think about an occasion when you sold a product or service to someone, or when you convinced someone to do something. What contributed to your success?

1 Green Financial Services provides financing solutions to allow companies to update to more energy efficient equipment and buildings. Scan the flyer and check your understanding using the true/false statements below.

Green Financial *Services*

Protecting the environment can be rewarding

Trade in
We take your used equipment as payment for state-of-the-art technology, at attractive conditions. As part of this 'asset buyback', we resell your old models and incorporate the income generated by the sale into the financing calculation.

Operating lease
As the lessee of our equipment, you pay only the costs associated with the use and depreciation of the capital goods – that is, less than the purchase price. This allows you to save on expenditures.

Retrofit financing
We buy your used equipment and lease it back to you at reasonable rates after upgrading. The costs for upgrading are covered by your gains in energy efficiency.

Hire purchase
You pay off the purchase in instalments but, from the beginning, are the owner of the capital goods and can thus take advantage of tax breaks and depreciation opportunities.

Energy-saving performance contract
When you upgrade your existing building, you will recoup your investment within the term of the agreement through guaranteed savings in energy and operating costs.

True or false? Justify your answer and correct the false statements.

		true	false
1	'Trade in' means that you can exchange your old equipment and get new, more modern equipment for free.	☐	☐
2	Under the 'operating lease', you pay less for the technology than if you had to buy it.	☐	☐
3	In 'retrofit financing', you do not own the upgraded equipment.	☐	☐
4	Under a 'hire purchase' contract, you pay a lump sum at the beginning.	☐	☐
5	The service provider guarantees under contract that you will fully finance your investment.	☐	☐

2 Daniel Fox from Green Financial Services is meeting prospective customers at the Berlin offices of a South African trading company. Kate Nel is the head accountant and Rick Reed is the chief controller there. Read the opening proposal, which Daniel has sent to outline the agenda. What will happen at this initial meeting?

Green Financial *Services*

Opening proposal for energy-saving performance contracting
We will:
1. review your needs, requirements and interests, and outline what we can provide.
2. demonstrate our baseline cost model to act as a ceiling for our cost proposal.
3. outline cost planning in short-, mid- and long-term models.

🎧25 **Now listen to the beginning of the meeting, and answer the questions below.**

1 Does Daniel start pitching his services straight away? Why or why not?
2 Had the customer already looked at the service portfolio before the meeting?
3 What kind of a financial solution is the customer interested in?
4 What assurance does Kate require before she will agree to any offer of this kind?
5 How does Daniel incorporate this when he pitches his proposal?

3 **Compare the sentences below. How does the use of phrasal verbs change the tone?**

We guarantee that our clients will **recoup** more than they **invest**.
We guarantee that you will **get back** more than you **put in**.

Link words from the two lists to form phrasal verbs that can be used to replace the words in bold below.

bring · draw · ~~look~~ · put · turn · work   down · out · together · ~~up~~ · up · up

1 We **made contact with you** because we liked your website.
   We looked you up because we liked your website.
2 If you want a model investment plan, we'll be happy to **create** one for you.
3 It may be a good offer, but without references, I'm afraid we'd have to **refuse** it.
4 I'm glad you **mentioned** it.
5 This sum is just an example. We **calculated** it using model figures.
6 We can **organize** it for you.

4 **Match the columns to complete the phrases used in the meeting.**

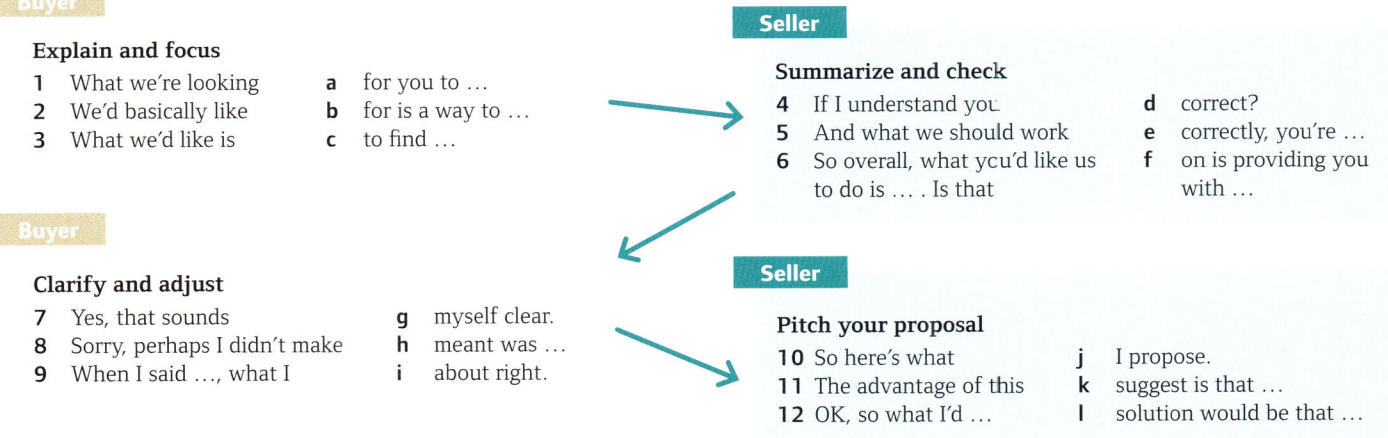

Buyer

Explain and focus
1 What we're looking   a for you to …
2 We'd basically like   b for is a way to …
3 What we'd like is   c to find …

Seller

Summarize and check
4 If I understand you   d correct?
5 And what we should work   e correctly, you're …
6 So overall, what you'd like us   f on is providing you
   to do is … . Is that   with …

Buyer

Clarify and adjust
7 Yes, that sounds   g myself clear.
8 Sorry, perhaps I didn't make   h meant was …
9 When I said …, what I   i about right.

Seller

Pitch your proposal
10 So here's what   j I propose.
11 The advantage of this   k suggest is that …
12 OK, so what I'd …   l solution would be that …

5 👥 **With a partner, think of a service that one of you could provide to the other (e.g. bookkeeping, proofreading or an actual service you offer). Choose a role and use the information in your file to organize your thoughts. Then follow the flow chart below to have a meeting.**

➔ *Partner A (Buyer): file 31, page 110*   ➔ *Partner B (Seller): file 38, page 113*

Buyer → **Seller** → **Buyer** → **Seller**
Explain and   Summarize   Clarify   Acknowledge
focus   and check   and adjust and pitch

Framing a proposal

Frame your proposal by beginning with your bottom line.

➔ *Skills file, page 127*

Part C Describe business strategy

▶ Can you think of companies which develop their products very long term (e.g. aerospace, defence, pharmaceuticals …)? What special challenges do you think they face in terms of raising capital and retaining staff long term? What kind of stories can they publish to persuade their stakeholders of the benefit of staying involved?

1 Biopharmaceutical companies are responsible for developing medicines – a socially beneficial but very costly and long-term proposition. How much do you know about the industry and the challenges its companies face? Do this quiz.

1

In drug discovery, how many years of study using test tubes and laboratory mice does it normally take before a drug candidate – a potential, yet untested cure – is tested on humans?

a about 22 months

b over 10 years

2

The average failure rate in the third clinical phase is (testing for therapeutic effect) is …

a minimal.

b roughly 10%.

c up to 50%.

3

Of new medicines that enter human clinical trials, the most successful are …

a small molecules (which most drugs are).

b antibodies.

→ *Check your answers: file 5, page 99*

2 Read this synopsis of a business study about the biotech firm MorphoSys to find out:

1 what the company produces and what services it provides.

2 what strategy it has used to build a sustainable business model.

MorphoSys:
Building a sustainable business through licensing and technology transfer

Munich-based MorphoSys, founded in 1992 and publicly traded since 1999, is one of the few biopharmaceuticals to have been consistently profitable in a volatile business environment. The company's business model is based, not on the development and sale of their own drugs, but on the formation of strategic alliances and lucrative partnerships with large pharmaceuticals firms. MorphoSys licenses out access to its propriety technology, HuCAL, a platform that generates 100 % human therapeutic antibodies, 81 of which are currently lined up in the clinical pipeline. In exchange for these services, MorphoSys receives steady revenue streams from licensing fees, R&D funding, milestone payments and royalties from its partners.

In recent years this business model has provided MorphoSys with the revenue required for investment in proprietary 'MOR' drug development and technological expansion. Significant expenditures for R&D result in lower revenues

Share Price and Volume Graph for MorphoSys from 2000–2013

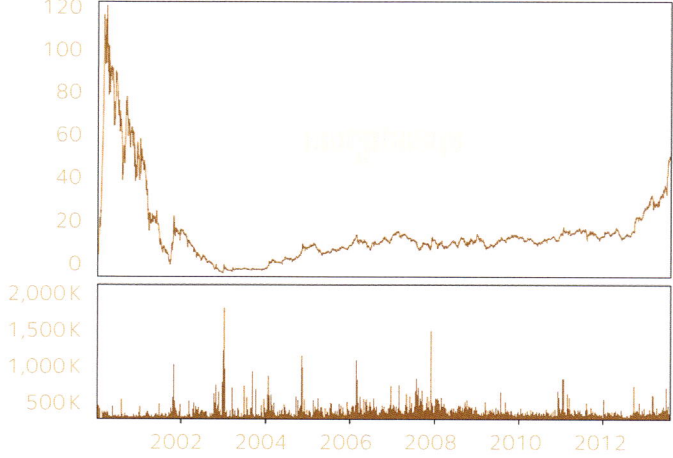

and margins as well as fewer initial short-term capital gains for shareholders. To build sustainable shareholder support, MorphoSys has over the years systematically shifted towards institutional investors more willing to wait for potential capital gains from long-term value creation. Within the next year, the current clinical trials are expected to impact MorphoSys's share prices. If successful, the market may see newer pharmaceutical companies follow suit towards a MorphoSys-inspired model.

3 Find words and phrases in the synopsis that mean the following:

1   contributing different but complementary resources to achieve a common objective
2   making contracts that promise good returns
3   predictable money coming into a company from a particular activity
4   sums paid for the contractual use of an invention under intellectual property rights
5   lump-sum payments by a licensee to the licensor when agreed events take place
6   a percentage of the sale price of products that are sold by the licensee
7   the earnings realized when an asset is sold minus the initial investment
8   increasing the value of goods, services and the business that provides them

4 Study two corporate media releases from the MorphoSys website. How does the company differentiate its business model from other biopharmaceuticals? Who is the intended audience for these two reports?

 Statement about company strategy

Strategy: Business Model with Balanced Risk/Reward Profile

MorphoSys's distinctive and sustainable business model has put the Company in a very strong financial position. This strength provides the foundations for a substantially increased investment in proprietary product and technology development, which, in turn, will drive growth and value generation. The Company's ability to fund all internal development activities while remaining profitable is a unique feature of its business model, setting it apart from the majority of high-risk, cash-burning biopharmaceutical companies.   *Extract from www.morphosys.com/company/strategy*

 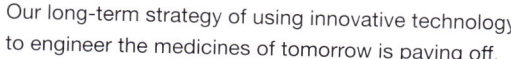 Introduction to the 2012 Annual Report by CEO Dr Simon Moroney

Dr Simon Moroney
CEO, MorphoSys

5 How do business reports and media releases portray corporate success? Look at these excerpts from Simon Moroney's introduction to the 2012 Annual Report. How does his language reflect his subjectivity and wish to persuade his audience?

The year 2012 was certainly one of the most successful in our history.

What we've seen is a fundamental re-rating of the company, as investors start to attribute real value to our pipeline.

Our long-term strategy of using innovative technology to engineer the medicines of tomorrow is paying off.

Corporate statements like the ones above are usually more persuasive and subjective than external studies and reports, such as the one on page 58, which tend to be more descriptive and neutral. Find examples to contrast the two types of reporting, e.g.:

descriptive/neutral

... one of the few biopharmaceuticals to have been consistently profitable ...

persuasive/subjective

... a very strong financial position This strength ...

6 Look at a business report and a media release for a company of your choice. What typical similarities and differences do you find?

7 Write a persuasive description of your department's or company's strategy.

❶ Which is the odd one out? Cross out the one word or phrase per line that doesn't collocate.

1 fund · raise · invest · seek   capital

2 license out · cut · invest in · default on   production

3 damage · default on · make · miss   payments

4 sustain · take advantage of · affect · bail out   developments

5 take advantages of · license · damage · affect   the company's reputation

6 sell · have · gain · invest   a stake in the company

❷ Test yourself. A colleague is relating an anecdote. Put the events in chronological order (1–4).

"Last year I was planning to apply for a new job in a utility company in the US. I had made some interesting American contacts at a trade fair and at the time was feeling like a change. I had already worked in wind power here at KBP for several years and was looking for a new challenge. In the end I was offered a promotion, which I decided to accept, and so here I still am today."

met some interesting people at a trade fair
started working for KBP
decided he needed a change
accepted a promotion

Relating past events: simple past, past continuous and past perfect

1 The company **reported** an increase in energy production in 2013.
First we **upgraded** the equipment, then we **increased** the output and finally we **started** to make a profit.
2 At the time, the economic conditions **were worsening**, and my company went bankrupt. Eight people **were working** at my father's company when I took over.
3 When the economy worsened last year, the company went bankrupt, although they **had already implemented** measures to save money. They got their share of the budget after they **had made** a good business case. (*First they made the business case, then they got their share.*)

The **simple past** is used to relate the main event/s that the speaker is focussing on. The events in the **simple past** follow in chronological order in the sentence (**1**).

The **past continuous** can be used together with the simple past to relate background events that were in progress at the time of the main event (**2**).

The **past perfect** is used to relate events that happened before the main event in the past. It is frequently used with words such as *after* and *already*. By using the **past perfect** you can relate events in non-chronological order (**3**).

❸ Put the verbs in brackets into the correct tense: simple past, past continuous or past perfect.

Last year everything seemed wonderful. We ....¹ (consistently have) growth rates in

the double digits for a period of over four years and were in the middle of planning our future strategy. At the time,

we ....² (plan) to expand into Asia and ....³ (even hope) to

further expand into North America eventually. We ....⁴ (already approach)

potential business partners, and interest ....⁵ (be) overwhelming, until August when disaster

.....................⁶ (strike). A competitor, who.....................⁷ (be) busy developing an innovative system that was both cheaper and more effective than ours, ...⁸ (launch) their new product. Within the space of a few months, expansion ....⁹ (become) financially unsustainable. We ....¹⁰ (have to) abandon our plans and ....¹¹ (decide) to refocus on our domestic market. To cut a long story short, all our ambitious efforts ....¹² (be) in vain!

4 Complete the statements by matching the sentence halves.

1 The company reported an increase
2 Earnings per share were up
3 The high share price reflects
4 Its operating result came to
5 The increase in profit was
6 Unfortunately, the question of sustainability remains

a roughly $2.3 million, up 5% over the previous year.
b in profitability of 2.4% last year.
c mainly due to the increased confidence in the market.
d an unresolved issue.
e the upturn in trading in this market.
f by over 21% to $4.20.

5 Which words below can be used to complete the sentence pairs 1–7?

asset/assets · balance · equity · liability/liabilities · net · return · sustainable

1 The company issued .equity.. shares to raise cash.
Equity.. ensures that funds, goods and services are fairly divided.

2 Windcraft AG has reported third quarter .... profits of €1.3 m.
We were able to .... a substantial return on our investment.

3 Fixed .... are what a company owns or uses in the production of its income.
Well-trained staff is a great .... to a company.

4 After the takeover, all assets and .... were absorbed into the new concern.
The partners assume unlimited personal .... for the debts and obligations of the firm.

5 The .... sheet shows our current accounts, i.e. what a business has and owes.
It is difficult to strike the right .... between different sources of energy.

6 The government wants to promote strong and .... economic growth.
.... energy serves present needs without compromising future generations.

7 We should start seeing a .... on our investment next year.
We can offer you company shares in .... for your services.

6 Complete the sentences with phrasal verbs from the list below and the words in brackets.
Use the clues in *italics* to help you choose the right phrasal verbs.

bring up · ~~get back~~ · get over · look into · look over · put off · set back

1 They lost money but they expect to .get.it.back. (it) next year. *recoup*

2 How much would the payments .... (us)? *cost*

3 The crisis? It was hard, but we .... (it) fairly quickly. *overcome*

4 Can you .... (it) and find a solution? *investigate*

5 Ah, the price. I'm glad you .... (that). *mention*

6 They made a bad pitch. It really .... (me) working with them. *cause to lose interest*

7 The accounts? I .... (them) last week and found nothing wrong. *examine*

> Phrasal verbs can be separable
> • **get** your point **across** ...
> or inseparable
> • **look after** a project
> Not: ~~look a project after~~

Discussing past decisions with hindsight: third conditional and *should / could have done*

1 We **wouldn't have suffered** so much in the crisis if we **had invested** more in R&D.
(But, in reality, we didn't invest, so we did suffer.)
If we **hadn't taken** that risk, we **would have failed**.

2 If we **hadn't taken** that risk, we **wouldn't be** here now.
NOT: … ~~we wouldn't have been here now~~.

3 In retrospect, we **shouldn't have relied** on experts; we **should have trusted** our own instincts instead.
All things considered, we **could have spent** more time on marketing.

The **third conditional** is used to imagine a past scenario which is the opposite of what actually took place. It is formed with *would have* + past participle in the main clause, and past perfect in the *if*-clause (**1**).

A **mixed conditional** can be used if we want to show how an imagined past event or decision would have affected the present. Note that *would (not)* + infinitive is used in the main clause (**2**).

Should have and *could have* + past participle can be used to talk about past events that did not happen or decisions that were not made (**3**).

7 Complete these third conditional and mixed conditional sentences with the verb pairs below.

continue / make   not have to / not develop   handle / now have

realize / not be   not default / have   ~~not overlook~~ / ~~not spend~~

1 If we .hadn't.spent. so much money on training, we .wouldn't.have.overlooked. certain trends.

2 If sales .... to increase as in the previous year, we .... plans for expansion.

3 We .... so deeply in debt now if we .... earlier how severe the situation was.

4 We .... a much better credit rating last year if our management team .... the changes more skillfully.

5 If our partners .... on planned payments, our shareholders .... the capital needed to bail out the company now.

6 The CEO .... file for insolvency if we .... risky long-term liabilities.

Now match a suitable comment to the situations 1–6.

a   We could have prevented this but now we owe too much.

b   We couldn't have foreseen this fall in demand so we shouldn't blame ourselves.

c   We should have placed less emphasis on improving skills, but now it's too late.

d   I couldn't have done anything about it, but I have to find a new job quickly.

e   Our leadership could have reacted differently and we would be much better placed now.

f   We couldn't have anticipated this failure, and despite all our efforts we have a cash-flow issue.

8 **Translate into English.**

1   Als ich anfing bei der Firma zu arbeiten, wurde ich nach Tarif bezahlt.

2   Wir haben letztes Jahr Verluste von knapp einer Milliarde Euro verzeichnet.

3   Die Firma hat letztes Jahr ungefähr 3,5 Millionen Einheiten verkauft.

4   Sie haben es nicht geschafft, genug Kapital für die Rettung der Firma aufzubringen.

5   Er hat die Rechnungen geprüft und dabei Unstimmigkeiten festgestellt.

Typical mistakes

1   They pay their managers **above the pay scale**. *(außertariflich)*
NOT   … *out of the tarif.*

2   a billion ≠ *eine Billion*
1,000,000,000 = one billion *(eine Milliarde)*
1,000,000,000,000 = one trillion *(eine Billion)*

3   They invested two **million** in the programme.
NOT   *They invested two ~~millions~~ …*

4   He has **raised** enough capital for the start-up.
NOT   *He has ~~brought up~~ enough capital …*

5   The accounts were **audited** by a firm in Bonn.
NOT   *The accounts were ~~proved~~ …*

Outside view

Anne Hodgson on … Speaking

Can you convince others by selling your strong points? No, says screenwriter guru Robert McKee, because your listeners will instinctively know that you are only giving them half of the story. Instead, build trust by telling a story that will persuade others to see the problem as you do.

Storylines

According to McKee, stories tell us about changes in our lives and why they happen. All stories follow a basic pattern. They start off showing a situation where life is more or less in balance. But then an event occurs that introduces a complication. The plot thickens as the protagonist tries to restore balance, working with whatever means available and taking action in the face of risks. In a personal story, that protagonist is you.

In a nutshell

Start your story like this: *That reminds me of when …* or *Something similar happened to me …* Bring it to life in a concrete setting with engaging details, using evocative words like *wonderful, unique* or *horrible*. Introduce both the objective challenge you rose to meet and your subjective reaction. Present the decisions and discoveries that you made in order to turn your listeners into participants in the story. Finally, be authentic … and know when to quit: a good rule of thumb for a purposeful story is to wind up quickly, saying *To make a long story short, …*

the plot thickens	die Handlung verdichtet sich
in a nutshell	kurz und bündig
evocative	aufrüttelnd
to wind up	etw zu Ende führen

6

Managing people

In this unit you will …

- debate the pros and cons of workplace conditions
- recount an HR incident
- practise giving feedback
- discuss assessment methods

Part A Discuss workplace conditions

▶ If you were thinking about leaving your company, what single most important factor would make you stay? If you could have one perk (non-monetary benefit) that would make your work more satisfying, what would it be? Survey your class. Do you have the same preferences?

1 👥 Draw lines between the words to find terms for work-related benefits. Which ones are monetary? Select three benefits that are important to you, and explain why.

paidholidayretirementfundsavingsplanhealthinsuranceworkerscompensationbuildingloansubsidylongservicebonus

commissionstockoptionsmealvoucherssubsidizedcanteencompanycartrainingopportunitiesparentalleave

2 🎧27-30 Listen to how these four employees describe their places of work. List what they like and dislike. Which of the workplaces do you find most appealing? Why?

1 Carla

2 Doris

3 Binh

4 Simon

Listen again and find the words the speakers use for the following:

1 a place where pre-school children can go during the day
2 work from home
3 pay that increases when you're successful at your job and decreases when you're not
4 additional pay connected to your employment contract
5 reductions in wages and salaries
6 lack of bureaucracy
7 formal assessments of how you work

Weighing the pros and cons

There are a lot of positive things to say … The downside is …
On the one hand … On the other hand …
To me, the biggest perk is …
On the whole / Generally …
So, for example / for instance …
Overall, … makes a big difference / makes up for a lot.

bullying: harassment of an individual (Not: ~~Mobbing~~)

3 Describe the pros and cons of working at your company or other companies you know well. Include terms from exercises 1 and 2.

4 🎧31 Listen to Carla's description of a conflict she had at work, then summarize using the keywords below.

team leader ➜ pregnant ➜ childcare ➜ 9 to 5 ➜ telework ➜ out of the loop ➜
behind her back ➜ bullying ➜ reprimand ➜ on probation ➜ breadwinner ➜ meeting

What is your impression of the overall situation? Have you heard of similar cases? What would you advise Carla to do?

5 How did Carla report on what happened? Listen again and complete these extracts.

1   I told my boss right away that I .... determined to keep the position

and .... childcare.

2   HR confirmed that I .... the right to return to the same job.

3   My boss asked me whether I .... that something

....

Now rephrase. What did the speakers actually say at the time?

Carla: I am determined …

6 Here are some things said at the meeting Carla scheduled. How did she later report them to her partner?

1   **Team:** 'We're working overtime because we can't reach you.'
    The team complained that they ...
2   **Team:** 'Do you know how many issues we have to decide on the spot every day?'
    They asked / wanted to know whether I ...
3   **Carla:** 'I need your support, because I have to do some of my work at home.'
4   **Carla:** 'Do you realize that you won't solve anything if you talk behind my back instead of to my face?'
5   **Carla:** 'We'll try defining new short-term targets for the team. From now on, we're going to monitor how well we can achieve them.'
6   **Carla:** 'While we can't solve all of our communication problems right away, my door will always be open.'

Finish telling Carla's story. Was Carla able to win the support of her team? Why (not)? Use the ideas below or some of your own to report what you think happened.

delegated more responsibility, settled for reduced contractual hours / pay?

re-evaluated team tasks and responsibilities, improved communication practices?

was unfairly dismissed, made a claim to the employment tribunal, negotiated a severance settlement?

7 Read the contrasting arguments below. Which do you agree with? Argue your opinion, supporting and justifying it based on your experience or knowledge.

1 Employees should not have the right to telework. Productivity may increase in the short term, but it may prevent teams from working effectively.

Teleworking is the key to maintaining a diversified workforce over time. The more diverse a company's workforce is, the more loyal and productive its employees will be.

2 Women with young children should not be team leaders. Teams need 'management by walking around', and young mothers are too busy for that.

Women with young children are natural team leaders. Their time management skills can help teams become more effective.

Did you know?
EU law guarantees:
'After taking parental leave, workers shall have the right to return to the same job. If that is not possible, the employer must offer them an equivalent or similar job consistent with their employment contract or employment relationship.'

Reporting what was said

'I'll have you transferred.'
He said (that) he would have me transferred.
'Have you heard the news?'
She asked me whether I had heard the news.
'She's not pulling her weight.'
Someone supposedly said that I wasn't pulling my weight.

Arguing your opinion

I feel / I think / I believe …
Personally, …
In other words, …
It seems clear that …
All things considered, …
I realize that …, but …
I am aware that … However, …
I understand that …
Nevertheless, …

Part B Give employee feedback

▶ What type of feedback do you give and receive at your place of work?

1 Hugh Johnson is going to his annual performance review next week, his first at Mores AG. Read this extract from an email that his boss, Doris Jelinek, has sent him. What has she asked him to do?

> You'll find attached (a) your **development plan** for the past year for review, along with (b) your **self-appraisal form**. Please take the time to review the objectives you set yourself in (a) and give yourself a score on each one for us to discuss. Your overall score must be in the permitted range of 80–120%. The final score will go into calculating your performance-based pay. Then make notes to prepare (c) your **new development plan** for the coming year, which we will finalize together.

Now read the development plan Hugh set up one year ago and some of the notes he has made for his self-appraisal. What had he planned to accomplish and how well does he feel he has succeeded?

DEVELOPMENT PLAN

M!

Goals	Measures	Due	Notes	
Assist team, HR Dept	meet w / boss to review progress	every 3 months	acquire basic key skills + knowledge	*100%*
Redesign staff induction procedure	present new model	March	1st update in 6 yrs; may be adopted	*100% (despite receiving no help from Beate!)*
Set up online counselling portal	Training: IT + video production Milestones: video + portal	May Sept	liaise w / counsellors, external partners / outsource	*great project 110%*
Draft anti-bullying policy	Survey, study, first draft	Dec	no precedent, must be reviewed by Legal Dept	

didn't work out – score?

1 In my role as a new hire, I successfully conducted a staff survey on the induction procedure to see how it could be improved.

2 The new counselling portal I introduced resulted in a 230% increase in enquiries about our services.

3 With respect to the anti-bullying policy, I have learned that getting enough responses to an internal survey requires effective collaboration across departments. This is an area I want to develop.

4 More training in German and a sparring partner to test my questionnaires would enable me to improve my surveys.

Assessing your performance

I was able to improve …
I succeeded in developing …
The changes I introduced resulted in …
I could benefit from …

2 Self-appraisal statements should be positive and honest. Here are four tips. Match them with statements from Hugh's self-appraisal above.

a Talk about performance in terms of concrete outcomes or standards.
b Acknowledge mistakes as areas for development.
c Don't criticize others; keep the focus on yourself.
d Ask for specific training and support to reach your aims.

Now use the tips to write statements about your own performance.

3 🔊32 **Read Doris's tips on giving feedback. Then listen to an extract from Hugh's performance review. Does Doris practise what she preaches?**

> Appraising employees
> 1) Focus on their behaviour, not their attitude.
> 2) Build trust, then cut straight to unresolved issues.
> 3) Be direct and concise. Make sure they understand.
> 4) Elicit their response and listen closely.
> 5) Let them propose a solution.

What points from the development plan do Doris and Hugh discuss?

4 **Doris uses communicative feedback skills to guide Hugh's responses. In which of the phrases a–e below does she …**

1 paraphrase to check and focus understanding?
2 summarize for analytical clarity?
3 ask open questions to get more information?
4 give positive feedback to create trust?
5 give evidence to stay concrete?

a I'm particularly impressed by the way you …

b So what you're saying is that …

c How do you see …?

d From what I'm hearing, there seem to be two main problems. … Is that correct?

e For example, when you … you could have … instead.

Can you complete the sentences? Listen again to check.

5 **Doris and Hugh used modifiers to fine-tune the message. Choose the most appropriate modifier and mark where it could go in the sentence.**

1 I've enjoyed being part of the team.   thoroughly / quite
2 I'm actually pleased with how things are going.   absolutely / quite
3 You had some good ideas.   really / thoroughly
4 I didn't get far with that.   too / rather
5 The case we had last month has proved you right.   clearly / really
6 Your people skills are first-rate.   absolutely / particularly

The results of the survey were **absolutely** fascinating.
I'm **particularly** pleased with this project.
Oh yes, well that was **rather a** disappointment.

6 👥 **Look at these observations a team leader has made about some members of the team. How can you make the feedback more constructive? Working with a partner, role-play the feedback sessions between the team leader and the people in question.**

Zoë is too quiet. It's hard to know what she is thinking. It would be interesting and helpful to hear her perspective more often.

Jake is always concerned about what others think. He doesn't focus on the most important priorities, since he's concerned with what he perceives upper management wants.

Mirko's presentation today was a mess. It was badly organized, and the print on the slides was too small. That's not how presentations are done.

Giving feedback

Overall, you've done a great job.
I would say …
It seems to me …
You might want to think about how …
It might have been better if …
Have you considered …?

➜ *Skills file, page 128*

Part C Profile competencies

■ **Did you know?**

Competence is the ability to do something, especially as measured against a standard. In HR, **a competency** is the measurable or observable set of knowledge, skills, abilities, attitudes and behaviours critical to a successful job.

▶ What specific skills and soft skills do you need to do your job well? What can you learn from people who are particularly good at what you do?

❶ Read the interview below and answer these questions.

1 What assessment methods (psychometric tests, standardized exams, interviews, etc.) are employed by STEIN12 MANAGER SICHTEN?
2 How does the consultancy determine what competencies to assess?
3 What do they measure performance against?
4 How can the candidates influence the assessment?

Successful Business: In conversation with Franz-Josef Nuß

Fitting the man – or the woman – to the job

HR can be a partner in personal career development. Yet firms are under pressure to reduce HR costs. How can these interests be reconciled? We asked Franz-Josef Nuß, Managing Director and owner of STEIN12 MANAGER SICHTEN, how their integrated HR audit works.

Franz-Josef Nuß, Managing Director, STEIN12 MANAGER SICHTEN, www.stein12.de

Successful Business: How can an external partner support HR in such a sensitive matter?

Franz-Josef Nuß: Our outside perspective is actually an enormous advantage. We're not entangled in internal relationships, so we can hold up an unbiased mirror and benchmark in-house candidates against the unified, industry-wide standards required in global markets. At the same time, we assess candidates using the corporate competency model developed by that specific company and focussing on the skills and behaviours that the company finds most valuable. So, assessing management competency might include systems thinking and emotional intelligence as well as influencing and negotiation skills. One of our recent clients defined 'entrepreneurial competency' as the key asset that their managers were supposed to have; they felt managers at their company should be more like independent entrepreneurs.

SB: What happens in an assessment?

FN: Every management audit includes a two-hour personal interview with two consultants. We combine it with a psychometric test that measures the value and the risks connected with each candidate. Other modules include a business case team simulation and a critical incident presentation. Or, in the 'Job-Man Fitting', first the candidate profiles the type of competencies required in his or her job, then our consultants assess the degree to which the candidate has those competencies, and the results – the candidate's self-profile and the assessment by the consultants – are contrasted in a diagram. Since each of the eight modules measures a different aspect, the aggregate result, compiled in an extensive report, is information-rich and quite reliable.

SB: Do you brief the candidate on his or her development potential afterwards?

FN: Absolutely. In the feedback session we go through the document, and try to make sure the candidate really gets the message. It's not always easy to get the candidate to accept the results, so we present the most obvious critical points, and try to convince the candidate to call for action. Then we ask: Which strengths do you need to focus on, and which critical areas should you develop?

SB: Is it possible to prepare for this audit?

FN: Yes, by reflecting on yourself. The worst thing you can do is to say what you think you are expected to say. There is no right or wrong. So ask yourself: What have I done in the past few years, and why and how? A key question is: How am I different from others around me, what makes me special? The better people know themselves, the easier it will be for them to be completely authentic in the audit. An authentic manner is really all that is called for. ▶ SB

2 Study the two 'Job-man fitting' diagrams below. Each profiles a candidate for the position of General Manager. Look at the key competencies and qualities (e.g. Leader / Elitism). Which do you think a manager needs? Which does an administrator need? Whose self-image (blue) most closely matches the assessment (green)?

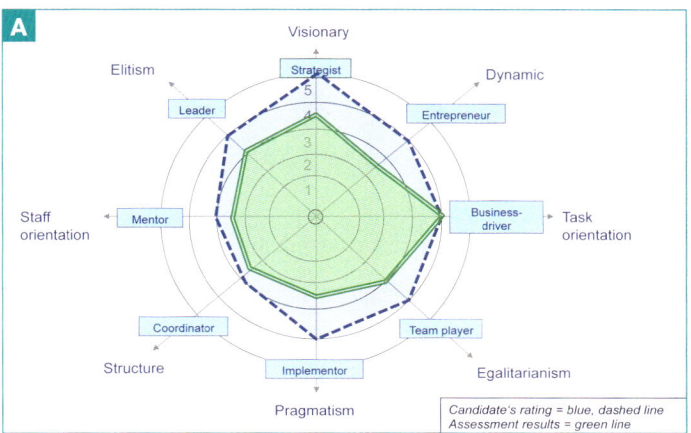

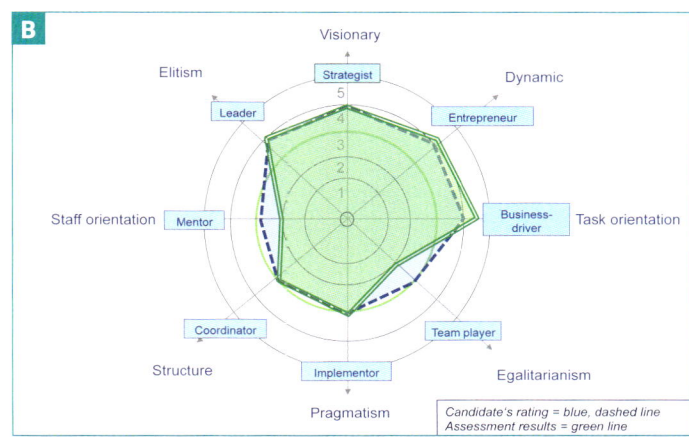

3 Look at these excerpts from a report describing one of the above candidates. First, match each sentence to the competency it describes (a–d). Then, decide which diagram the report refers to.

1 Ms Lin's own rating compared to the assessment results highlights her rather exaggerated perception of her managerial competencies.

2 Although she has not been in a leadership role for very long, she clearly stakes a claim to power.

3 Ms Lin can look back on many years of experience as a marketing expert. She has, however, done very little for her further education.

4 For all her highly infectious enthusiasm, she obviously could not get the others on board. She was far too focussed on herself to be willing or able to pay attention to her teammates.

a Professional / Methodological competency (Educational background, abilities?)

b Leadership competency (Does he / she want to lead, pursue goals?)

c Social competency (Good with people, convincing in the interview?)

d Job-Man Fitting (How well does self-image match assessment?)

4 Now use notes on Mr Bendar, the second profiled candidate, to formulate statements on his competencies. Use softeners and intensifiers where appropriate.

1 **Professional / Methodological:** good background, ideal combination technical knowledge studies in engineering + commercial expertise (finance, controlling, etc.), open to new ideas, intellectually inquisitive, prefers a challenge over routine work

2 **Leadership:** interest in people, happy to lead, pragmatic, has set his sights on taking on a general management role

3 **Social:** nervous in the audit, 'eager to please', wanted to do a good job, likeable, wins others through enthusiasm, energy, sparkling sense of humour, too enthusiastic, forgets to listen – nobody else gets a chance; too energetic, gets ahead of himself

4 **Job-Man Fitting:** degree of convergence self-image and assessment! top values for managerial skills

5 Rate yourself and describe your own competencies.

Food for thought

One of the partners in your company shares your values. The other doesn't, but is a genius.
Whom do you trust more?

1 **Match the collocations, then use them to complete the sentences below.**

> red   heavy   performance   voucher   evaluation   tape
>
> meal   parental   dress   code   workload   pay
>
> performance-based   retirement   fund   leave

1 My .... is due soon. Luckily, I've met most of my targets.

2 How long is .... in your country? Over here you only have six months to stay home with your child.

3 He has an extremely .... now because a huge order has just come in.

4 I need to go to lunch now but I can't find my ....

5 They don't have a formal .... here: just wear something smart but casual.

6 I hate all this bureaucracy! Can't we somehow just cut through the ....?

7 Do you offer .... or just a basic salary?

8 I'm still a bit too young to worry about the size of the ....!

Reporting what was said: reported speech

1 'I did my traineeship here.'
He said (that) he **had done** his traineeship there.
'I'm seeing Janet next Thursday and will discuss things with her then.'
She told me that she **was seeing** Janet the following Thursday and **would discuss** things with her then.
'They had left the office by ten o'clock.'
She explained that they **had left** the office by ten o'clock.

2 'She says that Tom was late with his last report.'
(Not: ~~had been~~)
They've noticed that we prefer cash. (Not: ~~preferred~~)

3 I said that it's fine like that. (Or: it was)
She pointed out that the accounts **are** always **processed** this way. (Or: were always processed)

4 'Have you worked for this company?'
They asked me if / whether I **had worked** for that company.
'When will you be finished?'
She asked me when **I would** be finished.
(Not: ... ~~when would I be finished~~)

We use **reported speech** to report what was said earlier. Reporting verbs include not only *say, tell (sb)* or *ask (sb),* but also *explain, announce, point out, advise, complain, think, wonder, etc.*

When the reporting verb is in the past tense *(he said that),* the verbs in **reported speech** change tense, e. g.:
'I go' – he said that he went;
'I went' – he said that he had gone;
'I'll go' – he said that he would go.
Note that there is no change with the past perfect and modal verbs like *might* and *could* (**1**).

Sometimes other changes are necessary, e. g.:
next Thursday – the following Thursday
this company – that company
with me – with him

There is no change in tense when you use a reporting verb in a present tense *(I hear / I've heard)* (**2**).

Some speakers do not shift the tense of the verb in informal communications or if the topic being reported still holds true at the time of reporting (**3**).

To report on yes / no questions use *ask sb if / whether* (not *that*). When reporting on questions with *who, where,* etc., note the change in word order (**4**).

2 Complete this text on giving feedback using these verbs.

announce · ask · complain · explain · insist · not apologize · promise · tell

I attended an interesting workshop last week on how to give feedback effectively. Tom, the workshop leader,

..................................¹ that feedback should be given as soon as possible; he was 100 % certain on that point.

A woman in the group ....² why he thought it was so important. He ....³ to us that

feedback could only be truly effective when delivered early. He ....⁴ us that most people can't remember

their experiences in detail for longer than 24 hours! He ....⁵ that he would prove it to us and

..........................⁶ that he would give us all a memory test the following day, which he did. Most of us failed

miserably and we ....⁷ that it was unfair because the test had had over 20 questions, but Tom

......................................⁸ for making it so long. He merely smiled and thanked us for the immediate feedback!

3 A few months ago you interviewed a woman who wanted a job at your company and made a note of what was said. Read through your notes, then complete the sentences about the interview using reported speech with *said*, *asked* and *told*.

Do you have any childcare facilities?

Can I start next month?

How often do you have a performance evaluation in your department?

I have never worked in advertising.

I didn't enjoy my last job because it wasn't very challenging.

Will I get a company car?

Last year we handled nine major projects.

1 She doesn't have a job at the moment and ..asked me whether she could start the following month..........

2 She has a two-year-old and so she ....
....

3 We had been very busy back then. I ....
....

4 I was speaking about possibilities for promotion and she ....
....

5 I asked about her previous experience in that branch and she ....
....

6 She wasn't very enthusiastic about her previous employer. She ....
....

7 Her jeep had just broken down, so she ....

Fine-tuning the message: adverbs

1 Your sense of timing is **absolutely** amazing. (Not: absolute amazing)
The new policy on bullying has been **remarkably** effective.
The staff does their job **extremely** well.

2 Our unexpected success in the USA last year was **quite** / **rather** surprising.

3 It was **rather a** surprise / **quite a** shock to our competitors. (Not: so a shock)
His performance is **a bit of** / **rather a** disappointment.

You can use adverbs to modify adjectives and other adverbs to fine-tune your message (**1**).

Words like *rather (a), quite (a)* can also be used as softeners or intensifiers (**2**).

Note that when you modify a noun, you need to use *a* or *an* (**3**).

> Quite can also mean 'completely'.
> • I quite agree!

4 Complete this dialogue about a performance review with words from the box. You will need to change some of them into adverbs.

> absolute · dependent · impressive · rather a(n) · remarkable · vast

Jill: Mike, I'm ....¹ thrilled with how the new portal you introduced has generated so many inquiries.

Mike: Thanks Jill. The number of inquiries has increased ....² quickly, hasn't it?

Jill: Yes, indeed. I must admit it was ....³ surprise for all concerned. What do you think you learned from the project?

Mike: Well firstly, that we are heavily ....⁴ on our online presence even more so than we thought. And secondly, I'm sure we can do ....⁵ better in the future.

Jill: Do you have any suggestions on how?

Mike: Sure, by focusing more on our customers' feedback, I think we can expect an immensely ....⁶ result by next year.

5 Complete the statements and questions from an appraisal by matching the sentence halves.

1 From what I'm hearing, it

2 Coming back to your assessment, you

3 I see what you

4 What do you

5 The projects I was involved in

6 I'm particularly

a were remarkably interesting and I learnt a lot.

b sounds like you are facing two main problems.

c impressed by your people skills.

d might want to rethink your approach to time management.

e mean, but I'm not sure how we can implement the changes.

f imagine we could do then?

Now match the sentences to a description.

A Build trust then cut straight to unresolved issues.
B Being positive to create trust
C Politely elicit a response.

D Paraphrasing to check and focus understanding
E Voicing constructive criticism
F Giving background on previous experience

6 **Translate into English.**

1 Ihren letzten Job hat sie gekündigt, weil ihre Vorgesetzte sie gemobbt hat.
2 Sie hat sich direkt nach dem Studium selbstständig gemacht und ist jetzt eine erfolgreiche Unternehmerin.
3 Biochemie hat mich immer interessiert. Es ist so ein spannendes Forschungsgebiet.
4 Ich mache mir Sorgen um die Kosten.
5 Das betrifft besonders die neue Produktreihe, die zurzeit in der Entwicklung ist.

Typical mistakes

1 She was **bullied** at work.
   NOT   *She was ~~mobbed~~ at work.*
2 He started out as an **entrepreneur**.
   NOT   *… as an ~~undertaker~~.*
3 This is **such an** interesting job.
   NOT   *This is ~~so an~~ interesting job.*
4 Note the differences:
   I am **concerned about** the issue. *(besorgt um)*
   I am **concerned with** the issue. *(involviert mit)*
   This **concerns** the organization. *(betrifft)*

Outside view

Anne Hodgson on … Power

The personal and team assistants I teach often tell me that they are treated poorly by some of their boss's foreign business partners. These callers and visitors, they say, don't seem to understand that they are in fact key coordinators and fail to show them the necessary respect.

Culture clash

Two separate issues play into this clash of business cultures. First of all, foreign visitors may not recognize the higher status the assistant enjoys in German companies, compared to assistants back home. Overall, subordinates may be more willing to submit to authority there, displaying something Dutch sociologist Geert Hofstede has referred to as greater 'power distance'. Secondly, foreigners may not appreciate the degree to which using official channels, a guarantee of transparency and stability, is part of the German business culture. By implicit agreement, the assistant is the first stop on the way to the boss.

How should you handle such a situation? Don't take it personally. Apologize first, because, after all, you are dictating rules your foreign visitor may not be accustomed to: *I'm sorry, but unfortunately* … Then explain the unwritten rules of the game politely, e.g. *The way we usually handle that here is* … and *I don't know whether Ms X has told you, but* … If something is officially off-limits, make sure that is absolutely clear, and use we, not I, to underscore that this is corporate policy: *I'm afraid we're not authorized to do that. I'm sorry.*

Making sure everyone knows and plays by the same rules is a major part of cross-cultural teamwork, a huge challenge to HR and, in the final account, the responsibility of the team leader. So an assistant who can provide real support towards this end can earn the boss's grateful trust.

off-limits	verboten
to underscore	unterstreichen
in the final account	letzten Endes

Business file 3

- discuss bonuses and benefits
- put forward a suggestion and argue your opinion
- relate how an agreement was reached

 ## An interdepartmental meeting

1 Read the memo from the management of Naxos AG. What is the issue? What are the department representatives supposed to do?

To all Department Representatives:

As you know, Naxos AG has gone through a very difficult year. Preliminary financial results have revealed a sharp decline in both the number of transactions per day and the average value of each transaction as compared to last year. After enjoying increases in sales and profits for over 20 years, we must now face the reality that, as a result of the economic crisis, we are going to miss our targets.

Our current remuneration policy is quite clear: If employees have met their individual performance targets and if the departments have met theirs, bonuses are paid out only if company growth targets are also met. Therefore, the Management Board has announced that this will be the first year since the bonus system was introduced 14 years ago that no one will be awarded a bonus.

This is cause for great concern. Many employees have viewed the bonuses as a part of their salary. For many, the bonus package adds one to two months' salary to the annual pay package, depending on length of service. We are committed to retaining talent and incentivizing our staff, and are therefore seeking a solution to reintroduce bonus payments as of next year.

In the coming week, Remuneration Officer Sunil Gupta will be meeting with you to discuss short-term solutions for alternative rewards to soften the edge this year and, more long-term, for ways to overhaul the bonus system so that bonus payments can be reintroduced next year. Please email Mr Gupta your suggestions ahead of the meeting next Thursday at gupta_s@naxos.com.

2 🎧 33 As the representative of your department, you are attending the meeting called by Sunil Gupta. Listen to Sunil present the situation, and fill in the missing words and figures on the handout below.

How can we incentivize our staff?

1 **To replace bonus payments this year:**
 1 ....[1] non-cash rewards like special vouchers and recognition
 2 ....[2] rewards for a job well done, e.g. training
 3 ....[3] stock options

2 **To improve the bonus system in the long term:**
 1 ....[4] some staff from the bonus system, as ....[5] % of companies that pay bonuses do

2 ....[6] oversight: the permitted range for bonuses is ....[7] %, but the average bonus is currently ....[8] %.

3 ....[9] individual performance ratings, leave choice entirely to manager – as ....[10] % of companies do

4 ....[11] non-performance related bonuses and replace through incentives

5 ....[12] non-essential positions

3 Do a role-play or a simulation of a meeting in which you must evaluate suggestions and reach agreement.

1   In groups of up to six, choose **Option 1** (a role-play based on the scenario in exercises 1 and 2) or **Option 2** (a simulation using your own work situation or ideas).

Option 1

Look again at the handout and decide which suggestion(s) you want to argue for at the meeting. Then choose a role (A–F) and be prepared to present the information in your file at the start of the discussion. Review phrases from Units 5 and 6 and the box below to help you prepare.

→ *Partner A (Sunil Gupta): file 28, page 109*
→ *Partner B (R&D): file 12, page 102*
→ *Partner C (HR): file 21, page 106*
→ *Partner D (Finance): file 25, page 108*
→ *Partner E (Sales): file 35, page 112*
→ *Partner F (Marketing): file 30, page 110*

Option 2

Come up with your own scenario in which you have to put forward your ideas and argue your opinion. Find an issue involving HR or Finance, e.g. a meeting to discuss cutting HR expenditures.

What's the situation? ⟶ Who's involved? ⟶ What vocabulary / phrases do you need?

What is the problem you need to solve? Write a short agenda outlining the issue, then come up with your own suggestion and arguments in support of your position.

Are you members of a team or a project? Are you from one or several departments? Who is going to run the meeting?

Review phrases from Units 5 and 6 and the box below to help you prepare.

2   Now hold the meeting.

4 Looking back on this meeting weeks later, tell the story (orally or in writing) of how and why you reached the agreement you did. Use phrases from below to relate what happened.

Reaching agreement at a meeting	Relating what happened
Putting forward your suggestion / argument	**Setting the scene**
There are a number of reasons why I think we should …	Back when we were …, we started off by …
The first / second / … reason / point is …	We were asked to bear … in mind.
Therefore, I think / feel / believe …	We were about to try … but then we remembered …
Adding arguments	**Developing the conflict**
What's more … Not only that …	After quite a bit of back and forth, …
If we don't …, then … After all, …	I was absolutely convinced that …
Disagreeing and standing your ground	**Describing the climax and resolution**
Let's get back to the real issue here …	Things really came to a head when we …
I don't really see why we can't …	That's when someone suggested …
I would have a bit of a problem with that.	Not only did we find …, we also solved …
Seeking and expressing agreement	**Analysing with hindsight**
How do you feel about …?	If we had …, we probably would have …
I could see that working.	We could have … but then we would have …

7 Meeting demand

Part A Market products and services

In this unit you will …

- contrast marketing practices
- practise networking
- discuss intellectual property issues
- handle formal correspondence
- discuss brands and social marketing

▶ What do you need to consider when marketing a product or service? Select a product you know well, and explain how it is marketed to consumers or to other businesses using the 4 Ps.

product	price	place	promotion
design, quality, features, image, branding, warranty, packaging, …	list price, discounts, credit terms, terms of payment, vouchers, …	market segment, distribution channels, points of sale, …	advertising, PR, sales promotion, social media, trade shows, …

1 🎧34 Engineer Udo Beier is at a trade fair having lunch and 'talking shop' with Pat Baldwin, a sales rep for a power tool company. Listen to the first part of the conversation. What does Udo do, and what did his father do?

Speculate about the differences there might be in the way the two men made or make purchasing decisions. Consider these aspects:

product quality · brand loyalty · price structure · compliance · distribution channels · points of sale · advertising

2 🎧35 Now listen to the rest of the conversation and answer these questions.

1 Were you right about the differences? How have the way purchasing decisions are made changed between then and now?
2 What liberties did Udo's father have as a buyer that Udo does not have?
3 What are the challenges for a company entering this market?

3 👥 Contrast the word pairs below. (The words on the left are from the conversation.) How do the words differ in meaning?

1 conscientious / conscious
2 warranty / guarantee
3 detrimental / instrumental
4 deficiencies / deficits
5 satisfactory / satisfying

6 on the spot / on the site
7 exacting / exact
8 cut corners / cut costs
9 priceless / free
10 flimsy / cheap

4 Think of how a product or service you know used to be marketed and how it is marketed now. Tell the story from the perspective of the buyer or the seller. What has changed?

Note that 'would' (like 'used to') can be used to talk about typical behaviours in the past.

The internet has changed everything. We used to broadcast information about our products, but now it's much more about building a dialogue..

I used to go to bookshops and I would stay there for hours, but now I only ever buy books at the train station.

5 Compare sentences A and B. What words have been left out or moved to make sentence B more succinct?

A   You won't get that kind of service, which is great and has been tailored to your needs, from a discounter who operates online and who is just interested in making one sale.

B   You won't get that kind of great service tailored to your needs from an online discounter just interested in making one sale.

Now make these sentences more succinct in a similar way.

1   The company that has just been selected to handle the sales promotion which was prepared by the marketing department is starting next week.

2   The sales reps have to convince managers who are responsible for decisions but who are not interested in the technology.

3   These tools have been introduced recently, but they don't have the durability and quality that we require.

6 👥 You have been invited to pitch your product or service to win the Sustainable Living Products and Services Award and are meeting with your co-competitors at a B2B speed-networking event to practise your pitch. Make sure your product or service complies with the award criteria below, then follow steps 1–3.

1   Divide the class into two equal groups of Product Developers and Service Providers. Working alone, take 10 minutes to write down everything you know about your product or service. Complete this sentence: *People used to have to … but now with our product / service they can … .* Then prepare a set of business cards with your name and the name of your product or service.

Sustainable Living Award

How does your service or product promote sustainability? Does it:

1   improve health and well-being (e.g. nutrition, health care)?

2   reduce environmental hazards (e.g. water scarcity, waste)?

3   enhance livelihoods (e.g. sustainable sourcing, fair working conditions)?

2   Meet for the B2B speed-networking event. Product Developers pair up with Service Providers. Sitting in pairs, each of you has two minutes to pitch to the other. When you both have completed your pitches, exchange business cards. Product Developers move on to a new Service Provider, and both pitch again.

3   After the event, decide which of the contacts was most interesting in connection with your own product or service. As a group, select the three best products and services, and award the winners.

7 👥 Write a 100-word description of how your product or service, or one of the winning products or services in your contest, meets the criteria of the Sustainable Living Award.

Adding information succinctly

We might have a **recently developed** tool **perfect for a specific job**.

Careful:
A responsible person is not always the person responsible, and the parts used are not automatically used parts!

■ **Did you know?**

Speed networking – a trend that first surfaced in the UK around 2004 – is an effective way of making new business contacts. Typically, people have up to five minutes to talk to another participant and exchange contact details before a buzzer signals them to move on to the next person in the group.

Speed networking

For effective speed networking, polish your socializing and pitching skills.

→ *Skills file, pages 129 and 130*

Part B   Protect brands

▶ **Discuss with a partner.**

- What kinds of products are typically available as counterfeits, and where?
- What damage is caused by the sale of these articles, and to whom?
- What aspects of your brand – for example, a design, an idea or a technology – is protected at your company?

1 Read about the four intellectual property cases below and say which company …

1 alleged that a competitor's product, and not just its packaging, infringed its trademark.
2 opened the door to widespread copyright infringement and cut artists out of royalties.
3 tried to protect its logo from being used by someone with very different products.
4 was ordered to temporarily stop production for the alleged use of patented technology.

How did the disputes affect both parties involved? Do you know of any similar cases in the news? Describe what happened and discuss who you think was in the right.

Disrupting the industry

Napster introduced a system that allowed music fans to share MP3 files for free. Not only did this undermine the music industry's business model, it also initially cut out royalties for artists. Within a few years the site was shut down for copyright infringement. Today, cloud-based file-sharing has become a part of 21st century life.

Gold bunny wars

Only rarely does an SME win a legal battle against an industry giant. After 12 years in court, Swiss chocolate maker Lindt lost its final appeal to trademark its gold foil wrapped chocolate Easter bunny. Family-run Confiserie Riegelein contested the claim and was able to show that a seated gold bunny had been a firm part of their offering for at least half a century – and won the case.

Race for innovation

In a race to the 2012 Olympics, Adidas introduced 'Primeknit' as 'a first-of-its-kind running shoe' five months after Nike had unveiled its nearly identical 'Flyknit' technology. Nike claimed Adidas had infringed their patent, and Adidas was ordered to cease production of their 'Primeknit' footwear in Germany. Although Adidas was able to settle the claim after proving that they had been using the technology for 70 years, Nike had already won in terms of sales and sponsorship volume. In 2013, *Fast Company* designated Nike 'The World's Most Innovative Company'.

Apfelkind vs. Apple

No sooner had Christin Römer, the owner of a café in Bonn, filed a trademark application for her company logo showing a child's face within a red apple than she received a letter from Apple asking her to withdraw the application, since customers could potentially confuse the two logos in online marketing. But she succeeded where the Beatles failed: she stood her ground, and after two years of legal correspondence, won the right to use her very own apple trademark.

Adding emphasis

Not only did this undermine the business model, it **also** …
No sooner had she filed **than** she received …
Under no circumstances should you ignore …
Never before have we seen so many …

2 Find words in the texts that fit these definitions.

1 to say something without proof
2 to formally question a decision
3 to violate the law or the rights of another
4 to reach an agreement
5 to remain firm and not give up
6 to interrupt something or prevent it from continuing

3 Compare these two sentences. What is emphasized in the second one?

An SME rarely wins a legal battle against an industry giant.
Only rarely does an SME win a legal battle against an industry giant.

4 Vera Kuhl is the office manager at Wholly Divine Chocolates, a small 'fair trade' charity located in Germany and managed by a priest called Father Steven. Read the letter she has received and answer the questions.

1 What is the purpose of the letter?
2 Who exactly is it addressed to?
3 What kind of action does it require, and by when?
4 What are the consequences of not complying?

Dear Sir or Madam

We are writing on behalf of our client, Catchoo. It has come to our attention that you have been marketing chocolates through your website www.whollydivine.com under the name "Chocolate Advent Calendar" using the colour Purple 365. We wish to notify you that Catchoo is the rightful owner of the trademark Purple 365 under European law. Catchoo insists on the sole use of its trademark to ensure that its European customers are not under the assumption that other similar products are in fact produced by Catchoo. Your use thereof infringes upon our client's trademark. Accordingly, you are hereby directed to

CEASE AND DESIST ALL TRADEMARK INFRINGEMENT

We demand that you immediately (A) cease and desist from the use of Purple 365 and (B) provide us with written assurance within ten (10) days that you will immediately withdraw from sale any product or packaging using Purple 365. Please sign and return the attached Agreement to us within ten (10) days. Should you fail to comply, Catchoo is entitled to seek monetary damages and equitable remedies.

Yours faithfully

■ Did you know?

Several companies have successfully registered the use of a colour as their trademark, including Milka (lilac for chocolates) and Deutsche Telekom (magenta). A colour can only be trademarked if the owner can prove that it has a 'distinctive character' strongly associated with the product that sets it apart from others in its class.

5 Vera is meeting Father Steven to discuss the letter. Look at these quotes from the meeting and explain what they mean. Do you think Vera and Father Steven have the situation under control?

1 We have a problem on our hands.
2 We're on exceedingly dodgy ground.
3 I don't quite know what's at stake.
4 I haven't the foggiest idea.
5 Our hands are tied.
6 Catchoo would see right through that.
7 We were acting in good faith.
8 Should we just play for time?

🔊36 Now listen to the conversation. What does Vera need to tell Robert Jameson, the charity's lawyer, and what questions do you think she should ask?

6 Robert gets Vera's text message and sends her this response. Use his tips and the phrases from the box to write Vera's letter for her.

> Lots of formal errors. They don't state when + where trademark was registered, or give title no. or list of goods and services covered. Pls write short letter + query those details! Don't acknowledge responsibility or make promises. Ask for extension of 1 wk. Refer to me. If they send you an injunction – i.e. an order to stop production + sales immediately – take website offline. Best, Robert

7 What areas of business life do you think require strict protection of intellectual property, and where do you think other interests are more important? Why?

Writing formal letters

We hereby confirm receipt of your … dated …
We were surprised to receive …
We were unaware of any such …
We have been advised by our legal department to ask for clarification regarding …
Could you kindly inform us when and where …?
We shall have our lawyer look into the matter upon his return on (date).

Part C Control the image

▶ Who are your customers and clients? Is your brand known outside a specialized segment? Does the brand have fans? If so, what do they like about it?

1 Match the characteristics below on the left with their opposites on the right. Which brands do you connect with each image?

1 spontaneous, high energy	a corporate, professional
2 personable, friendly	b established, tried and tested
3 contemporary	c careful, planned
4 cutting edge, novel	d traditional, classic
5 accessible to all	e scientific, high tech
6 crafted, authentic	f upscale, exclusive

■ **Did you know?**

Not everything can or should be translated. Two automotive brands use German slogans in their international ads: Audi – *Vorsprung durch Technik* and VW – *Das Auto*.

2 Many companies outline their brand's essence and values in three key characteristics, for example:

Audi: sporty, progressive, sophisticated

VW: innovative, offering enduring value, responsible

What three characteristics would you use to describe your brand? Create a short brand presentation.

3 Touchpoints are a company's customer contact points. Present how a company you know well communicates its brand image at each touchpoint. Consider:

1 the visual presentation (logo, corporate colours, graphic style, typefaces)
2 the brand 'voice' (slogans, buzzwords, copywriting tone, letter and email style)

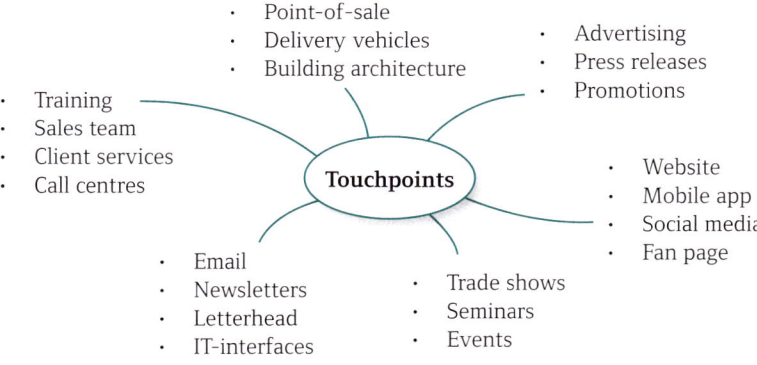

· Point-of-sale
· Delivery vehicles
· Building architecture

· Advertising
· Press releases
· Promotions

· Training
· Sales team
· Client services
· Call centres

Touchpoints

· Website
· Mobile app
· Social media
· Fan page

· Email
· Newsletters
· Letterhead
· IT-interfaces

· Trade shows
· Seminars
· Events

At trade shows we feature our corporate colour on details like … so the overall effect is …

The look and feel of our mobile app is a little different from … because its purpose is …

Every email contains an extensive footer with … which allows our customers to …

4 Companies alone do not control the brand; customers also have a major impact thanks to social media, fan pages, reviews and protests. Read the case study below, then answer these questions.

1 Why did social media experts criticize Ferrero for its actions?
2 How did the company get the tone wrong in its communications?

Nutella Exemplifies How Not to Use Social Media

Cameron Scott on May 21, 2013 6:53 PM

Facing an online revolt, Ferrero, the company that makes Nutella, rescinded a cease-and-desist letter it had sent to the organizer of World Nutella Day, an online event to celebrate the delicious chocolate-hazelnut spread.

"I'm relieved to say there's been a positive resolution to the situation. Ferrero employees reached out to me directly after I had posted my fan letter online and sent my formal reply to their C&D [cease-and-desist letter]. They were very gracious and supportive and we were able to have a productive discussion about World Nutella Day living on for the fans, which is the whole point," said the event's organizer Sara Rosso.

But even in its Facebook post apologizing for the fiasco, Ferrero still showed a lack of social grace.

"The case arose from a routine brand defense procedure that was activated as a result of some misuse of the Nutella brand on the fan page," the post said.

The case is what Brian Solis, author of *What's the Future of Business*, would call a classic example of a company not keeping up with the changes social media have brought to marketing. Brands need to create a unified experience around their brand that applies regardless of how consumers first learn about it, the

book argues. Many might learn about Nutella through World Nutella Day, and Nutella surely doesn't want to be a brand with phrases like "cease-and-desist order" and "routine brand defense procedure" associated with it.

Social media users stepped in to educate Ferrero on marketing in the social age after Rosso said on her blog that she may have to cancel World Nutella Day in 2014.

"Unbelievable – who made the idiotic decision to send a cease and desist letter to Sara Rosso, who did a better job of promoting your product than your company does??," Kim Trujillo posted on Nutella's Facebook page, which boasts 17 million fans.

"I always bought an extra jar to celebrate Nutella Day. After hearing about cease & desist letter sent to your 'superfan' Sara Rosso, I plan to stop buying. Should have given her a nice promotion, like Free Nutella for Year, not nasty lawyer letter. Don't you want to support efforts to get customers to buy your product?" asked Karen Genberg Larosa.

The company appears to have sort of gotten it.

"Ferrero considers itself fortunate to have such devoted and loyal fans of its Nutella spread, like Sara Rosso," it said in its Facebook post.

5 👥 Discuss: How do brand recommendations shared by your loyal customers and fans differ from the advertising generated by your company? Perform a SWOT analysis, then present the results of your analysis to another group.

➡ *SWOT analysis: skills file, page 131*

Strengths
The positive attributes within your control: What do you do well? What advantages do you have? How can you use them more effectively?

Weaknesses
The factors within your control that detract from your competitive edge: How can you enhance these areas to compete with your best competitor?

Opportunities
External factors in your market or in the environment providing potential benefit: What opportunities can you benefit from?

Threats
Potential hazards beyond your control. What factors must you watch, and what contingency plans are required?

Food for thought
Which recommendations do you prefer: those you get from your peers, friends and family, or those given by management gurus and consumer reports?

Adding information succinctly: reduced relative clauses

1 We have a tool ~~that is~~ **perfect for the job**.
We have a **perfect** tool **for the job**.

2 Customers **buying** high quality tools expect to pay more.
(Instead of: Customers who buy …)
Brands **moving** down market were examined.
(Instead of: Brands that moved …)
The supplier **presenting** that item was new.
(Instead of: The supplier that was presenting …)

3 The tools **purchased** were defective.
(Instead of: The tools that had been purchased …)
The pitch **made** persuaded us.
(Instead of: The pitch that was made …)

4 The **newly purchased** tools were defective.
Not: ~~The tools newly purchased~~ …

In reduced relative clauses we leave out the relative pronoun (*who*, *which*, *that*) and verb. Adjectives (such as *available*, *possible*) can be placed either before or after the noun (**1**).

The relative pronoun and verb can often be replaced by a participle. Notice that active tenses change to the present participle (*-ing*) (**2**) and passive tenses change to the past participle (*-ed*, or an irregular form) (**3**).

When we modify the past participle with an adverb, the adverbial phrase (e.g. *newly purchased*) must be placed before the noun (**4**).

① **Reduce these phrases using a present participle, a past participle or an adjective, and place them in a suitable sentence.**

> that is tailored to · ~~that was filed~~ · that was unavailable · which have approached · who wants to · who was negotiating · who was responsible for · who work

1 Have you heard about the claim ….*filed*…. against us last week?

2 Do you think the companies ……………………………………………………… us can really offer us a service …………………………………… our needs?

3 I tried to get through to the person …………………………………… copyright law but of course he was the only one …………………………………… at that time.

4 I thought the man …………………………………… the deal was violating some rules and regulations.

5 Anyone …………………………………… sell anything here must first convince the staff …………………………… in the legal department.

② **Make the sentences below more succinct. The first one has been done for you.**

1 I recommend that you order your products from this company, which has been recently established and which supplies goods that have been produced to the highest standards.

..*I recommend that you order your products from this recently established company which*…………..
..*supplies goods produced to the highest standards.*……………………………………………………………

2 We offer software packages which are highly reliable and provide innovative solutions that are needed in specialist branches such as yours.

………

………

3 I can show you some online catalogues that are illustrated in a beautiful way and which are produced in-house and showcase our product lines that are most popular.

....

....

4 They told me about some products that have been recently developed and which appeal to target groups that are highly attractive.

....

....

❸ **Test yourself: Tick the statement that most emphasizes the speaker's surprise.**

A ☐ We were not informed at any point of the change in policy.
B ☐ At no point were we informed of the change in policy.
C ☐ We were not informed of the change in policy.

Adding emphasis using inverted word order

Not only did we give a great pitch, (**but**) we also won the contract!
Not: ~~Not only we gave a great pitch …~~
Never before had they been able to settle more promptly.
In no way should this be taken as an invitation.
Under no circumstances are you to contest the claim.
Rarely does this sort of thing happen.
No sooner had he made the phone call **than** he received an offer.

Expressions that have a restrictive or negative meaning (e.g. *not only … but also, never before, in no way, under no circumstances, rarely*) can be used at the beginning of a sentence if we want to add emphasis, especially if what we are talking about is surprising or unexpected. Whenever these expressions start a sentence, inversion is necessary.

❹ **Give the sentences below more emphasis by rewriting them using appropriate expressions from the box and inverted word order.**

in no way · never before · no sooner · not only · rarely · under no circumstances

1 You shouldn't file charges whatever happens.

....

2 People rarely confuse the two logos.

....

3 The company accused us of copyright infringement as soon as we launched the product.

....

4 We had never been ordered to cease production before that.

....

5 We simply can't agree to any of your demands.

....

6 This isn't just a bad idea; it's probably also illegal.

....

5 **Select the appropriate word to complete the sentences below.**

1 We have had no complaints. These parts aren't as   cheap / flimsy   as they used to be.

2 How might diversification be   detrimental / instrumental   ? Can you name one negative effect?

3 This task requires close attention and is very   exact / exacting   .

4 Jack is the engineer who was   detrimental / instrumental   in the development of the process. Without him we'd be lost.

5 By cutting unnecessary   corners / costs   we hope to make our products as   cheap / flimsy   as possible for the consumer.

6 We want to react more quickly so we respond to complaints   on site / on the spot   , in other words, as soon as they are reported.

7 Please include the   exact / exacting   specifications with your next order.

8 We can't settle for this standard of quality. The number of   deficiencies / deficits   must be reduced.

9 This model is simply not   satisfactory / satisfying   .

10 The machine was still under   guarantee / warranty   so the repair was   free / priceless   .

6 **Complete the statements from a formal letter by matching the sentence halves.**

1	We hereby confirm	a	our legal department respond to that claim.
2	We are unable to respond as	b	learn that fact.
3	We shall have	c	receipt of your letter.
4	We have been advised to	d	of any infringement.
5	We were surprised to	e	cease and desist.
6	We were unaware	f	requested due to unforeseen circumstances.

Now match them to their less formal equivalents.

A We will have to stop.
B We have received your letter.
C We can't do anything now because something unexpected has come up.
D We will forward this to Peter who deals with things like this.
E We didn't realize we were doing anything wrong.
F We didn't expect this.

7 **Which words or phrases don't make sense? Cross out one word or phrase per line.**

1 They   withdrew / filed / confused   the application for a company logo showing a unique design.

2 He   failed / settled / contested   the claim made by the competing company.

3 The company stood its ground and ordered us to   stop / infringe / cease   production.

4 They won   in terms of sales / the right to use the logo / the decision   .

5 He used to be paid   an offering / royalties / a salary   .

6 The site was shut down   due to copyright infringement / after the final appeal was lost / as intellectual property   .

8 **Translate into English.**

1 Für die Steuer ist es wichtig, alle Quittungen aufzuheben.
2 Ist das ein kompliziertes Rezept?
3 Man gewinnt neue Kunden am besten, indem man verschiedene Vertriebskanäle nutzt.
4 Früher hat sie in der Rechtsabteilung gearbeitet, aber jetzt leitet sie die Personalabteilung.
5 Sie versuchen gerade mit der Einführung einer zweiten Marke den Markt zu dominieren.
6 Wir sollten keine Inhalte veröffentlichen, die Urheberrechte verletzen.

Typical mistakes

1 *Rezept* ≠ receipt
Can you please give me a **receipt**? (*Quittung*)
She likes to follow **recipes**. (*Rezepte*)
2 They use various distribution **channels**.
NOT … distribution ~~canals~~.
3 He **used to** buy his products in shops.
NOT ~~In former times he bought~~ …
4 They launched a new **brand** last year.
NOT They launched a new ~~mark~~ …
5 We accused them of copyright **infringement**.
NOT … copyright ~~injury~~.

Outside view

Anne Hodgson on … Reading

For decades marketing meant broadcasting brand messages. As a result, people have become very choosy about what they read and hear. As marketing expert Seth Godin has pointed out, the primary goal of marketers is to deliver their messages to the consumer, no matter what; in fact, their survival depends on it. But, he maintains, people are no longer interested in getting all those messages. As a consequence, companies are now widely adopting permission marketing, leaving it to potential customers to ask for the newsletter or catalogue. Still, the question remains: Do those customers really *want* another newsletter? What exactly will motivate them to read about the brand?

Why do we read?

Think for a moment about why you read. You may need information, and reading lets you get at it independently, at your own pace. Or you may read to experience the gift of serendipity, of learning something new and unexpected, of being invited to see the world from a different angle, of reconnecting to forgotten experience, of losing yourself to the pleasure of an excursion in your mind. Good marketers know this, and produce copy that caters to the needs and wants of their target audience.

To improve your own writing, be a good reader. Study and learn to contrast the various genres of writing, e.g. a customer review compared to an advertisement for the same product, or a press release about a campaign as compared to a blogpost written by someone whose expertise you trust. To describe products and services, follow the great writers and do away with empty words, like the buzzwords that cause readers to switch off. Keep it real by providing examples and quoting your customers, and cut vague and subjective words like *powerful* or *flexible*. Avoid hyperbole, like *epic* and *awesome,* or clichés that will age quickly, like *thinking outside the box* and *being a game changer*. Most importantly, be your own most critical reader. If you really love a word or phrase, you may be overusing it.
So go into thriller mode. Kill your darlings.

serendipity   glücklicher Zufall
hyperbole   Übertreibung

Part A Manage a crisis

▶ **Read the definition on the right and discuss these questions with a partner.**

- discuss codes of business conduct
- handle difficult questions
- explore corporate social responsibility
- write a press release
- deal with social media for PR

- Who and what is subject to compliance at your place of work?
- How can you report a concern about a possible violation?
- What would be your worst-case compliance scenario, and how would your company handle it?

Compliance is about acting in accordance with the rules that govern behaviour. These rules can be externally imposed through laws or regulations, or internally defined through policies. Compliance auditing ranges from technical compliance and process safety management to business ethics.

1 👥 **Bernd Jung, compliance officer at A&G Fashion, is dealing with a compliance crisis. He has printed out some documentation and highlighted key information. Summarize what has happened and predict what will happen next.**

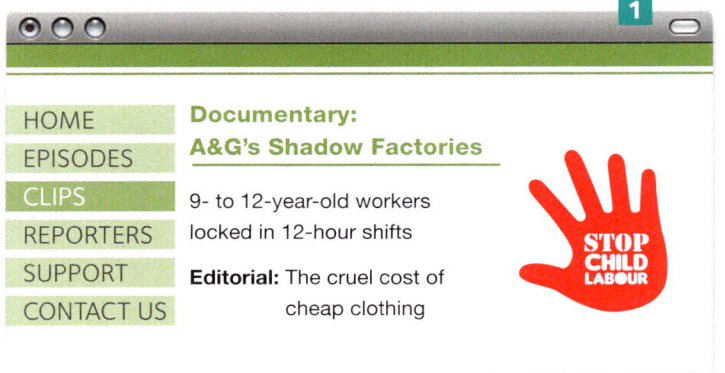

1

HOME
EPISODES
CLIPS
REPORTERS
SUPPORT
CONTACT US

Documentary:
A&G's Shadow Factories

9- to 12-year-old workers locked in 12-hour shifts

Editorial: The cruel cost of cheap clothing

STOP CHILD LABOUR

2

Stop Shadow Factories
20 October

Pressure to meet fast fashion deadlines is making suppliers cook their books, keeping two sets of records—the real ones, and a clean version for compliance auditors. In exchange for bribes, corrupt auditors will adjust questionable figures to pass compliance audits. The failure to stamp out fraud in the auditing system amounts to criminal negligence.

Like · Comment · Share

 3

Legal Department Memo to Department Heads

Strictly confidential: The documentary just released alleges that A&G subcontracted production to a network of sweatshops where half of the workers were found to be under the legal age of 15. Notices allegedly found throughout the factory district in question state that an 'ethics officer' from A&G flagged the premises as 'high risk' and warned that orders would be cancelled unless conditions improved by a given date. This allegation implies that the sweatshops were under A&G oversight.

In fact A&G had no prior knowledge of the existence of any such unregulated 'shadow factories'. It is feasible, however, that one of our vendors may have subcontracted production in collaboration with a third-party auditor.

The parties involved failed to meet A&G compliance standards, which require full documentation of our line of production including subcontracting. Anyone with knowledge relating to this case is expected to assist us in the investigation. Disclosure is subject to protection under the corporate whistleblower programme.

2 👥 **A&G is holding a press conference at its headquarters in Hamburg that same afternoon. Discuss the perspectives taken by the company and the press.**

1 How would you expect A&G to spin the story, and why?
2 What questions would you anticipate the press asking?

🔊 37 **Now listen to compliance officer Bernd Jung field questions at the press conference. How right were you?**

3 Listen again and complete what Bernd said to maintain control in the Q&A. What techniques did he use to answer the reporters' questions?

1 You're .... that we were monitoring the factory, but ...., we were not even aware of its existence.

2 I'm afraid I .... until we know more.

3 If you're .... our customers to accept practices that we condemn, then the answer is clearly 'no'.

4 I'm afraid I don't know ...., but let me ....

4 Complete these extracts from the press conference with the correct form of the verbs.

employ · get · lose · meet · work

1 Sweatshops fail .... our safety standards.

2 We most definitely do not endorse .... children.

3 We don't deny .... oversight of this vendor.

4 How do you reconcile .... at both ends of the ethical spectrum?

5 We pledge .... to the bottom of this.

5 👥 A&G Fashion has an SMS compliance hotline, i.e. a discrete reporting channel that employees can use. Read the question received. Which area does it relate to? How does the response reflect the hotline rules?

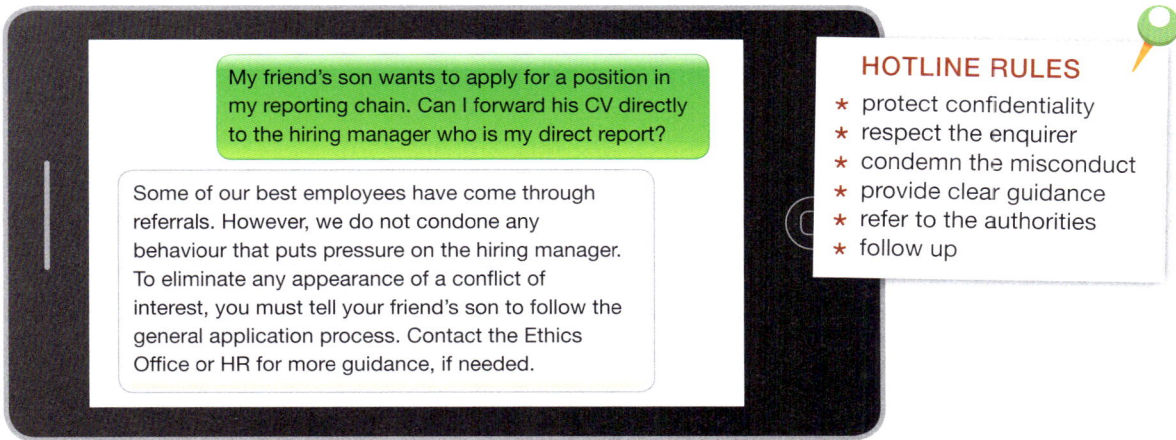

Read and discuss the other questions below. How would you respond? What would happen if a whistleblower leaked one of these compliance issues to the press?

1 If a supplier offers me tickets to a rugby match, may I accept them?

2 I attended a lavish dinner on a recent business trip. Now our hosts are visiting. My budget won't allow me to reciprocate. What should I do?

3 I think a consultant of ours is bribing local officials. What should I do?

4 What can I do if my manager is exerting pressure to 'make the numbers work'?

■ Did you know?

In public relations, **spin** is a form of propaganda to persuade public opinion. The term generally implies manipulative tactics, such as selectively presenting facts, burying bad news, being vague and beating around the bush. By contrast, in the age of social media, experts advocate telling it all, telling it fast and telling the truth.

Assessing and acting on issues

We don't endorse using such methods.
We don't encourage solving it on your own.
That fails to solve the problem.

Part B Communicate CSR

▶ Does your company promote any kind of corporate social or environmental responsibility? How do these initiatives relate to your company's core operation?

1 🔊38 Manu Khullar is an IT consultant dedicated to improving compliance in the garment industry. Listen. What does he say about compliance?

Listen again and complete the sentences. How does Manu use caution when evaluating?

1 Classical compliance is an approach that provides a solution ....

2 The overall effort .... aligned with the industry.

3 The whole approach .... a bit short-sighted.

4 ...., the only real outcome is illegal subcontracting.

2 There are many approaches to CSR. Read about three model cases and put the company names in the correct position in the table.

Three clothing companies want to stop the local use of child labour in cotton farming, textile production and clothes manufacturing. To guarantee the success of their policy, …

• TDS Garments Ltd conducts frequent visits to factories, coordinates oversight with industry competitors, and collaborates with local authorities to monitor indicators such as school absenteeism.

• Garma Ltd provides microfinance to family-owned organic cotton farms to source the majority of its raw materials. It also works directly with all main actors in its supply chain to assure traceability.

• Arcol Ltd donates to a charity with an orphanage that provides outreach programmes to slum children to prevent them from working in sweatshops.

	Company	Type of CSR	Purpose	Benefit
1		engages in philanthropy	provides funding and skills	has limited, short-term effects, is not aligned with industry, provides tax breaks
2		manages risk	assures compliance	mitigates operational impact and risks
3		creates value and assures transparency	innovates and promotes sustainable business	integrates competitive business into the community

Compare the approaches. As you do not know all the facts, evaluate cautiously.

> Company X is taking an approach that provides a solution of sorts. They provide certain benefits, but …

> Company Y's approach does not seem to be … I would say, …

3 🔊39 Now listen to Manu present the work he does in CSR, and answer the questions.

1 Which key performance indicator (KPI) does he consider most important Why?
2 What services did his company provide to Alpia?
3 What are his arguments against traditional compliance reporting?
4 Where does he see the real responsibility for holding companies accountable?

4 What did Manu actually say? Reformulate more cautiously.

Pride is a better invitation to suppliers to engage in good reporting than fear. Old-style compliance fails since it often forces vendors to <u>sweep things under the carpet</u> and to lie to get an order. It just <u>breeds contempt and prejudice</u>. That system is broken.

What do the underlined idioms mean?

5 Read this press release. What you think of the concept personally, and in terms of its effectiveness as a CSR initiative?

Alpia launches the 'Well Worn Initiative' – Encouraging Customers to Consume Less

Innsbruck, Austria, November 1, 20.. Alpia, a leading designer of outdoor clothing, today announces the launch of its Well Worn Initiative, a pact with its customers to reduce the negative impact of overconsumption on the environment.

"The Well Worn Initiative addresses a key issue – the footprint of producing clothing related to how long it is worn," explains VP Wolf Lang. "We are asking our customers to buy only what they need and to wear it for many years, to repair what breaks, to resell what is still wearable, and to recycle what is worn

out. In return, Alpia promises to make clothing that will wear well over the years, and to handle any repairs under a life-long warranty."

Alpia is joining forces with shopOn, the online marketplace, to launch a storefront for used Alpia clothes. The Well Worn Initiative marks the first time a major European retail brand has actively encouraged its customers to buy and sell used products online.

Customers selling used Alpia products become partners in the store. Alpia does not earn any associated profits.

The collaboration between Alpia and shopOn is based on their common interest in extending the useful life of products. The store is not only the latest example of shopOn's commitment to sustainable commerce, it is also a new model for consumption within the apparel industry.

"We want our customers to go to their closets, find the Alpia gear they don't need, and extend its useful life", Lang says. "The Well Worn Initiative will provide our customers with the satisfaction of knowing that they are helping the planet."

Now work with a partner to answer these questions.

1 Look at the title and the first sentence. What is the main message? What keywords are repeated?
2 What basic information immediately follows the title?
3 Identify the key information relating to the 6 w's: Who? What? When? Where? Why? How?
4 Where do you find the most important information? Why?
5 What is the purpose of this press release? Who is it written for? What effects does the company hope it will have?

6 Prepare a press release relating to news at your company. Choose one of the ideas on the cards, then follow these steps.

1 Brainstorm the details and keywords using the 6 w's.
2 Consider what effect you want to achieve.
3 Sort the details in order of importance.
4 Write a stand-alone summary containing the key message.
5 Add details in descending order of importance.

report on the successful completion of a project

announce a forthcoming event or a change in your company

notify the public of an ongoing event

???

Writing a press release

When writing a press release, be interesting, timely, accurate, precise, clear and brief. Inform, but don't advertise.

Food for thought

If environmentally controversial companies are sometimes found at the top of sustainability ratings, what use are the ratings in the first place?

Part C   Engage with the public

▶ Look at these cases of greenwashing. What similar cases can you think of? Why do you think companies do this? How successful is this use of spin in both the short and long term?

> Unilever, the biggest single buyer of palm oil in the world, is a founding member of the Roundtable of Sustainable Palm Oil (RSPO) certification scheme, established in 2004. While the scheme aims to move the industry towards sustainability, and awards best practice, it has continued to allow the conversion of rainforests into new palm oil plantations.
>
> Many clothing companies have failed to live up to their heavily publicized toxic-free production commitments. The Greenpeace Detox Catwalk campaign of 2013 challenged the garment industry to 'walk the talk' and labelled them Leaders (e.g. Puma), Greenwashers (e.g. Adidas), and Laggards (e.g. Diesel).

1 Read the blog post about CSR and social media. Then answer these questions.

    1   What impact does social media have on companies? What evidence is given?
    2   How exactly does the article say companies should use social media? Why?

How the Voice of the People Is Driving Corporate Social Responsibility

by Jen Boynton | HBR Blog Network | 8:00 AM July 17, 2013

The business case for corporate social responsibility (CSR) is becoming easier and easier to make. You can argue that it boosts a company's brand, manages risk, and just plain saves money. But perhaps most importantly the general public is clamoring for companies to enact good, fair business practices — and most of that public pressure comes through social media.

There are plenty of (very public) examples of businesses moved into more sustainable practices by a social media backlash: Immediately following the factory collapse disaster in Bangladesh in 2013, companies who sourced materials from the country quickly came under fire; now several retailers have banded together to create a safety plan to improve conditions in Bangladeshi factories.

Feedback through social media is immediate, permanent, and extremely public. When individuals feel strongly about a company's performance on social or environmental issues, one small voice can quickly become a swarm, difficult for even the most shielded executive to ignore. For this reason, social media has become a driving force in many companies' CSR agendas.

One of the easiest ways to be on the right side of the social media tide is to be proactive – and personal – by listening to feedback and responding in an authentic way. Firms that are excelling in this regard have active, branded Twitter accounts, but they also encourage their executives to use Twitter as well. Make sure that the people in charge of your social media accounts understand what your CSR efforts mean for your brand, and empower them to act in a positive way to support your company.

One company that is leading the way on using social media to inform its sustainability program and communicate about its CSR agenda is Unilever. The personal care product and food conglomerate has dozens of brands and thousands of products, which makes its sustainability program both extremely important and difficult to communicate, because it spans issues from health and hygiene to greenhouse gas reductions. Yet, Unilever has managed to bundle them all under one umbrella, the Unilever Sustainable Living Plan. The plan includes a multifaceted plan for communicating progress through a wide variety of methods, from video to Facebook to Twitter chats. It also includes traditional advertising tactics and public awareness campaigns from Dove's Real Beauty Sketches to a Lifebuoy hand-washing campaign delivered by roti in India.

Ultimately, social media is just a communication tool like any other. But it is one consumers use to talk about brands, and the world is listening. It is easy to fear the tide of social media for the risks it can bring, but this onslaught of information can also be viewed as an opportunity. By listening to those early whispers of complaint, companies can act quickly to minimize the fallout – while also gaining important knowledge that can inform and improve a company's internal CSR report.

blogs.hbr.org/2013/07/how-the-voice-of-the-people-is/

2 **Find phrases in the article that mean the following:**

1 to be very aggressive in requesting sth
2 to adopt as official policy
3 a strong negative reaction
4 to be attacked

5 to be very good at sth in a particular way
6 to include a wide range of issues
7 a huge mass of incoming details
8 to keep the negative outcome small

3 **The article mentions Unilever as one of the recognized leaders in using social media. Look at this series of tweets on the company's Twitter page and answer the questions.**

1 What hashtags (#) are used to keep the topic of the conversation searchable?
2 Who is addressed directly using @ and their username? Why?
3 Which tweets by others have been forwarded (retweeted) to followers to read?
4 Which tweets use 'via' to quote the information source?
5 What abbreviations are used here? Why?

---

1 "Palm oil market transformation can only happen if everyone involved takes responsibility" bit.ly... #SustLiving #traceability via @OlgaToto   *3min*

2 DYK you can trace any forest product from the forest of origin to the marketplace? unilever... #SustLiving #traceability RT by   *8min*

3 Paul Polman, Unilever CEO, shares thoughts on business values, trust and giving to society – streaming live youtu.be... #SustLiving   *10min*

4 Unilever and @Ferrero palm oil pledges show 'an industry in transformation' foodna...via @foodnavigator #traceability #SustLiving   *23h*

5 Join our live chat w/ experts including @Olga Toto tomorrow 9-11am EST youtu. be... Use the hashtag #SustLiving   *23h*

6 Proud that @NextDrop Anu Sridharan, 26, from India has made it to the Final 7 of #SustLiving Young Entrepreneur Award bit.ly... RT by   *23h*

---

4 **Update your stakeholders using Twitter. Work with a partner to create a series of tweets.**

1 First, develop a hashtag for the issue you want to create a conversation about.
2 Research related articles and write a tweet summarizing them, and publish them with the link and your hashtag.

5 **Discuss with a partner.**

1 What kind of news at your company or in connection with your brands are of interest to your customers or other stakeholders? How do you communicate it to them?
2 What companies do you follow, and why? How well do these companies connect with the public, in your opinion? How do they do it?

How to tweet

Be short and make your tweet easy to read.
Be human even as a business.
Be topical and react promptly.
Reply to one, but address all.
Tweet anything interesting.

1 Complete this excerpt from an invitation to a compliance workshop with the infinitive or gerund form of the verbs in the box.

> attend · comply · cover · happen · hear · improve · increase · promote · read · submit · violate

You have to memorize which verbs are followed by the infinitive ('to do') and which by a gerund ('doing'), but after a preposition always use the gerund.

It is with great regret that we inform you that we have been penalized for ....[1] the Anti-monopoly Law. To prevent this from ....[2] in the future we are holding compliance workshops throughout the company. We intend ....[3] the compliance awareness of all individuals by ....[4] auditing and education. This also means ....[5] legal compliance and screening for subcontractors and third parties. Please do not fail ....[6]. We strongly recommend ....[7] the Code of Conduct ahead of the training, since we intend ....[8] as much as possible during the workshop. We are extending training to business sites and are asking managers ....[9] a written statement confirming that they have taken the course and that they pledge ....[10] with the Code of Conduct. We look forward to ....[11] from you soon.

2 Unscramble these answers to a reporter's questions at a press conference.

1 I'm afraid / of our inquiry / comment / until the results / I can't / on that / are in

....

2 I don't / have / as soon / at this point / pass it on / but I will / as I do / that information

....

3 You are / previous / implying / which isn't / knowledge / the case / that we had

....

4 Let me / in turn / down / and answer / break that / each question / just

....

5 So, you're / this is part / really asking / is not / whether / and no, it / of our policy, / most definitely

....
....

Now match the answers to these guidelines on dealing with questions.

a If the question contains an unproven assumption, point that out before answering.
b If you are not authorized to answer, give a straightforward reason why not.
c If the question is unclear, rephrase it to check understanding before answering.
d If you don't know the answer, admit it and offer to get back to the questioner.
e Divide a complicated question into sub-questions, and answer them in turn.

3 Match the sentence halves to make cautious evaluations.

1	They appear to have	a	that the study does indeed suggest this.
2	This solution does help	b	condoned the use cf dodgy chemicals.
3	While we do not condone this practice	c	than a legal loophole.
4	You must admit that it is a way forward	d	to some extent.
5	For all practical purposes this is little more	e	of sorts.
6	I would say	f	we would like to point out that it is widespread.

4 Reformulate these statements to make them more cautious by using the verbs or phrases in brackets.

1   This system is broken. (not / seem / work)

   ....

2   We condemn this practice. (not / condone)

   ....

3   They pay low wages. (tend to)

   ....

4   Unclear ethical guidelines cause bad practice. (The evidence / suggest)

   ....

5   This proves I'm right. (suggest)

   ....

6   This is a KPI. (generally / consider)

   ....

5 Complete the idioms by adding an appropriate noun.

book · bush · carpet · conclusions · head · light · numbers

1   Although they tried to sweep things under the ...., the truth came to

   .... in the end.

2   They desperately tried to make the .... work but it was impossible.

3   Before you jump to any ...., please hear me out!

4   I'm afraid I can't answer that off the top of my ....

5   This doesn't look right. I think this company has been cooking the ....

6   He's always beating around the .... and never coming to the point.

Now match the phrases above to the expressions that mean the same.

a   to be revealed
b   to make assumptions
c   to never come to the point
d   to make a profit
e   to engage in fraud
f   without consulting something
g   to ignore the facts

6   Match the sentence halves.

1 Please make sure you adhere to	**a** this misconduct.
2 I'm sure they will try to exert	**b** condone the use of dodgy chemicals.
3 We strongly condemn	**c** than a legal loophole.
4 You must admit that it is a way	**d** the standards we set out.
5 For all practical purposes this is little more	**e** forward of sorts.
6 We would never	**f** pressure but make sure you stay firm.

7   Which words or phrases don't make sense? Cross out one word or phrase per line.

1   Sustainable practices   ensure / guarantee / generate   that we achieve positive environmental effects.

2   Compliance means acting   according to / after / in accordance with   set rules.

3   He is   alleging / implying / aligning   that we deliberately engaged in unethical practices.

4   Experts on ethics   condemn / advocate / advise   telling the whole truth quickly.

5   Actually, these rules are   imposed / specified / fulfilled   by an external party.

6   We   pledge / endorse / promise   to clarify this issue.

8   Match the collocations, then use them to complete the sentences below.

condone   protect   behaviour   confidentiality

assess   live up to   pressure   the life   the extent

exert   extend   its commitments

1   The company patented a method that can substantially .... of the product.

2   We cannot .... and are cancelling the contract immediately.

3   The government is trying to .... on companies unwilling to go green.

4   We promise to .... and will never sell your data to third parties.

5   Are you able to .... of the damage yet?

6   The company has not managed to .... as far as compliance is concerned.

9   Complete the text with six suitable words or expressions from the box below.

a backlash · clamours for · come under fire · enact · excel · minimize the fallout · an onslaught · spans

Last year BSG was falsely promoting its cereals as having 'natural ingredients' when, in fact, the corn used in the cereal was genetically engineered. The company faced ....[1] from their customers when the news leaked out last spring and sales were affected. BSG attempted to boost sales and ....[2] by pledging to ....[3] a more stringent ethical policy. This had the desired effect, but now the company has again ....[4], as it has become known that their so-called 'all-natural' chickens are treated with antibiotics. The company is now dealing with ....[5] of criticism, which ....[6] a wide range of issues including everything from CSR to truth in marketing.

10 Translate into English.

1 Ich finde es unhöflich, wenn Leute sich in Meetings gegenseitig simsen.
2 Wir garantieren diskreten Umgang mit sensiblen Kundendaten.
3 Die Anleitung ist in drei separate Abschnitte unterteilt.
4 Die Anwohner in der Nähe des Flughafens sind eine wichtige Interessengruppe. Deshalb müssen sie vor dem Bau einer neuen Startbahn befragt werden.
5 Zu diesem Punkt wird es bei der nächsten Versammlung der Aktionäre eine Abstimmung geben.

Typical mistakes

1 Can you **text** me later?
   NOT   *Can you ~~sms~~ me later?*
2 discreet ≠ discrete
   We ask you to be **discreet**. (*diskret*)
   We have **discrete** product categories. (*eigenständig, separat*)
3 stakeholders ≠ shareholders
   Some **stakeholders** don't own shares. (*Interessengruppen, Beteiligte*)
   The **shareholders** have voted against the plan. (*Aktionäre*)

Outside view

Anne Hodgson on … Uncertainty

When the Deepwater Horizon oil rig exploded, killing eleven workers and spilling oil into the Gulf of Mexico for three long months, BP, the licensing company, made a series of PR blunders. First, they failed to express genuine concern for those affected. When BP's CEO Tony Hayward told reporters that he too wanted the affair to be resolved as it was impacting his life so much, he was criticized for being selfish. In addition, BP's management was widely perceived as indifferent, and did nothing to earn the public's belief in their dedication to rectifying the situation.

Communicating in the face of uncertainty

Will Rogers once said, 'When people are stressed and upset, they want to know that you care before they care what you know.' This is especially important when the situation is complex and you have to make and communicate decisions based on incomplete evidence. Your listeners want certainty, or at least to know that you will do your best in the face of uncertainty. Not getting their support sets you up for failure.

It doesn't make sense to attempt – and then fail – to reassure the public by making false claims about the limited impact of a disaster. It is much better to be honest and to say, for example: *At the moment no one can foresee how this disaster will impact the environment, but we will work with the best experts to help mitigate the damage*. Show you care by saying *We understand what you are going through*. Provide reassurance by explaining the steps you are taking, e.g. *At the moment we are bringing in technicians …* and update people on what you have achieved, explaining its significance: *We have identified the source …, which means …*

In a crisis, presenting the risks you see without exaggeration or understatement, being open about the extent of your uncertainty, and explaining why you think a certain action is called for will provide the public with the assurance they need to trust in you to solve the problems as they arise.

blunder	grober Fehler
to rectify sth	etw in Ordnung bringen
to mitigate	mildern
understatement	Untertreibung

Business file 4

- handle a recall crisis
- prepare for and hold a press conference
- write a press release

📁 A press conference

1 Read the news story about Sonnenschein and the notice the company has sent to retailers. What has happened, and what is going to happen next?

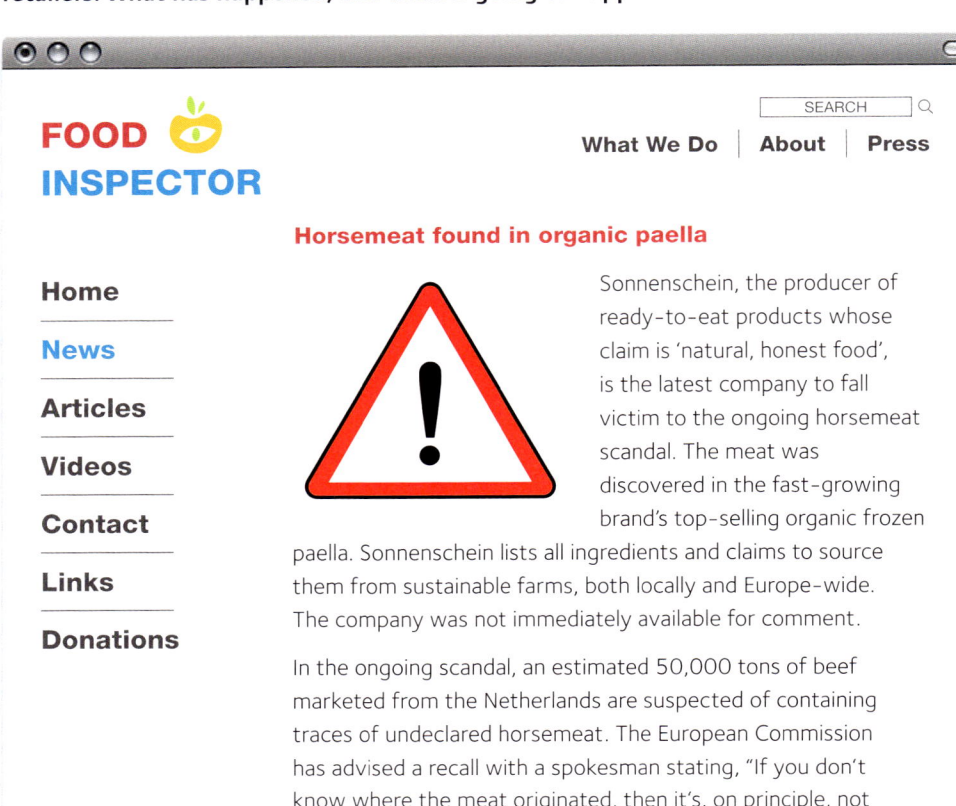

FOOD INSPECTOR

SEARCH 🔍

What We Do | About | Press

Home

News

Articles

Videos

Contact

Links

Donations

Horsemeat found in organic paella

Sonnenschein, the producer of ready-to-eat products whose claim is 'natural, honest food', is the latest company to fall victim to the ongoing horsemeat scandal. The meat was discovered in the fast-growing brand's top-selling organic frozen paella. Sonnenschein lists all ingredients and claims to source them from sustainable farms, both locally and Europe-wide. The company was not immediately available for comment.

In the ongoing scandal, an estimated 50,000 tons of beef marketed from the Netherlands are suspected of containing traces of undeclared horsemeat. The European Commission has advised a recall with a spokesman stating, "If you don't know where the meat originated, then it's, on principle, not suitable for human consumption."

More on this story: Food scandal triggers widespread call for change

---

Notice to retailers

This is to inform you that a batch of Sonnenschein Organic Paella is being recalled after traces of horsemeat were identified in samples of the product. This recall affects only the batch of this product with the expiry date 1 March 20.. and the lot number 139-3467. Please cease sale immediately.

In the next few days, consumers will be notified via public announcements and advised to return the product to the store where they purchased it. For any questions and to arrange refunds, please contact your Sonnenschein sales rep.

Please post the enclosed notice in your store on or near the freezer where Sonnenschein products are sold.

Sonnenschein take matters of safety and quality extremely seriously. It is our top concern. Please note that no illnesses connected to any of the products identified as containing undeclared horsemeat have been reported to date. We wish to apologize to our customers for this regrettable incident. We are doing all that we can to pinpoint how the horsemeat entered our production system and have intensified inspections to eradicate any possibility of the contamination reoccurring. For more information, please contact Sonnenschein's Retail Hotline (Tel: 0800 6799271 or +49 180 234400) from 8 am–8 pm CET) or visit the Sonnenschein website: www.sonnenschein.com

Thank you for your support.

2 🔊 40 Now listen to an interview with a key supplier. What is at stake, and who are the stakeholders? How well are Sonnenschein and Fresh and Fair Seafood handling the crisis so far? What does Sonnenschein have to do to improve the situation?

3 Do a role-play or a simulation to prepare and then hold a press conference.

1 In groups of four, choose **Option 1** (a role-play based on the scenario in exercises 1 and 2) or **Option 2** (a simulation using your own ideas).

Option 1

Choose a role (A–D) and use the information in your file to prepare and then hold the press conference. Review phrases from Unit 8 and the language box below to help you prepare.

→ *Partner A (CEO + spokesperson): file 9, page 101*
→ *Partner B (COO + spokesperson): file 17, page 105*
→ *Partner C (Marketing Manager + reporter): file 37, page 113*
→ *Partner D (CFO + reporter): file 27, page 109*

Option 2

Come up with your own scenario in which you have to hold a press conference in response to a crisis of some sort.

What's the situation? →

What are you informing the press about and how will the news affect your stakeholders? Draft an opening statement.

Who's involved? →

Are you members of a team or a project, from one or several departments? Share your different perspectives and anticipate reporter questions.

What vocabulary / phrases do you need?

Review phrases from Unit 8 and the language box below to help you prepare.

2 Now hold the press conference. If you chose **Option 1**, take on the second role on your cards (spokesperson or reporter). If you chose **Option 2**, decide who will represent the company and who will ask the tough questions.

4 Issue a formal press release to respond to the crisis while summarizing or reformulating your brand identity and your policies.

Holding a press conference	Issuing a press release
We take matters of safety and quality extremely seriously. It's our top concern / of utmost importance to us.	Our company is deeply committed to matters of safety and quality.
We're committed today to being absolutely open and transparent with you and the public.	Our commitment to openness and transparency …
As you may know, we have been asked to recall …	At the request of …, we are recalling …
The batches in question are: …	The recalled products are: …
We're going to be complying with this request, and we expect that it will be completed within the next 48 hours.	Compliance with the recall is expected to be effected within 48 hours from release of this statement.
There's widespread confusion amongst the public who believe that all of our products …	We wish to reassure the public that …
So I really want to stress today that this directive is restricted to only one …	This recall directive is strictly limited to only one …

→ *File 1*

Partner A

You are the 'analytical' type. You want to do things right and avoid mistakes. Ask lots of questions during the discussion of the topics below.

Discussion topics:

1 Should you introduce the practice of shadowing colleagues from other departments?
2 Should you extend a delivery deadline by a week, as several people are off sick?
3 Should you switch from company phones to private mobiles?

Use phrases like these to make suggestions:
· Do we have all the facts we need?
· Let's look at the details first. What do we know about …?
· Let's get this right. How can we be sure (that) …?

Use phrases like these to respond to other suggestions:
· I'd prefer not to rush into things.
· I think we need more information before we can decide.
· I'm not sure that will work without doing more research.

→ *File 2*

Proposal A

You are going to give a 2–4-minute oral report at your next team meeting. Follow the steps below to prepare.

1 First read the consultant's brief below.
2 Then add your own ideas (advantages / disadvantages) and be ready to discuss them after giving your report.

Hold regular 10-minute video conferences

What:	Hold 10-minute video conferences to connect teams in Birmingham and Leipzig.
	Do this regularly, either daily or weekly (to be discussed).
Why:	Update each other as needed.
	Know what the others are doing to avoid overlap.
	Build trust and strengthen rapport, especially in difficult times.
	Save time.
How:	Meet for exactly ten minutes. Time your agenda by the clock.
	Hold the meeting standing up to help everyone focus.
	Talk about the same things each time, e.g.:
	– Did we meet last week's target? What are we aiming at this week?
	– What should we look out for?
	– What is going well? What is not going so well?
	– Who will be out of the office?
Critical note:	Possible technical problems & delays

Own Project

First complete the status overview of your ongoing projects.

Projects	Issues	Milestones / date	Status ✔ 🟢 🟡 🔴
1			
2			
3			
4			

Then, on behalf of your department, write an email to the project coordinator, answering these questions.

- Can you take part in the kick-off next Friday to coordinate projects across departments?
- What projects are ongoing in your department? What are their aims and status?
- What cross-departmental project support would benefit your department's aims?
- Could your department contribute to projects in other departments? How?

Partner A

You are Ian, an account manager at Medtec Hamburg. First, look at the agenda and your notes below.

Agenda

typical, but all suppliers like this

Loglab is in breach of contract.

Conference Call   Wednesday 10.00 CET   Call-in number: …

Objective: To discuss plan of action re Loglab

Attendees: Jan + Johanna (Vienna), Ian (Hamburg), Valerie (Warsaw)

Action item: Delayed delivery yesterday with Loglab is one in a series. Meet to discuss options / decide plan of action

talk to legal department, put pressure on Loglab, maybe set up new contractual terms? Call Christian Karg in the Legal Dept? (he handled the contract with Loglab)

Now take part in the telecon while keeping the following information in mind.

- People keep coming into your office and interrupting you.
- Construction outside your window is making a lot of noise.
- You have a cold. (You got caught in the rain yesterday.)
- You can manage a meeting any morning except Thursday.

Answers to the quiz

1 b   **2** c   **3** b

→ File 6

You provide specialized services (for the type of project you have defined with Partner A). Use the questions below to make notes about your services.

- If you have a standard package, what is it?
- What else do you recommend / offer, and why?
- What are your fees?
- Can you offer (more) attractive terms to win this new client?

Then take a phone call from a potential client and negotiate the best possible terms.

→ File 7

Present the information below to your partner, using your own words and explaining any terms as necessary.

Waterfall development is a traditional, established approach to project management in IT. As in a relay race, team members pass each other the baton when they have completed their part of the project.

Key features:
- planned ahead, defined timeline, budget, scope
- called 'waterfall' because it is visualized using a Gantt chart (critical path* in red):

| 23 Jul 20.. | 30 Jul 20.. | 6 Aug 20.. | 13 Aug 20.. |

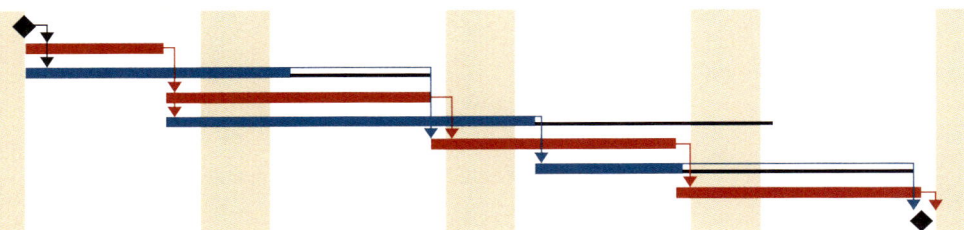

S M T W T F S S M T W T F S S M T W T F S S M T W T F S

- One phase (e.g. planning) is completed before the next (e.g. development) is started.
- There are standard procedures for the project manager to follow.
- This conventional project management method is in compliance with ISO standards.

Method and terminology:
- *'critical path' = the longest sequence of activities needed to complete a project on time. Each activity on the critical path has to be completed before the next one is begun.

Main drawbacks:
- Value is realized only at end of project, i.e. deployment.
- Testing at end leads to increased risk of failure or lower quality than hoped for.
- Stakeholders are not involved after the kick-off, so the project team is not informed when stakeholders' requirements change.
- Full responsibility lies with project manager: the power of one.

→ *File 8*

Partner B (consultant): negotiating intercultural workshops

You facilitate intercultural workshops. Use the information below (and your discretion) to negotiate the best possible terms with the person who calls.

The standard package:
- Three workshops within three months plus two reports, for a total of € 10,000.
  (This package is very effective, but you are flexible.)

You recommend / offer:
- Time between workshops for 'homework'.
- Two blocks of two days also possible, for the price of three separate days.

Your fees:
- Facilitation: € 1,000 / day
- Initial report (orientation): € 3,500
- Final report (road map): € 3,500
- Only offer a discount for projects with more than three workshops with both reports.
- Charge for additional reports if necessary.

→ *File 9*

Partner A

Step 1: Sonnenschein CEO
You are the spokesperson for global strategy and have called a meeting to prepare for the press conference. Using the expertise from the four participants, you want to write the opening statement and agree on strategies to deal with questions. Before you start the meeting, which you will chair, look at the agenda and your notes below.

AGENDA / Let's rethink these points:

Compliance overview system? Stakeholders? Speed of development? Price segment? Packaging? PR + co-branding with suppliers of meat products from organically farmed animals? Implement a new 'Purity Code' (to be defined)?

Notes

We are the largest, fastest-growing producer of organic frozen foods in Europe.
Since 1980s selling frozen ready meals, since 2004 rebranding with organic-or-local policy. Ongoing shift from local to more organically grown, which is more expensive, but price wars in organic food are forcing ready-to-eat products to become cheaper.

Step 2: Sonnenschein spokesperson
During the press conference, you will represent the company along with the COO, and field the reporters' questions.

➜ File 10

Proposal C

You are going to give a 2–4-minute oral report at your next team meeting. Follow the steps below to prepare.

1 First read the consultant's brief below.
2 Then add your own ideas (advantages / disadvantages) and be ready to discuss these ideas after giving your report.

Share information in a project wiki

What: Create a team wiki, i.e. an online platform that everyone has access to. A team wiki allows the team to upload and share key files and updates. It creates a well-structured information pool.

Why: Necessary information is quickly available.
Information is shared more effectively than at meetings.
It remains available for later use.
Easy to use and readily accessible for everyone working on a computer.

How: An expert will need to set it up.
We'll need to train team members to use it.

Critical note: Requires consistent use and additional time on the computer

---

➜ File 11

Partner B: Planning team

Take part in a short telecon to clarify the main issues of the upcoming trip.

- Your main focus is on coordinating the overall logistics.
- Talk about a specific document all participants should have copies of. This document is important because … (come up with your own ideas).
- The line is bad and you have problems understanding.

➜ File 12

Partner B

Present the situation in the R&D department. Afterwards, you are free to defend the special interests of 'your' department, or to argue your own opinions and ideas.

The staff in R&D regularly receive top bonuses. The head of department consistently awards 120 % performance-based pay, not simply to reward the staff, but also to ensure that, thanks to their good earnings, they stay with the company. Competition for talented staff is keen, as the work the employees do today ensures the company's market lead tomorrow.

The R&D department consistently reaches its targets. Your boss has told you that she's against any change in the bonus system in the coming year. Her advice: *'Never change a running system.'*

Facility Management

The Head of Facility Management has received an email from Ellen Wagner regarding the new cross-departmental project to reduce energy use at Schulze. (Ellen is the project coordinator.) This is the current status of the energy-related projects in your department:

Projects	Issues	Milestones / date	Status ✔ ● ● ●
1 Air conditioning		01 Dec	✔
2 Ventilation		30 Mar	●
3 Lighting system	cost	30 Jun	●
4 Insulation of roof	resources	01 Sep	●
5 installation of solar panels		pipeline	●

On behalf of your department, write an email to Ellen, answering her questions.

· Can you take part in the cross-departmental project kick-off on 25 January?
· What projects in your department aim to reduce energy use? What is their status?
· How could our cross-departmental Energy Project contribute to your goals?
· What resources (expertise, plans in the pipeline, unused staff potential) could you contribute to the Energy Project?

Partner C

You are the 'expressive' type. You are proactive and use enthusiasm to get everyone involved. Try to be enthusiastic during the discussion of the topics below.

Discussion topics:

1 Should you introduce the practice of shadowing colleagues from other departments?
2 Should you extend a delivery deadline by a week, as several people are off sick?
3 Should you switch from company phones to private mobiles?

Use phrases like these to make suggestions:
· I really want to try something out with you.
· We really need everyone on board, so let's try this: …
· I think a great way to do that would be …

Use phrases like these to respond to other suggestions:
· That's an excellent idea.
· Good, but we could also …
· I understand exactly what you're talking about.

→ File 15

Technical Services

The Head of Technical Services has received an email from Ellen Wagner regarding the new cross-departmental project to reduce energy use at Schulze. (Ellen is the project coordinator.) This is the current status of the energy-related projects in your department:

Projects	Issues	Milestones / date	Status ✔ ● ● ●
1 replace fleet or lease other models		01 Dec	✔
2 use public transport campaign	resources?	30 Mar	●
3 improve schedules in production		01 Mar	●
4 switch off copiers, printers at night	scope?	pipeline	●

On behalf of your department, write an email to Ellen, answering her questions:

· Can you take part in the cross-departmental project kick-off on 25 January?
· What projects in your department aim to reduce energy use? What is their status?
· How could our cross-departmental Energy Project contribute to your goals?
· What resources (expertise, plans in the pipeline, unused staff potential) could you contribute to the Energy Project?

→ File 16

Partner D

You are Jan, responsible for logistics at Medtec Vienna. You are leading the teleconference. First, look at the agenda and your notes below.

Agenda

Conference Call   Wednesday 10.00 CET   Call-in number: …

Objective: To discuss plan of action re Loglab

Attendees: Jan + Johanna (Vienna), Ian (Hamburg), Valerie (Warsaw)

Action item: Delayed delivery yesterday with Loglab is one in a series. Meet to discuss options / decide plan of action

> We need to talk to someone higher up at Loglab – explain what Medtec needs, why.
> I worked with Joe at Loglab to develop value added service.
> Loglab is good and cheap – replacing them might be expensive
> build trust, cultivate good communications – call Joe?

Now take part in the telecon while keeping the following information in mind.

· Manage the teleconference and make sure everyone has their say.
· Encourage everyone in the team to explain what their opinions are based on.
· Summarize what people say.
· Arrange a meeting to collect information and decide further steps.
· You can manage a meeting any day but Friday.

Step 1: Sonnenschein COO (Chief Operations Officer)
You have been invited to a meeting to prepare for the press conference. Look at the agenda and your notes below. At the meeting, suggest the next steps and possible changes in operations.

AGENDA / Let's rethink these points:

Compliance overview system? Stakeholders? Speed of development? Price segment? Packaging? PR + co-branding with suppliers of meat products from organically farmed animals? Implement a new 'Purity Code' (to be defined)?

Notes

Purchasing only from EU-certified companies, transparency about sources, 100% traceability guaranteed but not possible, suppliers prepared for visits from our inspectors at any time.
Incident involves buyer at organic market. Testing every batch not feasible, too expensive.
Sonnenschein labelling its ingredients since 2003 as organic or locally sourced. Limited space on package doesn't allow more than distinction between organic/local.
New 'Purity Code' would not be enough.
More consumer-friendly: Give exact source of ingredients with detailed machine-readable information on the package.

Step 2: Sonnenschein spokesperson
During the press conference, you will represent the company along with the CEO, and field the reporters' questions.

You are the 'amiable' type. You put people first. While discussing the topics below, use appropriate language to show others that you understand them.

Discussion topics:

1 Should you introduce the practice of shadowing colleagues from other departments?
2 Should you extend a delivery deadline by a week, as several people are off sick?
3 Should you switch from company phones to private mobiles?

Use phrases like these to make suggestions:
· What exactly do we need to do?
· Why don't we ask everyone what they think?

Use phrases like these to respond to other suggestions:
· That must be quite a lot of work. I'll be happy to help.
· Is everyone happy with that suggestion?

→ *File 19*

Partner A (client): own workplace scenario

You want to hire a contractor for a project in the next few months (make sure you have defined the type of project with Partner B) and were given a name by a business partner of yours. First answer the questions below and make notes to prepare for the phone call.

- What are your requirements?
- What is your budget?

Then call the contractor and negotiate the best possible terms.

→ *File 20*

Partner B

You are Valerie, an account administrator at Medtec Warsaw. First, look at the agenda and your notes below.

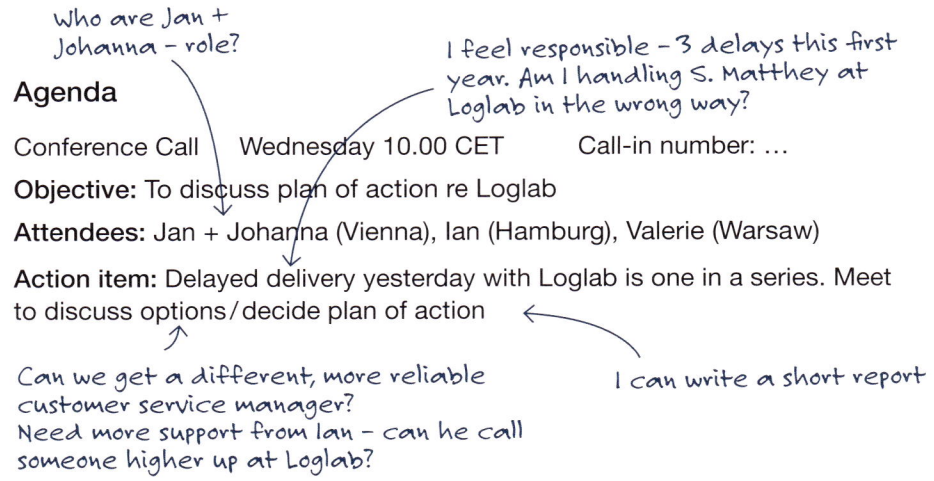

Who are Jan + Johanna – role?

I feel responsible – 3 delays this first year. Am I handling S. Matthey at Loglab in the wrong way?

Agenda

Conference Call   Wednesday 10.00 CET   Call-in number: …

Objective: To discuss plan of action re Loglab

Attendees: Jan + Johanna (Vienna), Ian (Hamburg), Valerie (Warsaw)

Action item: Delayed delivery yesterday with Loglab is one in a series. Meet to discuss options / decide plan of action

Can we get a different, more reliable customer service manager?
Need more support from Ian – can he call someone higher up at Loglab?

I can write a short report

Now take part in the telecon while keeping the following information in mind.

- You have a call with a customer at 11.10 (10.10 Central European Time).
- You are taking the minutes, so make sure everything is clear.
- You get disconnected and have to dial in again.
- You can have a meeting any morning except Tuesday.

→ *File 21*

Partner C

Present the situation in the HR Department. Afterwards, you are free to defend the special interests of 'your' department, or to argue your own opinions and ideas.

Your department is split between two groups; your payroll staff earns substantially lower bonuses than your HR development team. This has actually caused some major problems in the department. The head of department has briefed you to suggest a way out: outsource payroll and have the department focus solely on human resource development. As your boss says, *'Let's do what we do best.'*

Partner B

Present the information below to your partner, using your own words and explaining any terms as necessary.

Scrum development is one of several agile approaches to project management in IT. As in rugby, the team members work closely together, starting each working day with the 'daily Scrum', a stand-up meeting used for planning that day's work as a unit.

Model:

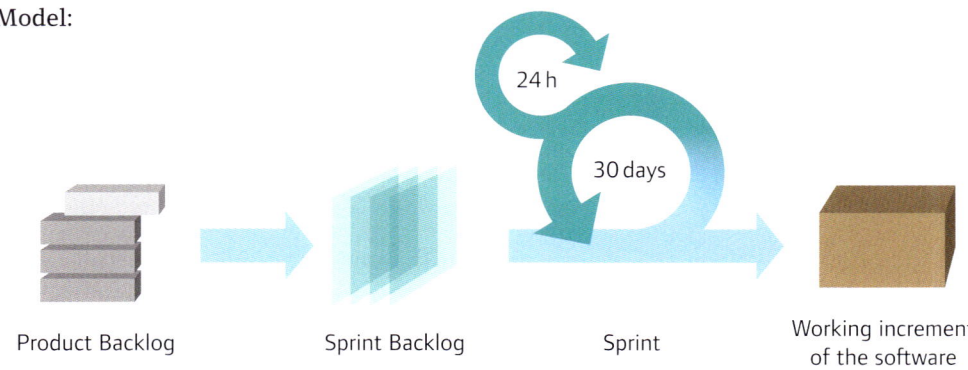

Product Backlog   Sprint Backlog   Sprint   Working increment of the software

Key features:
- Agile Project Management is more flexible and interactive than traditional PM.
- Deliverables are submitted in stages, and requirements adjusted as needed.
- Scrum coordinates the work in units of 30 days, broken into daily work cycles, with the workload defined by the team every morning.
- Testing is integrated, raising quality and reducing risk of outcomes not matching expectations.
- Stakeholders / users are involved to test and adjust product requirements.

Method and terminology:
- 'product backlog' = product requirements broken down into tasks of 4–16 hours.
- 'sprint backlog' = work selected from the backlog for the next sprint, i.e. to be completed within 30 days.
- 'daily stand-up' = short team meeting held every 24 hours during the sprint, where everyone reports on what's been done, what needs to be done, and what's stopping them or what they need help with.

Main drawbacks:
- It is difficult to implement within a hierarchical organization used to formal planning, since the team defines the workload during the sprint.
- Improving the deliverable incrementally (i.e., with gradual increases) invites 'scope creep', as the requirements change and expand to suit the stakeholders' needs.
- Stakeholders may not understand or accept their key and active role in the process.

Partner A: Planning team, telecon facilitator

Hold a short telecon to clarify the main issues of the upcoming trip.

- Invite each person to contribute.
- Your main focus is on the safety of the equipment / instruments / gear in transport. You think the best way to transport everything would be by … (come up with your own ideas).
- The telecon has been delayed due to technical problems and now you have to go another meeting in five minutes.

→ File 24

Partner C: Support on site

Take part in a short telecon to clarify the main issues of the upcoming trip.

- Your main focus is on the well-being of the travellers.
- Go off-topic occasionally. You have experience of a similar trip where something bad happened because of poor planning. Make up the details and inform the other participants.
- You have to leave briefly, but will come back.

→ File 25

Partner D

Present the situation in the Finance Department. Afterwards, you are free to defend the special interests of 'your' department, or to argue your own opinions and ideas.

Your department's performance-based remuneration averages to 100 %. This is a policy your boss suggests the whole company should adopt. He has also suggested reintroducing stock options. They were once a part of the pay package but were dropped when the shares didn't grow. Now that steady growth is established, being shareholders might be an attractive perk. As your boss says, *'No risk, no fun'.*

→ File 26

Partner C

You are Johanna, responsible for logistics at Medtec Vienna. First, look at the agenda and your notes below.

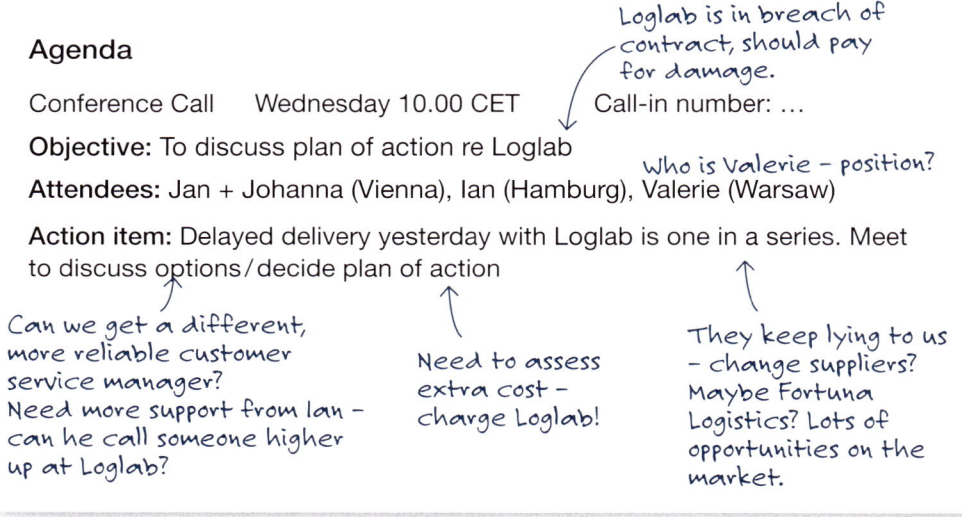

Agenda

Conference Call   Wednesday 10.00 CET   Call-in number: …

Objective: To discuss plan of action re Loglab

Attendees: Jan + Johanna (Vienna), Ian (Hamburg), Valerie (Warsaw)

Action item: Delayed delivery yesterday with Loglab is one in a series. Meet to discuss options/decide plan of action

Loglab is in breach of contract, should pay for damage.

Who is Valerie – position?

Can we get a different, more reliable customer service manager? Need more support from Ian – can he call someone higher up at Loglab?

Need to assess extra cost – charge Loglab!

They keep lying to us – change suppliers? Maybe Fortuna Logistics? Lots of opportunities on the market.

Now take part in the telecon while keeping the following information in mind.

- You have trouble dialling in the first time, and keep losing the connection.
- You have to leave for a meeting at 10.15 at the latest.
- You're waiting for an important call on your mobile, and have to interrupt the telecon to answer it.
- You can't attend meetings on Mondays and Wednesdays before 10 am.

Partner D

Step 1: Sonnenschein CFO (Chief Financial Officer)
You have been invited to a meeting to prepare for the press conference. Look at the agenda and your notes. At the meeting, your role is to introduce questions that the various corporate stakeholders will ask.

AGENDA / Let's rethink these points:

Compliance overview system? Stakeholders? Speed of development? Price segment? Packaging? PR + co-branding with suppliers of meat products from organically farmed animals? Implement a new 'Purity Code' (to be defined)?

Notes

Total expected cost of recall = ¼ of all profits incl. possible loss of key supplier.
Need to rebrand and improve CSR to grow!
Expecting new markets in emerging economies in Eastern / Southern Europe.
Sources / Guaranteed quality: New regulations on compliance next year; redefine 'Purity code' for specific target markets.

Step 2: Reporter

During the press conference, you will act as a reporter. Use your notes below to formulate questions.

Notes

What happened? Where? When did they find out? What are they doing about it? Who's responsible / to blame? Were there any warning signs? How will consumers be protected / compensated? If ... then why ...?
Research has shown: Definition of 'Purity' varies from country to country, e.g. China is stricter about transparency requirements and the levels of bacteria permitted in products; there is more trust in local production in Europe. How will Sonnenschein handle this?

Partner A

You are Sunil Gupta, remunerations officer and head of the committee to agree on:

1 a short-term solution to replace bonuses in the current year; and
2 a solution to improve the bonus system in the long term.

Start the meeting and keep it on track. Make sure all members have their say, and summarize the results. Remember, compromise means that everyone benefits in some way and can be happy with the results.

➜ File 29

You are a 'driver'. You focus on the task and want to get the job done. During the discussion of the topics in the box, use phrases from below to make sure the others focus on getting the job done too.

Discussion topics:

1 Should you introduce the practice of shadowing colleagues from other departments?
2 Should you extend a delivery deadline by a week, as several people are off sick?
3 Should you switch from company phones to private mobiles?

Use phrases like these to make suggestions:
· Come on, let's get started.
· The first thing we need to do is …
· When can you have this ready?

Use phrases like these to respond to other suggestions:
· The sooner, the better.
· If that works, fine.
· OK, but let everyone know if there are any problems.

➜ File 30

Partner F

Present the situation in the Marketing Department. Afterwards, you are free to defend the special interests of 'your' department, or to argue your own opinions and ideas.

The staff in your department enjoys perks like company cars and other non-financial rewards such as free tickets to sporting events and fashion shows.

Your boss has suggested more such perks would benefit the company and that, with some imagination, more cost-effective online training or 'free' team-building activities could replace payments. Your boss likes to quote Henry Ford: *'A business that makes nothing but money is a poor business.'*

➜ File 31

Partner A: Buyer

Partner B is going to pitch his / her services to you. Use the questions and tips below to organize your thoughts and prepare for the meeting.

Before the meeting:
· Think about the service you are interested in. What exactly do you want or need?
· Why aren't you doing it yourself? (e.g. time, risk, ability)
· What details are important to you? Why?
· What assurance would you need to agree to buy this service?
· What is this service worth to you in general?
· Determine the price range you would be willing to pay.
· What are your terms and conditions?

At the meeting:
· Explain exactly what you are looking for, and why.
· If the seller hasn't understood your needs, correct him or her.
· Then listen closely: Is the service this seller is offering you what you want?

→ *File 32*

Partner A (client): negotiating intercultural workshops

You want to hire a facilitator for intercultural workshops to be held over the next few months. Look at the information below from someone who was recommended by a customer of yours, then call him / her and negotiate the best possible terms.

The standard package:
· Three workshops within three months plus two reports, for a total of € 10,000. (This package does not suit your needs.)

Your requirements:
· You prefer two workshops, or two compact blocks of two days.
· You could reduce the scope of the project, e.g. drop the initial report.
· Suggest two project phases, perhaps additional workshops later?

Your budget:
· € 15,000 for facilitation of the entire project.

→ *File 33*

Proposal B

You are going to give a 2–4-minute oral report at your next team meeting. Follow the steps below to prepare.

1 First read the consultant's brief below.
2 Then add your own ideas (advantages / disadvantages) and be ready to discuss these ideas after giving your report.

Specify roles in the team more clearly

What:	Assign specific roles to each team member and make sure they understand and act accordingly.
Why:	Collaboration improves when the roles are clearly defined and understood, and when individuals can do most of their work independently. (Studies prove this.) People should focus on their task, not protect their role.
How:	Define roles. Inform everyone.
Critical note:	If there is no overlap, it may be more difficult to jump in when a co-worker is ill, etc.

→ *File 34*

Proposal D

You are going to give a 2–4-minute oral report at your next team meeting. Follow the steps below to prepare.

1 First read the consultant's brief below.
2 Then add your own ideas (advantages / disadvantages) and be ready to discuss these ideas after giving your report.

Build better relationships in the team

What:	Ensure that the team has a more effective working relationship. Create opportunities to communicate on the job (go to lunch together, secondment, …). Offer after-work activities (team building, networking, …).
Why:	'All work and no play makes Jack a dull boy.' Intercultural problems can only be solved personally. Motivation is key: people need to enjoy working together. Trust and team spirit are built on shared experience.
How:	Create opportunities (events, etc.) and delegate responsibilities (who coordinates, who invites, and so on).
Critical note:	No direct and measurable effect; additional time required

---

→ *File 35*

Partner E

Present the situation in the Sales Department. Afterwards, you are free to defend the special interests of 'your' department, or to argue your own opinions and ideas.

Your department does not participate in the pay-for-performance scheme. Your bonus comes through actual sales performance. The difference in salaries within your department is higher than elsewhere in the company. Your department is the first to feel that sales are down due to the crisis.

Your boss has said to you that the company would benefit from being more careful about 'performance evaluations' and thinks it is right to cut bonuses for everyone. Your boss has also reminded you not to confuse lots of activity with actual achievement.

→ *File 36*

Partner D: Support on site

Take part in a short telecon to clarify the main issues of the upcoming trip.

· Your main focus is on practical details: dates, times, etc.
· You can't always identify who is speaking – ask speakers to repeat their names.
· Interrupt someone to try and clarify details.

Partner C

Step 1: Sonnenschein Marketing Manager

You have been invited to a meeting to prepare for the press conference. Look at the agenda and your notes. At the meeting, your role is to introduce questions that consumers will ask.

AGENDA / Let's rethink these points:

Compliance overview system? Stakeholders? Speed of development? Price segment? Packaging? PR + co-branding with suppliers of meat products from organically farmed animals? Implement a new 'Purity Code' (to be defined)?

Notes

Absolute transparency required; survey shows that organically grown high quality + good price more important than local source. Increase visibility of sources

Step 2: Reporter

During the press conference, you will act as a reporter. Use your notes below to formulate questions.

Notes

What happened? Where? When did they find out? What are they doing about it? Who's responsible / to blame? Were there any warning signs? How will consumers be protected / compensated? If ... then why ...?
Research has shown: Price for home-made paella w/ingredients from organic supermarket (seafood, meats and vegetables, rice, olive oil, herbs and spices) = over EUR 6 per person;
Price for regular frozen paella at a discounter = EUR 2.10 per person.
Price for Sonnenschein Organic Paella = EUR 3.20 per person. Too cheap to be real?

Partner B: Seller

You are going to pitch your services to Partner A. Use the questions and tips below to organize your thoughts and prepare for the meeting.

Before the meeting:
- Think about your range of services. What different demands and needs do they serve?
- What is your target group? What details set you apart from the competition?
- What credentials do you have to win the buyer's trust? (e.g. transparency, case studies)
- What is your bottom line for a price, and what are you aiming for?
- What are your conditions?

At the meeting:
- Find out what the buyer wants or needs. Listen carefully, then summarize and check.
- Once everything is clarified, pitch your services.

Unit 1   pages 16–19

1

A, **C** and **D** still have a connection to the company. **B** doesn't.

2

1   have just submitted
2   have … been living, For
3   have been researching, since
4   did … design, conducted, ago
5   has … negotiated, have been discussing, for
6   Has … drafted, haven't spoken, finished
7   completed, ago, has been working / has worked, since
8   has he been auditing, has been doing, for

3

1   have … made (or: have … been making)
2   has become
3   designed
4   have been drafting (or: have drafted)
5   took part
6   ran

4

The following words should be crossed out:

2   accounts
3   customers
4   negotiations
5   budgets, emails
6   to attend
7   to arrange, to process
8   to process
9   to conduct
10 to participate in, to conduct

5

1 f F		**3** a E		**5** c C	
2 e B		**4** b D		**6** d A	

6

1 d		**3** a		**5** c	
2 e		**4** f		**6** b	

7

Suggested answers:

1   Excuse me, I was just thinking that we could take a short break.
2   John and I were hoping we could have a video conference next time.

3   Uhm, I was just wondering if anyone / someone could give me a lift to the airport after the meeting?

8

Suggested answers:

1   The new member of our team has excellent knowledge in the field / area of consumer (packaged) goods.
2   Look. Here is the proof that the product has been / is successful.
3   We haven't tested the ingredient / substance in the laboratory yet, but we are confident (that) it will be effective.
4   The customers had to fill in several forms as part of the survey.
5   What sector / field / industry do you work in?
6   He's (already) been working in this branch for a few months but will soon move to our head office in Vienna.
7   We use the customer surveys / feedback reports to carry out various analyses.

Unit 2   pages 26–29

1

C

2

1 is received		**3** are met		**5** are remitted	
2 is reviewed		**4** is placed		**6** is returned	

3

1   we were taken
2   makes
3   we were greeted
4   informed
5   we had arrived
6   he had handed / he handed
7   told
8   were employed
9   wasn't mentioned
10 is going to be downsized / will be downsized
11 is currently being built

4

2   d   The interface has been streamlined in order to simplify the system.
3   b   No staff leave is being scheduled at key times to avoid being short-staffed.

4 f Their clients will be offered immediate refunds to prevent further complaints.
OR Immediate refunds will be offered to their clients to prevent further complaints.
5 c A marketing campaign will be launched in order to win more clients.
6 a A series of workshops is being organized in order to train our staff.

5
1	log on	**8**	pinpoint
2	access	**a**	because of
3	led	**b**	then
4	allowed	**c**	though
5	enter	**d**	but
6	was notified	**e**	in the end
7	have been instructed	**f**	at first

6
1	c	**3**	e	**5**	d
2	a	**4**	f	**6**	b

very formal recommendations: **1**c, **3**e, **5**d

7
1 First of all, we noticed
2 so we decided to
3 secondly
4 finally
5 actually
6 so overall this meant that
7 resulting in
8 the next steps

8
1 I suggest (that) new machines be bought.
2 We propose that the manager hire highly skilled staff.
3 I suggest (that) costs be cut radically.
4 I propose that the workers be given better training courses.

9
1 The bad economic situation probably won't / isn't going to affect us.
2 As soon as / Once payment has been effected, the goods will be sent / dispatched.
3 We must / have to live with the effects of the changes.
4 I always make a note of the names of new colleagues.
5 He made some notes beforehand.
6 She advised me to check the system.

7 He can give very good advice.
8 How can you ensure that the processes will improve?

Unit 3   pages 38–41

1
B

2
Complete sentences in the correct sequence:
2 e This afternoon our group is holding a meeting.
5 c I won't be going, though, because I am flying to Switzerland in a couple of hours.
4 a I'm not sure what they'll be discussing either because I haven't seen the agenda.
3 d However, I'm pretty sure they wouldn't be talking about Project Excellence.
6 f The reason I say that is because, as far as I know, that particular project won't be starting until next year.
1 b That's why I'm sure they won't be going into that matter in any depth.

3
The following tenses are correct:
1 will be laying / would be laying
2 would be running
3 are you meeting / will you be meeting
4 will you be joining
5 will you be discussing
6 would you be going over / will you be going over

4
Suggested answers:
2 What we are probably supposed to do is ask head office first.
3 High-quality products – that's what this company is well known for.
4 What we don't know yet is the scope of the project.
5 A firm commitment from your side – that's what we're hoping for.
6 What we will definitely agree (to do) is not to disclose any confidential material.
7 What we really appreciate is your confidence in us.

5

1 Before we go any further
2 Assuming
3 would you be willing
4 step by step
5 if I have understood you correctly
6 Just thinking aloud for a moment

6

1	otherwise	b	**4**	never	a
2	exclusively, thus	c	**5**	accordingly	e
3	Presumably	d			

7

Suggested answers:

1 The firm / company has implemented the new measures quickly and consistently.
2 They didn't sign the contract yesterday. Consequently, we now need to rethink everything.
3 He has overseen the whole process up to now but he has overlooked an important detail.
4 That was an oversight. It won't happen again.
5 We need to develop efficient oversight measures, otherwise we won't get the contract.
6 Unfortunately, I don't have much spare time at the moment.
7 We need the spare parts urgently.
8 We (have) saved a lot of money with the new energy plan.

Unit 4   pages 48–51

1

1 point of sale
2 incoming goods
3 tagged
4 RFID technology
5 temperature-controlled
6 shipped
7 track and trace
8 outgoing goods

2

1	c	C	**3**	b	F	**5**	d	B
2	e	A	**4**	f	E	**6**	a	D

3

1	off	**3**	put	**5**	over
2	out of	**4**	piece	**6**	off

4

1 d I've noticed that you don't seem to provide overnight deliveries.
2 c Keep things as simple as possible please, because …
3 a You might want to keep your voice down.
4 f I have the impression that you sometimes don't fill in the right form.
5 b One thing that puzzles me is that you hardly ever get back to me.
6 e If you could just use the surname first …

5

1	a	**3**	a	**5**	b
2	b	**4**	a	**6**	b

6

1 I suppose we might just be misunderstanding one another.
2 I'd appreciate it if we could communicate more often in the future.
3 It would help if I had more time to prepare next time.
4 It seems we might have got off on the wrong foot.
5 Can you try and send it to me by the end of the day at the latest?
6 That certainly has taken me a bit by surprise.

7

1	a	**5**	b	**9**	e
2	i	**6**	g	**10**	j
3	h	**7**	c		
4	f	**8**	d		

8

Suggested answers:

1 It was not proper / right to pass on that confidential information by email. / Passing on that information by email was not the right thing to do.
2 The logistics are rather / quite / very complex, but I'm convinced / sure (that) we will soon (be able to) find a good solution.
3 You can't blame him for that; he just didn't have all the information (he needed).
4 She knocked over a glass of wine at the dinner with her business partner and made a complete fool of herself.
5 Our competition really messed up / failed miserably in the presentation of / when presenting their new product.

6 We were all a bit / a little confused after the telephone conference. Who is (now) responsible for the delivery / shipment (now)?

7 It irritates me when people don't respond to their emails straight away / quickly.

Unit 5 pages 60–63

1

These words are the odd ones out:

1	fund	**3**	damage	**5**	license
2	default on	**4**	bail out	**6**	invest

2

Correct order:

1 started working for KBP

2 wanted a change

3 met some interesting people at a trade fair

4 accepted a promotion

3

1 had consistently had

2 were planning / planned

3 were even hoping / even hoped

4 had already approached

5 had been / was

6 struck

7 had been

8 launched

9 had become / became

10 had to

11 decided

12 had been

4

1	c	**3**	e	**5**	c
2	a	**4**	a	**6**	d

5

2 net; net

3 assets; asset

4 liabilities; liability

5 balance; balance

6 sustainable; Sustainable

7 return; return

6

2 set us back

3 got over it

4 look into it

5 (have) brought that up

6 put me off

7 looked them over

7

2 had continued, would have made

3 wouldn't be, had realized

4 would have had, had handled

5 hadn't defaulted, would have

6 wouldn't have had to, hadn't developed

1	c	**3**	a	**5**	f
2	b	**4**	e	**6**	d

8

Suggested answers:

1 When I first started at the company, I was paid according to the pay scale.

2 We made losses of just under a billion euros last year.

3 The company sold approximately / roughly 3.5 million units last year.

4 They were unable to raise enough capital to bail out the company / to bail the company out.

5 While auditing the accounts, he discovered discrepancies / problems / inconsistencies.

Unit 6 pages 70–73

1

1 performance evaluation

2 parental leave

3 heavy workload

4 meal voucher

5 dress code

6 red tape

7 performance-based pay

8 retirement fund

2

1 insisted

2 asked

3 explained

4 told

5 promised

6 announced

7 complained

8 didn't apologize

3

2 asked me whether we had any childcare facilities

3 told her / said (that) we had handled nine major projects in the previous year

4 asked me how often we had a performance evaluation

5 told me / said (that) she had never worked in advertising before

6 told her / said (that) she hadn't enjoyed her previous job because it hadn't been very challenging

7 asked me whether / if she would get a company car

4

| 1 | absolutely | 3 | rather a | 5 | vastly |
| 2 | remarkably | 4 | dependent | 6 | impressive |

5

| 1 | b – D | 3 | e – A | 5 | a – F |
| 2 | d – E | 4 | f – C | 6 | c – B |

6

Suggested answers:

1 She quit / left her last job because her boss (had) bullied her.

2 She started her own business directly after university and is now a successful entrepreneur.

3 Biochemistry has always interested me / been of interest to me. It is such an exciting area of research.

4 I am very concerned about the costs.

5 This especially concerns the new line of products that is currently being developed / in development.

Unit 7 pages 82–85

1

2 approaching, tailored to

3 responsible for, unavailable

4 negotiating

5 wanting to, working

2

2 We offer highly reliable software packages providing innovative solutions needed in specialist branches such as yours.

3 I can show you some beautifully illustrated online catalogues produced in-house and showcasing our most popular product lines.

4 They told me about some recently developed products appealing to highly attractive target groups.

3

B

4

1 Under no circumstances should you file charges.

2 Rarely do people confuse the two logos.

3 No sooner had we launched the product than the company accused us of copyright infringement.

4 Never before had we been ordered to cease production.

5 In no way can we agree to your demands.

6 Not only might this be a bad idea, it's probably also illegal.

5

1	flimsy	6	on the spot
2	detrimental	7	exact
3	exacting	8	deficits
4	instrumental	9	satisfactory
5	costs, cheap	10	warranty, free

6

| 1 | c – B | 3 | a – D | 5 | b – F |
| 2 | f – C | 4 | e – A | 6 | d – E |

7

The following words should be crossed out:

1 confused

2 failed

3 infringe

4 the decision

5 an offering

6 as intellectual property

8

Suggested answers:

1 It's important to keep all your receipts for tax purposes.

2 Is that a complicated recipe?

3 You get more customers by using different sales channels.

4 She used to work in the legal department but now heads (up) / is head of the HR / personnel department.

5 They are trying to dominate the market by launching a second brand.

6 We shouldn't publish any content that infringes / violates copyright.

Unit 8   pages 92–95

1
1	violating	7	reading
2	happening	8	to cover
3	to improve	9	to submit
4	increasing	10	to comply
5	promoting	11	hearing
6	to attend		

2
1 b I'm afraid I can't comment on that until the results of our inquiry are in.

2 d I don't have that information at this point but I will pass it on as soon as I do.

3 a You are implying that we had previous knowledge, which isn't the case.

4 e Let me just break that down and answer each question in turn.

5 c So, you're really asking whether this is part of our policy, and no, it most definitely is not.

3
1	b	3	f	5	c
2	d	4	e	6	a

4
1 This system doesn't seem to work.
2 We do not condone this practice.
3 They tend to pay low wages.
4 The evidence suggests that unclear ethical guidelines cause bad practice.
5 This suggests that I am right.
6 This is generally considered to be a KPI.

5
1	carpet, light	3	conclusions	5	books
2	numbers	4	head	6	bush

a 1 to come to light
b 3 to jump to conclusions
c 6 to always beat around the bush
d 2 to make the numbers work
e 5 to cook the books
f 4 off the top of my head
g 1 to sweep things under the carpet

6
1	d	3	a	5	c
2	f	4	e	6	b

7
The following words should be crossed out:
1 generate
2 after
3 aligning
4 condemn
5 fulfilled
6 endorse

8
1 extend the life
2 condone this behaviour
3 exert pressure
4 protect confidentiality
5 assess the extent
6 live up to its commitments

9
1 a backlash
2 minimize the fallout
3 enact
4 come under fire
5 an onslaught
6 spans

10
Suggested answers:
1 I think it's impolite when people text each other in meetings.
2 We guarantee discrete handling of sensitive client data.
3 The manual is divided into three discrete sections.
4 The people living next to the airport are important stakeholders, so they must be / have to be consulted before building the runway.
5 This point will be put to the vote at the next shareholders' meeting.

Self-introductions

Whether you are preparing for a face-to-face meeting or a telephone conference, the more you know about the other participants and the purpose of the meeting, the easier it will be to make a link between what you *need to say* in your introduction and what the other attendees *need to hear*. Prepare several variations of your self-introduction for different types of meetings.

Tips
- Keep your introduction short and to the point.
- State your company or department name as clearly as your own.
- Smile, and in face-to-face meetings, make eye contact with the other participants.

Template

Before you prepare your introduction, identify your role and determine the context and purpose of the meeting.

My role is …
The context is …
The other participants are …
The purpose / objective of the meeting is to …

Greet your fellow participants by clearly pronouncing (and if necessary spelling) your name.
Explain how you would like to be addressed. In telephone conferences, state your location as well.
Telephone conferences
Good morning / afternoon from (city). / This is (both names) calling from … / I'm based in (city) / at HQ / the Linz subsidiary / branch … / Please call me (first name). / That's Stephen with a P-H, by the way …

Face-to-face meetings
Good morning / afternoon. My name is / I'm (both names) … / Please call me (first name).

Explain your role and function at the meeting.
I'm going to be chairing / facilitating / demonstrating / updating … / I'm standing in for … / I'm here to learn more about … / I'll be presenting the current status of … / I'm here as an observer today actually and am particularly interested in …

State key responsibilities that have a bearing on the issue at hand. Keep the message concise and upbeat.
Formal / Neutral
I'm the CIO / a member of the project team … / I ensure / see to it that …

Informal
I am the 'go-to person' around here … / I'm the first point of contact for … / By that I mean, … / It's my job to … / I look after the legal / technical / PR side of things.

(Optional)
Mention key past (relevant) professional achievements in a few words.
My team is a forerunner in … / I am a member of the team that developed … / My team and I set up the …

For conference calls: Finish by saying something personal to catch people's interest.
Hope the sun is shining where you are too! / … and I'd just like to congratulate you on your (national sports team / your company) winning the … / Looking forward to seeing you all in August …

Effective report writing

Writing effective reports to communicate information both internally and externally is a key business skill. Headings, subheadings and signposting enable both the initiated and uninitiated to grasp the content quickly. Succinct language, the appropriate use of the passive voice, linking words and parallel structures ensure that your report is clear and professional.

Template

Introduction

Terms of reference: Provide the reader with the background and rationale for your report.

The following is a report on ... commissioned by ... / This study was requested by ... / This business proposal was developed in response to ... / This is the half-year / quarterly report ... for the month ending (date).

Summary / Abstract: Present the main topic and the scope of the report in the first few lines.

This report is an investigation into / analysis of ... / The following defines the scope and limitations of ... / This survey was conducted by ... / Over the last three years the (group / department) has undertaken a structured review of ... / It was concluded that ... / The major findings were ... / The recommendations are the following: ...

Body

Procedure: State the analytical measures or principles used to gather the data.

The baseline data for this report was collated by means of a large scale survey ... / The methodology comprised ... / A SWOT analysis was conducted ...

Findings: Present the breakthroughs and results of your analysis or research. Include figures and tables.

The major findings are as follows: ... / The results of the analysis confirm that in the first quarter of the year ..., however ... / This may be due to ... / Surprisingly, ..., which was an unforeseen result of ... / This has laid the foundations for a successful long-term ...

Closing

Conclusions: Summarize your findings and make recommendations.

The main conclusion that can be drawn, therefore, is that ... / To sum up, it may be concluded that ... / In the light of these factors / In order to prevent future setbacks, it is recommended that ... / Thus we strongly recommend that ...

Short talks

Most effective talks, regardless of length, follow a basic and predictable outline: opening, body and conclusion. Use the template below, which contains tips from www.write-out-loud.com, to practise short talks and develop the techniques and phrases needed to do them off the cuff.

■ **Tips**
- Keep your talk brief, conversational and personal.
- Select one main point to focus on.
- Pause before you start. Smile and make eye contact with the audience.

Template

Begin with the first good idea that strikes you and make it the core of your speech.
Choose the framework you wish to hang your talk on:

☐ Past ➡ present ➡ future
☐ Cause ➡ effect ➡ solution
☐ Point ➡ reason ➡ example ➡ point …

Jot down one main point and two or three sub-points that you would like to cover in your talk.

Opening
Lead in with an effective opening.
When I was driving here today I …/How often do we find ourselves in a situation where …?/
I distinctly remember the first time I met (name), …, and he turned to me and asked/said …

State your topic and outline your agenda.
I've been asked to say a few words about …/I'm going to tell you about …/
I am only going to mention one main point …/We only have five minutes, so I will briefly fill you in on the one thing that everybody wants to know …

Body
Use one of the frameworks below to develop your brief talk.

Past ➡ present ➡ future
First talk about what happened in the past, then lead in to what is happening at the moment and conclude by saying what will happen next.

What happened in the past
In the past we focused chiefly on …/
Five years ago who would even have thought of …?

What is happening now
Now we have come to the conclusion that …/
Currently we are not only … but also …

What is going to happen next
In the future we will …/The next quarter will show …/Time will tell …

Cause ➜ effect ➜ solution

First get to the root of the issue, then state what the effects are and conclude with a solution or way out.

Cause
The cause of / reason for / source of the problem is … / We are confronted with / facing …

Effect
The effect / result / outcome / consequence / upshot is …

Solution
The solution / answer / way out as I see it is …

Point ➜ reason ➜ example ➜ point …

First make a point, then give a reason or reasons for it and conclude with a concrete example. Repeat this pattern for each point you make.

Point
The point I wish to make is that … / What I would like to draw your attention to is …

Reason
The reason for this is … / The explanation is quite simple really; it's …

Example
Let me give you an example … / I'll show exactly what I mean by that now …

Conclusion

End with a powerful statement or, if possible, a relevant quote.

So, before I hand over to (name), I'd like to ask you to … /
On that note, I'd like to … / And lastly, I leave you with this thought … /
To borrow a few words from Mohammed Ali, 'Float like a butterfly, sting like a bee!'

Effective emails

Email is undoubtedly the most important form of written communication in business today. Many emails, however, are unnecessary and ineffective. To avoid unproductive emails, ensure timely responses and reduce the number of emails returning with follow-up questions, summarize your message in the subject line and be specific about what action you want the recipient to take.

■ Tips
- Never leave the subject line blank.
- Keep your sentences concise and to the point.
- When writing complex emails that cover several points, add an introductory line and number the points.
- Use a spell checker or dictionary to avoid mistakes that could tarnish your professional image.

Template

Salutation and close

Personalize your message by including a pleasant (and appropriate) salutation and closing comment.
(Note that if you use a comma after the salutation, you should use one after the complimentary close as well.)

Neutral / Formal

Dear Ms Smith,   Dear Liz
Thank you for your email ...   It was nice to hear from you ...
Should you have any questions or queries, please do not hesitate to contact me. /
Please give my regards to ... / I look forward to hearing from you. / Wishing you a good week.
Kind regards / Best wishes (,)

Informal

Hi Tom,   Hello Sarah
Hope you are well.   How are things?

Please feel free to get in touch any time. / Have a good / great evening / weekend. /
Say hi to everyone from me.
All the best / Atb / Take care / Best (,)

Opening

State the point of reference for writing your email.

Neutral / formal

Further to your email ... / I am writing in response to ... / I was asked by (name) to contact you
regarding ... / I have a question concerning / regarding ... / I'm interested in ...

Informal

Re your comments, I'd just like to ... / This is just a short email to ... / Just a quick reminder ... /
Re the next meeting, I'm afraid ... / I need some info on ...

Body

State the purpose of your email in the first one or two lines. Say concisely what you want the recipient to do and state any deadlines clearly.

Informing

Neutral / Formal

I am pleased / I regret to announce that … / I would just like to give you an update on / confirm / respond to your request … / I am afraid there has been a change in circumstances / plan … / I have attached the … / No reply is necessary.

Informal

Here's the info you requested … / FYI, we've had to make some changes / adjustments re … / Good news, we … / Unfortunately, we have run into some difficulties … / Pls find the … attached. / No need to reply.

Requesting action

Neutral / Formal

Could you possibly revise / draw up / organize / ensure … by 12 August / no later than Thursday 12.00 p.m.? / I would be grateful / appreciate it very much if we could … / We ask that you keep us informed concerning … / Could you contact me regarding …?

Informal

Can you give me a hand with … / do me a favour … / check whether … / fit me in for a meeting? It would be great if you could let me know / keep me in the loop about … / Pls fill me in on … / Re …, what's the story?

Ask yourself the question 'so what?' after each point you make and then formulate the answer.

The reason we have decided to do this is … / This action is part of the … / The rationale behind this is … / We are doing this because … / This is a direct result of …

Etiquette

Answer all questions you have been asked, then anticipate further questions and answer them, too. Not answering all the questions in an email can generate a stream of superfluous follow-up emails and thus waste time.

I will answer your three questions in blue below. / The answer to your question is yes.

However, I do foresee … / I'm afraid I can't help you with this question but perhaps (name) can.

If time constraints do not allow a prompt response, let the recipient know when you will respond.

Formal / Neutral

Thank you for your email. I will respond to your queries on my return from … / once I have gathered the necessary information. / We have received your request and will process it by (date). / I will respond in full to your query on (date).

Informal

Thanks for your message. I will look into it and get back to you asap. / I got your query. Thnx. Once I hear back from (name) I will send out an email with …

Opening a conference call

At the beginning of a conference call, the call leader (who may or may not be the chair) should explain the importance of communicating as clearly as possible and set some ground rules to ensure the effectiveness of the meeting. As call leader, it is worthwhile going live with the call a few minutes before the actual meeting is due to start. This is the conference call equivalent of letting people engage in small talk before the official meeting begins; it also helps ensure proceedings begin on time.

■ Tips

- Know who you will be speaking to and address participants by name.
- Smile. Smiling has a positive effect on the tone of your voice and helps build rapport.

Template

Introduce yourself and welcome the participants. Say something about your location and something pleasant to get the meeting off to a good start.

Good afternoon from … / This is (both names). You are all very welcome … / I'm glad we are able to start on time today … / Thanks to all of you for being on time … / It's a beautiful day here in (city) … . I hope it is where you are too.

Refer to the agenda.

You should all have the agenda. / Let's take a quick look at / review / try to stick to our agenda. / Our agenda today is deliberately short as we want to spend most of our time developing ideas and brainstorming …

Highlight the goals of the meeting.

Our objective / main task / brief today is to … / As you all know, we are here today to …

Define the ground rules.

Let me go over the ground rules briefly. Please refrain from writing emails / interrupting other speakers … / I'd like to ask you to use headsets / not use your speakerphones … / Please speak clearly and keep your comments brief. / May I ask you to take into account that not all of our colleagues here today are native speakers of English? / Could I ask you to speak in turn / identify yourself and your location before you speak?

Framing a proposal

Whether a proposal put forward at a meeting or a point made in a negotiation is accepted or rejected depends very much on how it is presented or *framed*. What follows is an easy-to-remember framing method for getting your ideas across in a logical and convincing fashion.

■ **Tips**

· Make sure the benefits of your proposal are clear.
· Restate any objections in the form of a question and then answer the question.
· Listen actively to show interest in what the other party has to say.

Template

BLUP (Bottom Line Up Front): By putting your key message first, you get the other party's immediate attention and avoid misunderstandings.
I'd like to run something past you. / Here's what I've been thinking ... / Here's what I propose. Why don't we ...?

Link details and benefits.
The advantages of doing it like this are ... / I think it would be wise to ... /
Can I point out one great benefit? You see by doing this, it would take the pressure off ... /
Not only would this solve the problem of ..., it would also ...

Disarm anticipated objections.
I realize that there could be a drawback to this, namely ... But, on balance, I think the advantages of my proposal outweigh the disadvantages. / You might say ..., but I think that this particular objection might not be relevant in our / this case. I'll tell you why.

Ask for feedback.
OK, so that's the gist of it. What do you think? / That's the proposal in a nutshell. I'd appreciate your opinion on this. / I'm looking forward to hearing your feedback.

Giving feedback

Whether you are talking to a direct report, a peer or a superior, giving feedback can be a difficult task. The techniques and language below will help you keep your feedback constructive and non-threatening.

Template

Before addressing the weak points, make sure the person feels valued and respected. Focus on the value the person creates for the team / company and emphasize the positive.

Congratulations on … / That was a real coup … / Your personal effort led to … / You are a very valuable / key member of the team … / I must say, I have been very impressed by …

Set the tone. Use your people skills to decide which approach to take when voicing criticism.

Matter-of-fact approach

To be honest, this is … / Let's put our cards on the table … / This is the situation: … / There are three points I'd like to address: … / What we need to discuss is the following: …

Delicate approach

I'd like you to give me your opinion first … / So, your strengths clearly lie in … / Let's focus on what can be improved on now …

Emphasize the key points and be careful to describe the behaviour, and not the person. Give concrete examples.

What I have noticed is … / It is vital that we … / You see, when you roll your eyes, it … / I feel that this kind of behaviour is counterproductive. / Let me give you a concrete example. / I am referring to … in particular … / Allow me to be specific here …

Listen actively. Pay close attention to what the other party has to say, summarize periodically and address any questions calmly and thoughtfully.

That is a valid point … / I understand your concern; however, … / Let's summarize at this point … / Would you like to sum up your understanding of where we are now?

Reiterate the person's strengths and give (or ask for) suggestions for improvement.

I am quite confident that with your expertise / business acumen / customer savvy / technical know-how, you will be able to … / If I may make a suggestion, …

Offer support and the opportunity for follow-up.

Feel free to approach me at any time for a quick chat … / My door is always open …

Effective socializing

Social niceties and small talk are important not only to 'break the ice', but also to build relationships with business partners, colleagues and acquaintances. Good social skills such as selecting the appropriate choice of topic, listening actively and sharing common ground lead to conversations that flow naturally and reflect the interests of everybody involved.

■ Tips
- Ask 'open' questions to engage your partner.
- Comment on what you hear and ask follow-up questions.
- Establish common ground by sharing experiences but avoid 'one-upmanship'.

Template

When acting as a host, greet visitors, welcome them to your company or town and offer hospitality.

Meeting somebody for the first time

Hello, I'm … / Nice / It's a pleasure to meet you. / Welcome to (company or city). / Let me take your coat / your bag. / Can I offer you some refreshments / something to drink / a cup of coffee?

Greeting somebody you have met before

Hello / Hi (name). How nice to see you again. / Long time no see! (informal) / How have you been? / Can I take your coat? / Let me take that for you. / Can I get you something to drink? / How about a (cup of) coffee?

Ask standard questions – whether about the journey or where somebody's from – to build empathy and rapport.

Did you have any trouble finding us? / Where do come from originally, if you don't mind me asking? / How are you enjoying your stay? / So, is this the first time you've been to (town / country / the conference)? How do you like it so far?

Find common ground and share experiences.

That reminds me of … / I know exactly what you mean. / Now that you mention it, I also … / How interesting, I also happen to know someone who …. / How is (a mutual acquaintance)?

Develop the conversation by asking 'opinion' questions.

How did you find the …? / How do you see the development of …? / What do you think the chances of success for … are like?

Keep the conversation going by following up on remarks.

Interesting. And what did you do then? / I see what you mean. A similar thing happened to me … / Oh, you've been here before. When was that? / Really? / How interesting / funny / terrible / awful!

Close the conversation by commenting on the time spent together and looking ahead to future contact.

It's been great talking / interesting chatting to you … / I've really enjoyed our … / I was wondering if we could get together / meet up again to discuss this in more depth. / Why don't I give you a call next week and we can discuss this further?

Elevator pitch

An elevator pitch is a prepared self-introduction that says a great deal about you and your company in very few words – or in the time it takes you to go from the bottom to the top of a building in an elevator (or a lift)! It should grab the audience's attention and lead to follow-up questions and a conversation. This 'power statement' is as indispensable as a business card and is also a very effective networking tool.
Try to have several variations on hand for different situations.

Template

Before preparing your elevator pitch, identify your role and determine the context and purpose of the gathering.
My role is …
The context / venue is a / an …
The purpose of the gathering is to …

Who am I? Make an interesting and dynamic statement about what you do / your company does.
My name is (both names) / I am a (n) / the (job title) at (company) / I am based in … /
I am a link in the global logistics chain … / We provide peace of mind for … / By that I mean, …

What does my company offer? What problem does it solve?
Say what is unique or special about your products / services.
We help businesses to tell their stories to the people who need to hear them … /
We provide a way out for small businesses struggling with bureaucracy … /
We are the people to call when there is a crisis … / We deliver solutions …

What can I do personally?
My specific area of expertise is … / This is where I come in … / I can ease the burden of …

(Optional)
What should the person I am speaking to do next?
Perhaps you would like to come and see us some time. / Would you like to set up an appointment? /
Could you possibly pass on my details / refer me to …?

SWOT analysis

A SWOT analysis is an analytical strategic tool used to review a current strategy in order to determine what the next steps should be. It draws together enough information to clearly show what particular strengths, weaknesses, opportunities or threats exist in a company and also what the implications for the company are.

Template

Be very precise. Only put forward points that can be supported by hard figures or precise evidence quoted from reliable sources.

Based on empirical evidence / the current balance sheet / our customer survey results, I would like to put forward the following ...

Clarify why each point should be considered as a strength, weakness, opportunity or threat.

The reason we have identified ... as a strength / threat / ... is because of / due to / wholly dependent on the fact that ...

Strengths

We excel in / outclass / surpass our competition ... / We have the following key resources available to us: ... / We are positively perceived as being ...

Weaknesses

We could improve on ... / X certainly needs attention ... / The following resources are lacking: ... / We are negatively perceived as being ...

Opportunities

The following opportunities have presented themselves: ... / We could profit from the following trends: ... / We cannot afford to ignore the current development in ...

Threats

The following threats exist as a direct result of our weaknesses: ... / Our competition is currently dominant in the following fields: ...

Make a sound conclusion about the next steps.

Based on our discussion and the evidence presented, I would suggest that we ... / We could turn our strengths into opportunities / threats into opportunities by ...

Welcome Unit

Exercise 1

2 Jörg Sprung: I attend online meetings – teleconferences and so on – for example with international partners, mostly in Asia, and take notes and then write technical reports, so I have to be able to understand what people say, especially when they speak fast or are not really clear and I don't know what they mean. The most difficult situation is when I have to clarify technical issues and things like delivery details with other engineers on the phone. In my work, details are everything, so I try to focus on grammar details, too, so I sound professional. I sometimes think I'm not polite enough with native speakers. They use a lot of polite phrases like 'I'm afraid'. I want to be more polite, but I'm not so comfortable using those phrases."

3 Peter Glück: When I present or negotiate, I put the facts in perspective to help the people I'm talking to understand and trust me. That's not so easy! So I watch the best business presenters and study how they tell stories. Technical jargon and some basic financial and legal vocabulary is very important in business negotiations, but I don't worry about grammar, because my contacts in Vietnam and Ukraine are making mistakes, too. The main thing in these meetings is that we are being clear about the technical and business issues, not that we are speaking perfect English. But I don't want errors in my writing or on our website, so I think we will have to make some corrections to polish our international image!

4 Carla Lopez: We use English in our daily work, because the team is very international. At first my colleagues had trouble with my Spanish accent in English, as I did with their German accent, actually. I don't think they always understood me when I explained what I wanted, maybe also because of differences in culture. But that's better now. I lead meetings and telecons, so I have to moderate in English. It's not always easy to keep everyone on track. Another thing I have to do is write project reports and proposals for our American partners, to get the facts on paper. I think some of my formulations come from Spanish or maybe even German now. That's a little embarrassing. My writing should be more business-like, more professional.

Unit 1

5 Part A, Exercise 2

Azra: So, Ben, what do you do exactly?

Ben: Well, in Strategic Marketing, we mostly conduct market research.

Azra: I see. And where does your data come from?

Ben: Different sources. We study sales figures, conduct surveys, run focus groups, and also collect raw data from outside agencies. And then we filter data according to customer segment and see how much households and individuals actually spend on the various product groups. We also do a lot of data mining, you know, collecting consumer information from websites. My job has become a lot more data-driven than when I started out.

Azra: But do you ever go out and see actual consumers?

Ben: Well, you know, actually, I've just recently become head of the Shopper & Customer Marketing Division for the Asia-Pacific region.

Azra: Oh, congratulations!

Ben: Thank you. And so, last month I went to China and Vietnam to take a good look inside people's bathroom cabinets.

Azra: Really? How fascinating.

Ben: It was, actually. I learned so much about how people use cosmetics. While I was working there, I also researched claims and trademark issues and analysed packaging and displays.

Azra: Sounds like a great trip. Are you originally from Mainland China, then?

Ben: From Hong Kong.

Azra: Interesting. And what brought you here, if you don't mind me asking?

Ben: Well, after finishing my BA in Hong Kong, I completed a one-year Masters programme in London. And from there I went to Vitapharma in Geneva as a market research associate. I got the chance to shadow people in all the different departments there and learned all about organizing tests and conducting proof of efficacy trials.

Azra: Vitapharma. That's a good company.

Ben: Yes, it is. And in Geneva I was able to learn some French and found the industry I wanted to work in. That's when I got the invitation to come here, to Wilde.

6 Part A, Exercise 4

Ben: Azra, you're not from Germany either, are you?

Azra: No, I'm from Sarajevo originally.

Ben: Really?

Azra: Yeah, but this is home, really. My parents have long since moved back, but my husband is

German, and our three kids too, and so many friends are here. Also, I've been working for this company in various functions since 2000.

Ben: A long time. You studied Chemistry?

Azra: Exactly, on a work-study programme. My first job here was in Skin Research as a cosmetic formulations chemist, working on the active substances in the products. Normally I would have pursued a PhD, but I had children and was on parental leave for four years, which got me on the mommy track. I tried working part-time in my old department when I came back, but I was working in the lab, and it was very difficult to do. I mean, the hours are extremely irregular and I really couldn't leave the lab until the experiments were completed. So I decided to change departments to Final Skin Products. I've only recently started working full-time again. Now that I'm in charge of efficacy trials, I feel like I've just rebooted my career.

Ben: Sounds good. So you handle all the paperwork for regulatory compliance, then?

Azra: That's right.

Ben: I haven't dealt with compliance issues yet. I expect it's complicated?

Azra: Oh, yes. We're responsible for compliance with national and international regulations, and each country in the EU has an authority of its own. Lots of red tape.

Ben: I see. So, would you say this is your greatest challenge, then?

Azra: Compliance? No, it's designing the efficacy trials. You see, they've become much more complex recently. There's been a significant shift towards products that promise to do many different things for you at once. Just to give you an example: We recently conducted a 12-week study that looked at seven different effects on skin. Seven!

Ben: Wow.

Azra: At the same time we're working on tighter schedules and smaller budgets. We can't handle it ourselves anymore. That's why we've been outsourcing this kind of work to contract research institutes. In fact, we've just signed a big contract.

🔊₇ Part B, Exercise 1

Anna: Hello?

Azra: Hello.

Ben: Good morning!

Anna: Ah, you must be Azra Winter. Am I saying that correctly?

Azra: That's fine. And you're Anna Hattig?

Anna: Nice to meet you.

Anna: Benjamin Yong? It's nice to finally meet you in person.

Ben: And you!

Anna: I guess Dr Mehring isn't here yet?

Ralf: No, here I am. Hi everyone! Anna.

Anna: Ralf.

Ralf: Ms Winter, Mr Yong … Jörg, are you coming?

Anna: Jörg Sprung?

Jörg: Yes.

Anna: Hi, it's good to meet you. I'm Anna Hattig.

Jörg: Good to meet you too.

Azra: Um … Ben and I were just wondering if we could use first names. I mean, all of us, since we'll be working together.

Anna: Fine with me.

Ben: I think I called you Herr Spring by mistake, didn't I?

Jörg: Jörg is fine, no problem. And is it Benjamin or Ben?

Ben: Ben.

Jörg: OK.

Ben: Perfect. And thanks for using English, by the way. I'm still really rubbish at German.

Ralf: OK. Let's get started. I think a short round of introductions is in order. Let's start with you, Anna. So, Anna will be the project manager. She's currently taking part in our junior executive programme, and we're very fortunate to have her. She has an impressive track record in product marketing and has worked with several global players. Anna?

Anna: Well, since I'm new, I imagine all of you must be very curious about my background. So, I have an MBA from the University of Vienna, and I've worked both at home and abroad in Consumer Packaged Goods in two separate industries: media products and sports footwear. And in the two companies I worked for, we managed to get new products onto the shelves in record time.

Ben: That sounds really exciting.

Azra: It must be quite a challenge to move from one industry to another.

Anna: Well, in many ways they're similar, but you're right, many of the variables change from business to business …

Ben: Definitely, and from product to product. Different lead times, different degrees of flexibility …

Azra: Right.

Anna: Exactly, so I'll need your support.

Azra: OK. Well, I don't know if it's possible, but I was thinking that it might help if you came around to the departments and shadowed us for a day to see what we do. That is, if you have the time. Just to get a real impression of how we develop new products …

Anna: That's a great idea, Azra, thank you! So, Jörg, I hear you're the creative head of packaging.

Jörg: I'm not sure what you mean by 'creative'. I am a packaging engineer.

Anna: Yes, but you must be proud of your many patents.

Jörg: Oh, I see what you mean. Yes, the folding box with the adhesive seal, that's my design, yes. We're using four or five of my patents at the moment. But that's just part of the job. I've been developing packaging for Wilde since 1994.

Anna: A long time. And what was your most recent challenge?

Jörg: Well, things like the colour of the materials can be quite tricky, when you have to match different materials. For this new product line we could maybe try out some new materials. I have a few ideas … how do you say? … 'in the pipeline'.

Anna Great. I was thinking we might be able to implement a new kind of package in this project.

Ralf: Well, uh, actually, Anna, Jörg, we haven't finalized the arrangements yet. We're still negotiating the details internally with Jörg's line manager.

Jörg: That's right. My boss has to agree to any *new* design projects. But I can advise you about the options already available.

Anna: I see.

Jörg: I was hoping to hear more about the project timeline …

Ralf: Well, Jörg, Anna, we'll talk about that later. If we could just get back to the introductions. Ben, would you like to say a few words about yourself?

Unit 2

🔊 8　**Part A, Exercise 4**

Martin: Let me tell you about an issue we're facing in order processing. Last month we noticed that orders weren't being activated in the system, so people were entering orders that weren't being finalized, and they weren't being sent any kind of error message.

Maria: I see.

Martin: At first, this only happened a few times a week, but then last week we experienced a sudden spike. What triggered it was a system update. We'd set up a new interface to try to reduce the length of the initial wait. You know about the complaints we got about the long waiting time for processing orders, right? That sometimes it could take up to 15 minutes?

Maria: Yes, of course.

Martin: OK, so we thought this update would help to improve the user experience and minimize

response time. The suggestion came from one of our young trainees, by the way.

Maria: Great!

Martin. But after we went live we began seeing an increase in trouble tickets, you know, automatic error reports. We ran some diagnostic tests and luckily pinpointed the specific issues that were causing trouble. What we found was that almost all of the trouble tickets were coming from orders placed through tablet computers.

Maria: Interesting.

Martin: So, to make a long story short, we aborted the update and went back to the old interface.

Maria: Have you found out what caused the problem with the tablets? Was the update incompatible?

Martin: Well, it ran perfectly on all the tablets we tested here.

Maria: Hm. What about mobile connectivity? Did the update increase the risk of the connection being interrupted?

Martin: Well, that's possible, yes. When a user is on the move, there's always the chance they can lose the connection. But at this point we simply don't know for sure. In any case, what this does suggest is that maybe now would be a good time to look at applications for tablet users in general. Tablets are booming, and I don't think users of tablets are being given the right kind of service. They're used to apps that really simplify the process, you know, user-friendly ones.

Maria: So, you're saying that we have to develop something new for users who are switching to tablets or we'll lose their business, correct?

Martin: Exactly.

Maria: And do we really know for sure that our customers *are* switching to tablets?

Martin: Yes. I can get you the figures on that.

Maria: OK. The thing is, we have to maximize the efficiency of our operations overall. We can't afford to develop apps for tablets just for the fun of it.

Martin: Right, well, then I think what we need to do is to develop and provide a sustainable solution for the various mobile platforms. So that means multiple platforms. You know, why don't we talk to Rebecca … ?

🔊 9　**Part B, Exercise 2**

Hi, Jim. I just wanted to say thank you for helping with the special delivery to Toulouse. Everything has gone smoothly. It's always exciting to see things come together.

…

Well, we really don't have much time to play with. Our current lead time is 20 weeks and, quite frankly, with so many long lead items to build to specifications, we simply can't wait for all of the construction plans to be reviewed by Airbus before we start simulating them. They all come in at once, but of course we can't start on all of them at the same time. I know it poses a certain risk to start production before construction plans have been cleared, and we might have to change things later, but I don't see any alternative. The extra work of making the changes after CDR is less of a risk than falling behind schedule. So I still recommend starting the 3D simulation quite early on, the way we did this time, as soon as the designs have passed PDR. Then we fine-tune the simulations if the specifications are changed.

…

Definitely, very happy. We're producing in response to concrete demand, and that's very efficient. But of course any unexpected changes can put us behind schedule.

…

Well, yeah, actually, this time there *was* a problem that resulted from a change requested by Airbus. They changed the lamp system after we'd started building. And because several of our staff were on scheduled leave, we couldn't handle the extra work at short notice and had to outsource some of it to an OEM supplier. That's what delayed us, you see, so we couldn't complete that unit in time for the main transport to the construction site. Thanks again for the special delivery, by the way. I understand it's already been fitted in. And with your help we've actually managed to stay within budget and on schedule.

…

Lessons learned? Well for our next projects I'd strongly recommend not scheduling any staff leave at key times. I don't know if that's always possible, but being short-staffed is tough on everyone. And in addition I'd suggest sourcing some backup suppliers. And then, finally, since last minute external changes are the norm, I'd advise coordinating very closely with our external partners.

…

Yes, of course. I'll send you the report later today.

🔊10 Part B, Exercise 5
Marion: Marion Bender, Controlling.
Carole: Hi, Marion. Carole here.
Marion: Hi, Carole. Good to hear from you. How are things?
Carole: Actually, not too good.
Marion: Oh? Sorry to hear that. What's going on?
Carole: Well, basically, the warehouse is not going to be ready in time for the next delivery.
Marion: How come?
Carole: We've just lost a key IT services supplier. We've been directed not to use them anymore.

Marion: Yes, I heard about that. Zetcom, right? We're concerned that they may have been passing proprietary information on to a competitor.
Carole: It's just that we've always relied on Zetcom to jump in at short notice, and we knew that they'd have the capacities we need since they were counting on repeat orders. For all we know, those claims could be unsubstantiated.
Marion: No, sorry Carole, I'm afraid there is simply no way we can work with that supplier. What are your other options?
Carole: Well, our second supplier can't deliver because there's a strike going on down there.
Marion: Oh, dear.
Carole: If it weren't for that strike, we'd be OK. And the other supplier we were using has gone belly up.
Marion: That's terrible. You haven't been able to identify an alternative yet, then?
Carole: Not one who can provide the same quality at the same price.
Marion: What if you contacted the IT service suppliers at the Hamburg warehouse? You'd get top quality if you used them.
Carole: Well, they'd be great, but they'd also be much more expensive.
Marion: I frankly wouldn't prioritize cost at this point. Why don't you call them? Wait. Uhm … let me put this in a very short report first and send it around. And then we can all put our heads together to find a more strategic solution.

Business file 1

🔊11 Exercise 2
OK, so now to the last point on the agenda. As you all know, several people on the team have left recently, and Marius is going on parental leave for three months starting on Monday. What's more, it doesn't look like any new staff will be coming on board in the forseeable future.

This has put us under a lot of pressure, and we need to handle the extra work more efficiently. Losing staff has cost us some key knowledge. One of the problems, of course, is that we're working from two separate locations. Information that is common knowledge up in Birmingham isn't always shared with us here in Leipzig, and vice versa.

So I've asked a consultant to suggest some ways that we can improve the way we share and manage knowledge as a team. She's proposed four solutions, and I'd like for us to consider them in greater detail. So would four of you please each have a look at a different proposal and report on it at our next meeting? Feel free to add your own ideas and criticism. Keep your reports short, just two to four minutes, no more, since we just need something to start us off. And then we'll discuss the proposals and see what we think would be the most effective solution. OK? So, if you would just have a first quick look at these four ideas here, and decide now who is going to present which one, then we just need to decide on a time to meet …

Unit 3

🔊 12 Part A, Exercise 2

Yves: Hello, Ellen. How's it going?

Ellen: Hi, Yves. Fine, thanks. And thanks for your email. Your Project Portfolio looks really interesting. I don't think many people in the company know what you're doing, and why. And these three projects would fit in very well with the Energy Project goals.

Yves: Thanks! I think so too.

Ellen: The reason I'm calling is that I'm just looking at our available resources, and before we go any further, I wanted to make sure I've understood exactly what you'll be needing help with. I see that you're requesting staff to complete your mobile device management project, yet that's the one you've switched to yellow as being behind schedule. Are you understaffed in general? Or is this project outside the scope of your usual work?

Yves: Well, no, actually, the yellow light makes it look worse than it is. We've already fleshed out all the procedures in that project, and have lined up the steps we'll need to take, but implementing them is going to be very time-consuming.

Ellen: I'm not sure I really understand what that project is all about. Can you give me some background and a rough outline of what you have planned?

Yves: Sure. Last year, maintenance and energy costs skyrocketed when more and more employees started using multiple mobile devices. 'Bring Your Own Device' is allowed in some departments, you know, so people are bringing in their own phones, tablets and maybe their daughter's tablet and I don't know what …

Ellen Back in the States we say 'everything but the kitchen sink'.

Yves Haha, that's nice, yes, they are bringing in everything but the kitchen sink. It's a security nightmare. They fill their devices up at home with malware and infect our network, and they have confidential information on a device that they let their kids use. It's crazy. We've now created new guidelines for what to bring and

how to use it – we've got questionnaires and agreements all set up – but implementing all of that isn't going to be easy. I mean, we'll be telling people they can't use their little toys.

Ellen: People are funny about their gadgets.

Yves: Exactly! The thing is, we're tied up in other, highly complex technical projects that require our full attention, and can't really spare a lot of time for this. But if we had someone with good communication skills and a lot of patience to explain the guidelines and train the staff in compliance, and if we could highlight this effort as part of a popular campaign to save energy, well, that would be a huge help, and we could get back on track very quickly.

Ellen: And have you thought about the exact scope of the workload yet?

Yves: That really depends. If it were a part of a campaign, it might not be such a big job.

Ellen: OK, well, just thinking aloud for a moment: We're getting a student trainee for the duration of the project starting in January. We'll be sharing her across departments. I'm meeting with HR to hammer out the details tomorrow. What if we had the student assist you? Would that work?

Yves: Maybe. But that's a lot of responsibility for a student.

Ellen: Sure, but the Energy Project would be overseeing everything, so lots of support and guidance there. And even if the student was working for *you*, she'd still be reporting to *me*.

Yves: I see. Uhm, yes that would help. Still …

Ellen: Well, why don't we both think it over some more, and maybe you can figure out how many hours of support you'd need. And then, if you decided to go ahead with this, and I hope you do, do you think you could get a job description written up for me?

Yves: Sure, OK. But … uhm … not this week or next.

Ellen: No problem. I'll be talking to the other departments before I do anything else. You're leaving town for Christmas, right?

Yves: Yes.

Ellen: OK, well, you'll be hearing from me shortly. OK?

Yves: Fine. And I'll be sending you that job description right after Christmas.

Ellen: Super. Thanks again, Yves. Nice talking to you.

Yves: And you! And … uhm … happy holidays!

Ellen: The same to you. Bye now.

🔊 13 Part B, Exercise 2

Tom: Tom Stiller, Energy Consulting.

Ellen: Hello, Mr Stiller, this is Ellen Wagner, from Schulze in Attendorn. Your name was given to me by Uli Baum, a business partner of mine who I believe is a client of yours.

Tom: Ah yes, Uli. That's right, we did a project with him not too long ago after they merged with a Chinese company. How is he?

Ellen: Fine, I think. He told me about you when we met up at the trade fair in Hanover in September.

Tom: Really? That's nice. Well then, Ms … Wagner, was it? …

Ellen: That's right.

Tom: … what can I do for you?

Ellen: Well, the reason I'm calling is that we're interested in energy consulting and project facilitation for a big cross-departmental initiative of ours. I understand you did something very similar for Uli.

Tom: That's right. What we offer our clients, essentially, is a set of facilitated workshops to help them build collaboration across departments and develop concrete plans. In Uli's case, the company needed to align its energy policies across the German and Chinese plants. The results of the workshops are documented so they can be carried over into daily operations. What you get is essentially a road map to energy savings.

Ellen: Right.

Tom: So, could you tell me a little about your project, Ms Wagner?

Ellen: Well, we produce models and chassis structures for the car industry, with about 350 employees here and another 5,000 or so in our international subsidiaries. We're fully compliant with energy regulations and proud of our environmentally friendly operations, but we're feeling the pinch of rising costs and need to reduce our energy use even further. So the Energy Project is looking at ways to achieve additional savings. Better collaboration across departments and international benchmarks – that's essentially what we're looking for.

Tom: And what's your scope and timeline?

Ellen: The pilot phase kicks off on the 25th of January and we aim to have the projects evaluated and ready to go by the end of the year. What is really important for us is to see results. Management will be looking closely at the bottom line, and we're supposed to be able to show measurable improvement in two to five years.

Tom: Right.

Ellen: What we don't want to do is to outsource the project. We'd like to develop it with our own staff, building our knowledge close to operations using a facilitator.

Tom: That makes sense.

Ellen: So I understand from Uli that you generally begin by compiling a preliminary report. Why is that?

Tom: With a report, all of the participants are on the same page in terms of industry knowledge and best practice in similar companies. This makes the workshops more effective.

Ellen: OK. And you suggest three workshops, don't you?

Tom: That's what works best for most companies. But we're flexible and will adapt the offer to suit your needs. It's good to space the workshops about a month apart to allow participants to do their homework.

Ellen: OK, and what do you charge? Can you give me a ballpark figure?

Tom: Well, for a rough estimate we'd really need your specifications first. But generally speaking, with the initial and the final report and the three workshops, we'd be looking at roughly 10,000 euros, plus expenses.

Ellen: So, that would be travel expenses, mostly?

Tom: That's right, so from Bristol to Attendorn … let me see … I'd put that at about 1,500 euros for the three workshops together.

Ellen: Hmm. Well, we can cover expenses like that, provided they don't exceed 20 % of your overall fee. Our regulations for contracted services are quite strict in that point.

Tom Fine.

Ellen: What if we decided we needed an additional workshop later on, could you make us a special offer?

Tom: Well, assuming we didn't need an extra report, I could offer you that additional one-day workshop for 1,100 euros, again plus expenses.

Ellen: As I said, we're really not supposed to allow expenses over 20 %.

Tom: Right, well that shouldn't be too difficult to work around. We could agree on a flat fee of 1,500.

Ellen: OK, well, could I ask you to put those details into a proposal so we can think them over?

Tom: I'll be happy to. If you could just draft, in simple terms, what you aim to achieve in your workshops with us.

Ellen: OK, I'll do that after we finish this call. Uhm. How soon do you think you could get your proposal to me? We don't have much time to spare before the kick-off; there's just over a month left.

Tom: It shouldn't be a problem to get the proposal to you within 48 hours.

Ellen: Really? That would be great.

Tom: There's just one thing. If you did decide to go ahead with this, when would you want to schedule the first workshop?

Ellen: Er … well, would you be able to manage our kick-off date of the 25th of January?

Tom: Ah, that's a bit short notice, perhaps. I'd have to see … . Can I count on getting the materials from you within a week or two?

Ellen: Well actually, I'm not supposed to give out any unpublished information before we've got a confidentiality agreement in place, so we'd have to draft and get your contract signed first, and I doubt that will happen before Christmas. So, the earliest I could send you material would be in week one, so you'd have it probably around the 7th or the 8th. But it shouldn't be a problem to give you a firm commitment by the end of this week.

Tom: OK, well in that case, let me see … the 8th of January. That would give us just over two weeks. It's a bit tight, but it should work.

Ellen: Great! Well then, so, you'll be getting our Request for Proposal today, and then we'll look forward to receiving your proposal the day after tomorrow.

Tom: Right.

Ellen: Well, thank you for your time, Mr Stiller.

Tom: My pleasure, Ms Wagner. And thank you for calling. Goodbye.

Ellen: Goodbye.

Unit 4

🔊14 Part A, Exercise 3

Anke: Hi, this is Anke Kern in Eisenhüttenstadt, and with me here is Clara, our trainee. She'll be taking the minutes.

Clara: This is Clara. Hello everyone.

Anke: So, are we all on? Can everybody hear me all right? And can all of you identify yourselves before you speak?

Alisa: Alisa Petrova here in Sosnowiec. I can hear you just fine.

Anke: Good.

Alisa: Clara, are you enjoying your training?

Clara: Yes, Ms Petrova, thank you! And how is Sosnowiec?

Alisa: It's a very interesting assignment.

Anke: OK. Anke Kern here. Mr Henry, are you there?

Tim: Yes I am. So, it's Tim Henry in Luxembourg. How are you all this morning?

Anke: Uhm, Mr Henry, you're very quiet. I've turned the volume up here but I can hardly hear you. Can you try adjusting the volume? Or try speaking directly into the microphone.

Tim: OK, how does this sound?

Anke: Much better. How is the weather in Luxembourg?

Tim: A bit chilly for this time of year. Ms Petrova, can you hear me?

Alisa: Yes.

Tim: So you've left Eisenhüttenstadt and are in Sosnowiec now?

Alisa: That's right, I'm reviewing production logistics here for the next three months.

Tim: Excellent.

Anke: Alisa, is your operations manager, Mr Novak, there with you?

Alisa: No, he's dialling in from another office today.

Piotr: Hello? Good morning. I'm sorry I'm late.

Anke: No problem. Good morning, Anke Kern here. We're just getting started. How are you?

Piotr: Very fine, thank you.

Tim: Was that Mr Novak just now?

Anke: Yes, so Mr Novak, Tim Henry from Luxembourg and Alisa Petrova are here, too.

Tim: Hello Mr Novak, Tim Henry here.

Piotr: Good morning, Mr Henry.

Tim: Thank you for taking the time to attend this telecon.

Piotr: You are welcome. Sorry, my English is not so good.

Alisa: Alisa here. I'd just like to say that Piotr Novak and I met earlier to discuss the agenda. Could everyone please speak slowly? If necessary, I'll be happy to translate.

Anke: Good, Alisa, thank you.

🔊15 Part A, Exercise 4

Anke: So, did everybody get the agenda?

All: Yes.

Anke: OK, let's keep this short. We're meeting to discuss a change in the production and delivery schedule for the June deliveries. Mr Henry, you wanted to explain the changes?

Tim: That's right. So as you know, we're splitting production of hot rolled steel evenly between your two plants, with 1,000 coils per plant per week. But we have a special order for thinner steel sheets coming up on the 12th of June. This is a non-standard production.

Anke: Mr Henry? Hello? Can you hear me? I'm afraid the line is breaking up. Maybe if we hang up and try again, that will solve the problem.

Tim: Hello? Hello? Is it better now?

Anke: Yes the line seems OK again. So, let's go on. Could you just repeat that last part about the special order, please?

Tim: I was saying that the June 12th order for thinner steel sheets will require a different type of production. And although Sosnowiec is normally cheaper, in this special case Sosnowiec has not produced this type before. Eisenhüttenstadt has the necessary expertise. So I would like to order the entire consignment from there.

Anke: Mr Henry, just to clarify, what exactly do you mean by 'expertise'?

Tim: Well, Eisenhüttenstadt produced a small quantity of the thinner steel sheets last year, tested the settings and passed quality management. So the procedures are established.

Alisa: Sorry to butt in. Alisa Petrova here. I'm afraid I don't follow you, Mr Henry. Didn't you just say that Sosnowiec is normally cheaper? I frankly don't quite understand why things should be different now. Can't Sosnowiec run production using the settings tested for the thinner sheets?

Piotr: Exactly. Piotr Novak speaking. We can produce these thinner steel sheets in Sosnowiec. It's just some small changes. Investment is no problem.

Alisa: So what Mr Novak is saying is that it will mean an initial investment, but he told me that it is important to expand the range of products here to include those with potential for new markets. The plant has all of the expertise and capacities needed to expand the line, so …

Anke: Uhm, Alisa, can we keep on track here? Let's just focus on this particular consignment.

Alisa: Right. So we've calculated production and logistics and have found that the cost of producing thinner sheets will come down quickly once we start getting more orders.

Anke So to recap, what you are saying is that Sosnowiec is counting on repeat orders for this product?

Piotr: Excuse me, I don't understand 'recap'.

Anke: Sorry, uhm … to summarize.

Alisa: So, in other words, the Sosnowiec plant wants to secure more orders.

Anke: I see. Have you sent me your calculations, Alisa?

Alisa: Yes, by email.

Tim: Tim Henry here …

Anke: Could you just hang on a second, please, Mr Henry? Sorry! I just need to get something; I'll be right back. Alisa says she's sent me an email with her calculations. Could you go and check that for me, Clara? Yes, go ahead and print out a copy of the attachment while you're at it. And if you'd just bring me a glass of water … thank you! Sorry! Mr Henry, you were saying …

Tim: Yes. Mr Novak, the problem is that this order may be a one-off.

Piotr: A one-off? Could you explain that another way, please?

Tim I mean a one-time order. You see, we simply don't know yet whether the customer wants more of this type of steel.

Piotr: Oh. OK, I see. That's too bad.

Tim: Yes, so I really think it would be better if we left this to Eisenhüttenstadt. But what I'm suggesting is that you could handle the entire standard order the following week, for the 19th of June. Would that work?

Piotr: Hmm. But then we have no order for June 12th. So we send the workers home, but then the week after we have so much work we will need

overtime. That's not so good. So can we …

Tim: Yes but the customer …

Alisa: If we produced the consignment …

Anke: Sorry, Mr Henry, Alisa, can we just let Mr Novak finish, please?

Piotr: Thank you, Ms Kern! So can we deliver half of the order the week before, on June the 12th?

Tim: Well, our customer requires just-in-time delivery. They have a seamless supply chain. So we'd need interim storage for that week until shipment on the 19th of June.

Anke: Did you want to say something, Alisa?

Alisa: Yes, thank you. We don't have the right kind of storage space here. We'd have to outsource.

Anke: So, you're saying it would mean extra costs.

Piotr: Maybe we can use a storage company that we used before. They're cheap.

Tim: Yes, that's an excellent idea, Mr Novak. DB Schenker Rail provide multimodal transport, so I'll see what they can offer in combination with storage. But we should also know what local storage costs.

Alisa: I can find that out.

Tim: Thank you, Ms Petrova. Do you think you could get the quote by this afternoon, by around four?

Alisa: Sure.

Tim: Splendid. And then we'll look at the overall costs again.

Anke: OK, I think we're ready to sum up. Clara, if you'd just put this next part in the minutes, please. First, we've established that producing the June 12th consignment in Eisenhüttenstadt would save cost, but that Sosnowiec would need to produce a delivery for June the 12th to keep production levels up. In order to do that, the June 12th production in Sosnowiec will need to be put into storage. So Mr Henry will contact DB Schenker Rail about possible multimodal storage and transport, and Alisa will get a quote for local storage. They will phone around 4 pm today to look at the overall costs and then make a final decision about the production and delivery schedule. Have I left anything out?

Tim: No, I think that's all. Well done. Thank you, Ms Kern. And I'll update you all tomorrow, OK? Thanks, everyone. It was a pleasure meeting with you.

Anke: Likewise. OK let's wrap things up for now. Have a good day, everyone, and goodbye.

All: Goodbye.

🔊 16 Part B, Exercise 2

Bob: Hi, Ivo. What's up?

Ivo: Hello, Bob. Nice to see you. I wanted to ask you, can you give me feedback on these emails?

Bob: Sure.

Ivo: I'm having trouble with this guy, Doug, in Atlanta. We're working on the Mexican project together, and he's always asking me to do things for him, but then he criticizes how I do them. It's not correct.

Bob: What do you mean by 'correct'?

Ivo: Well, he can't do it, and asks for help, and then all he does is criticize.

Bob: Hmm. A real jerk, huh?

Ivo: A jerk? Like an idiot?

Bob: Well, more annoying.

Ivo: Aha. So, can you read these for me? I want to know your opinion.

Bob: Sure. Hm … right … mhm … hm… OK. So, he's writing about a purchase order, or rather two separate POs, right? So, what was this about exactly?

Ivo: Well, Atlanta needed parts and they couldn't get them from their supplier in the US. We use the same supplier in Germany, so Doug asked if we could get the part for him here, and he sent us an internal PO. When my colleague Rose contacted the supplier, they had the parts, but the strange thing was, they told her that they already had a purchase order from the US.

Bob: I see. So, Doug or the US supplier must have sent them a copy of the PO.

Ivo: It's so typical. Doug's always doing things and not telling me. He never copies me into his emails and then he attacks me for not 'fully understanding the situation'.

Bob: OK, so this is your reply … Hmm … scroll down a little … . You know, Ivo, both Doug's email and your reply sound like you might want to talk it over on the phone.

Ivo: Why should I phone? He wants something from me! No way. I'm really fed up with him.

Bob: Listen Ivo, I understand that you're angry, but your whole line here, 'I will not accept these kinds of emails from your side blaming Rose and me', is far too strong and angry for an email. You can give him a piece of your mind on the phone, but I wouldn't put it in writing. Besides, Ivo, by telling him off in writing, you're making a big thing out of this. You're putting him on the spot, you know. You might want to ease off a little. Play it cool.

Ivo: But he accused me!

Bob: OK, so what he said was 'It seems we have had several instances now where poor communication or confusion has caused some trouble for us with you'. He's being cautious, I'd say. How long have you known this guy?

Ivo: Too long. Three years.

Bob: So why didn't you call him up?

Ivo: On the phone it's always so difficult.

Bob: Why's that?

Ivo: He speaks so fast.

Bob: Well, slow him down! C'mon, Ivo! You don't know it all, and neither does he. Share a laugh about it. You really need to show him you're playing on the same team.

Ivo: Oh, I don't know …

Bob: Well, why don't you just call him up and say something like, 'Listen, Doug, OK, we've been having some problems, but I noticed that you didn't copy me into your email last time. So next time, could you copy me in to let me know what's going on?' Or you might want to tell him 'It would be nice if you could just give me a call when you need something. It would simplify things for me.' How about that?

🔊 17 **Part B, Exercise 5**

Uh, hello Ivo, I'm calling about our last few emails. I guess I may have misinterpreted the situation. Uh, I suppose we probably got off on the wrong foot about this matter. I was kind of surprised, after that last email. Anyway, give me a call when you get a chance, and we'll figure out a way to handle things from here on out. Oh, and thanks for your help so far. I appreciate it! Bye now.

Business file 2

Exercise 2
🔊 18 **Call 1**

Recording: Saved message, Tuesday, 9.12 am

Ian: Hello, Val, sorry, this is Ian from the Hamburg office. I can't seem to get hold of you this morning. I've just had a call from the haulier telling me that your 10 am consignment from Loglab due for cross-docking to Sweden this afternoon is probably going to be delayed by several hours. The haulier said that there was something wrong with the labelling devices so there was a backlog. I know you've been handling this particular consignment, so do you think you could call the service rep at Loglab – Sandra Matthey, I think you said it was – and try to speed things up a bit? Maybe you could remind her that delivery to Hamburg between 4 and 6 pm is guaranteed in the contract so we can promise our customers overnight shipment. Loglab would essentially be in breach of contract if they didn't get this consignment to us as scheduled. OK? Just give me a call if there's any trouble. Well, I hope the weather's nicer in Warsaw. It's pouring with rain here. Bye.

🔊19 Call 2

Recording: Saved message, Tuesday, 9.51 am
Sandra: Hi Valerie, Sandra Matthey here from Loglab Customer Service in Frankfurt returning your call and email. I'm sorry, I was speaking on the other line. So about your query about your consignment – uhm … that's 14/H1278 – I've checked in the system and with our logistics department, and it really looks like everything is in order. There was a technical issue a little earlier but that seems to be solved now and under control. The haulier is scheduled to pick up the consignment at 10 am, so delivery to Hamburg should be on schedule. There's no need to worry. OK? Thank you for calling! Goodbye!

🔊20 Call 3

Recording: Saved message, Tuesday, 7.15 pm
Ian: Valerie, Ian again in Hamburg. It's now past six and the consignment hasn't arrived. Like the haulier said, there was some technical trouble at the warehouse, so everything was delayed and they didn't finish loading until after lunch. They thought they'd be able to make up for lost time, but the heavy rain has really slowed them down. I find it quite annoying that the service rep gave you that rubbish about the pickup being on schedule. This is not the first time this has happened with Loglab. I really think we need to set things straight with them. Anyway, would you mind giving me a call in the morning? I think we need to review our contract. Well, I'm knackered. I'm packing it in. Bye.

🔊21 Call 4

Recording: Saved message, Wednesday, 8.42 am
Sandra: Hi, Valerie. This is Sandra from Loglab Customer Service. I want to say that I'm really, really sorry that things went wrong with the consignment. This sort of thing isn't supposed to happen. It turns out that there was a technical problem in the labelling down in Value Added Services, and someone forgot to report that in the WMS, sorry, the warehouse management system, so we didn't have the latest details. The haulier knew more than we did because they were there to pick up an early delivery and talked to the people at the warehouse who were fixing things. I should have double-checked with them.

Anyway, in the meantime the technical problem has been sorted out, so it shouldn't happen again. OK? Once again, please accept my apologies, and feel free to contact me. Bye for now.

🔊22 Call 5

Recording: Saved message, Wednesday, 9.34 am
Ian: Hi Val, Ian here. I was just calling to see whether you've received my email inviting you to the ten o'clock telecon, well eleven o'clock your time. Do you think you can manage to be there? I've asked Johanna and Jan in Central Logistics in Vienna to join us for a short call to discuss what steps to take about Loglab. It shouldn't take more than 15 minutes. Everyone will be dialling in from their own offices, and Jan will be leading the conference. If you can't attend for any reason, just let me know and maybe we can rearrange things. So, you'll find the dial-in number and the agenda in the email. OK, speak to you in a few minutes.

Unit 5

🔊23 Part A, exercise 3

The company reported an increase in electricity production of 10.4 % in 2012. Its operating result came to roughly € 6.4 billion, up 10 % over the previous year. This increase was mainly due to the absence of the exceptional burdens that had marked the year before, namely Fukushima and the subsequent nationwide 'energy transition' from nuclear and fossil fuels to renewable sources of energy.

In 2012, the company reported a decrease of 27.7 % in net income, with earnings dropping to roughly € 1.3 billion. Earnings per share were down by over 36 % to 23 euros. The low share price reflects the pessimistic outlook caused by the unresolved infrastructure issues that continued to plague the industry.

🔊24 Part A, Exercise 5

When I took over my father's metal works in the 1980s, we had a staff of eight. 20 years later, we had a staff of nearly 800 and I had turned the company into a trailblazer for wind power. The introduction of grid feed-in tariffs introduced in 1991 helped us build the business. We developed and sold our first wind turbine in 1991, just as people were beginning to produce their own electricity from renewables and to charge the utilities for it. We were there to supply the equipment.

It was my aim to run a business that was environmentally and socially sustainable, so I didn't just want to promote green energy; I also wanted to promote equal access to jobs, training, good health – in a word, social equity – for the socially disadvantaged. Our growth enabled us to pioneer social responsibility at home and permitted us to focus on training young people, including those who had not completed secondary school. Public policies enabled us to realize our own agenda and helped us make friends in high places. That meant that when we went public in 2001, we had some support raising equity capital.

For years the company had growth rates in the double digits. We set up branch offices and joint ventures, and licensed out production from Brazil to Vietnam. In 2007, high demand and favourable conditions encouraged us to venture a major investment. We were able to take advantage of generous government subsidies, which allowed us to build a new plant, where we could produce 200 turbines a year. By 2009 we had over 240 million euros in revenue. Other companies were suffering as a result of the financial crisis. This motivated us to invest in our trainee programme, taking on well over 400 young people, up from just over 100 the year before, giving at-risk teenagers access to vocational training.

I see now that these changes made me overlook certain trends that were beginning to undermine our growth as our competitors became stronger. Then, in 2010, disaster struck. A series of turbines demonstrated technical defects under strong winds. This damaged our reputation and caused us to lose most of our German business. In 2010 the bottom fell out on domestic sales, which dropped from 40 % to 7 %. Meanwhile, our international customers were still failing to get credit for energy projects. By 2011, sales had fallen by roughly 50 % to 150 million euros and we were forced to downsize. So, essentially, we had to cut our payroll in half. So there we were, deeply in debt, with a poor credit rating and no chance to get further loans. The bank had consultants come and advise the company. They considered me a liability to the company, and in the end, to cut a long story short, they convinced me to sell my 64 % stake in the company to a consortium of strategic investors from the Ukraine. In other words, I was out of the picture.

Sadly, and a bit ironically, I suppose, what caused the company to fail in the end were technical issues in our Ukrainian projects. Severe cash-flow problems resulted when our partners defaulted on payments. The shareholders decided not to raise further capital to bail the company out. Our CEO filed for insolvency immediately, but not even the drastic reorganization measures that followed saved the company. Windcraft was liquidated and later relaunched as a much smaller service unit.

Looking back, I now know that I made a number of mistakes. I think that if we hadn't opted for aggressive growth … if we hadn't developed risky long-term liabilities by expanding our operations … if we had kept our focus on keeping our business competitive, our balance sheet would have looked a lot better and we might have survived … we might still be in business today. With hindsight I know now that we really should have focused on the technical problems. On the other hand, I believe in social responsibility, and if I hadn't focused on our most important asset, our young talent, a lot of young people would not have had the opportunity we were able offer them … at least for a few years.

🔊25 **Part B, Exercise 2**

Daniel: So, thank you for giving me the opportunity to present our services to you. Before we go into what we could do for you, I'd just like to hear again from you what you are looking for.

Rick: Well, as I was saying earlier, what we're looking for is a way to make our operations more energy efficient. We have to invest in this building we're in now, so we looked you up because we're intrigued by the idea that with this financial package we would pay off our debts with energy savings. We'd basically like to find a solution that doesn't cut too deeply into our budget, because we're not in a position to spend a great deal of cash very soon. So we're especially interested in looking into long-term financing. What we'd like is for you to lay things out very clearly. We really need to know what we'd be getting into. Kate?

Kate: Exactly. So, for us the important thing at this stage is to understand how you operate so we can decide whether we want to go ahead with this. From what we've read so far, it looks like an attractive package.

Daniel: OK, if I understand you correctly, you're looking for a clear outline showing what steps and costs will be involved. And what we should work on is providing you with a long-term contract that represents a low initial investment. So overall, what you'd like us to do is draw up a model investment plan for your operations in this building and work out the payment structure. Is that correct?

Rick: Yes, that sounds about right.

Kate: Uhm, sorry, perhaps I didn't make myself clear. When I said I wanted to know how you operate, what I meant was I'd like to see some actual examples that show how you work with your clients, and get some references. Model calculations without a context put me off because variables like energy prices change. Without references, even if you made us a good offer, I'm afraid we'd have to turn it down.

Rick: Good point.

Daniel: Right, and I'm glad you brought that up. I'll be very happy to show you examples from our portfolio, and to give you the names of our clients that you can get in touch with. We have quite a number of case studies that might be interesting for you to look at, and I certainly understand your concern. OK, so here's what I propose. Let me give you a preview of what we can put together for you based on what you've told me. I won't bore you with lengthy model calculations, but I'd like to give you a rough idea of where the main potentials lie. Now, in terms of energy savings in your building, ventilation and lighting are normally the biggest energy consumers. Adding modern engineering and replacing old neon lamps with energy-saving lamps can raise your efficiency by 30 %. Of course, anything you invest can be set off against revenue when calculating your taxable profit, so you'll also save taxes at the end of the year. We can provide you with some *case studies* from companies that have used our services and have reported their results. Here, have a look. Here you see … The advantage of this solution would be that you would recoup your investment more quickly. How does that sound?

Rick: Very interesting. Well, what do you think, Kate?

Kate: I'm frankly very surprised that the performance contract guarantees that we will get back more than we put in. It sounds like this would not only make us able to afford to 'go green', which would be great in itself, but it would actually pay off in the end and leave us better off financially. That's still really hard to believe, frankly, but it sounds great. So let's hear some more. How much would this set us back in the first year?

Daniel: Well, OK, so what I'd suggest is that we start by looking at some actual examples …

🔊26 Part C, Exercise 4

The year 2012 was certainly one of the most successful in our history. Major advances in the development of several programmes in our clinical pipeline were the decisive events of the year. The positive reaction of our share price illustrates the importance of these programmes for the company's value proposition. What we've seen is a fundamental re-rating of the company, as investors start to attribute real value to our pipeline. Underscoring this point is the fact that, financially, 2012 was not a particularly noteworthy year for MorphoSys. This illustrates the reality that for us, as for other biopharmaceutical companies at a similar stage, value is much more closely linked to pipeline progress than to financial results. Our long-term strategy of using innovative technology to engineer the medicines of tomorrow is paying off as momentum builds in the pipeline.

Unit 6

Part A, exercise 2
🔊27 1

Hi there. I'm Carla. There are a lot of positive things to say about my company. First of all, the pay is good. Every two weeks there is a general staff meeting, so we are up to speed on our business development. Then we have some nice perks, like, for example, a health club discount, meal vouchers, language classes, that sort of thing. The company also offers on-site day care for our children, which I really appreciate since I have a small child.

The downside is that day care closes at five pm. My workload can be quite heavy at times and many tasks are time-critical, so I occasionally have to stay in the office until nine or ten in the evening. Overall I have found that I need to manage my time, my team, and my work-life balance very carefully so I'm not overstretched. It helps to be able to go home and telework.

🔊28 2

Hi, my name is Doris. Work-life balance is not too big a problem where I work. Neither, on the whole, is job security. Many of our staff have been with the company their entire working life, using the many opportunities for advancement, training and mobility. On top of performance-based pay, we get fringe benefits, including long-service bonuses and building loan subsidies. During the recent economic crisis, everyone took pay cuts and gave up their bonuses, and many departments had to switch to short-time work. That was tough, but the company avoided having to downsize. So, on the one hand, working here has many benefits. But on the other, you need to be able to negotiate your way through a big hierarchical corporation with a rigid chain of command. People tend to be somewhat unresponsive, so trying to change anything can be a lengthy process. In the end, it makes a big difference who you know and how well you network.

🔊29 3

My name is Binh, and I work for a company that ranks among the top employers in the US. This place is full of extremely capable people, and compensation is excellent. People who make an impact are rewarded regardless of their job title or level of experience. Teams enjoy a lot of autonomy. Reporting lines are short, and there's no red tape, so it's easy to get hold of the right person when you need them.

To me, the biggest perk is being able to take time off to volunteer. You're encouraged to schedule leave time to help with community work, for example after a disaster.

But with so much going on, it takes a great deal of energy and discipline to stay focused on the things that matter most. Also, we don't have the kind of employment protection or as much paid leave as you have in Europe.

🎧 30 4

Hello, I'm Simon. I work part-time, just 30 hours a week, but enjoy full benefits, including a retirement and savings plan and accidental death and disability insurance. Not too many people my age have that kind of security.

What I like best about my job is that this is a safe environment for taking risks and being creative. We're allowed to take decisions on our own; there's no micromanagement to speak of. But success is what counts in the end, isn't it, so people tend to work hard and play hard. Little things count for a lot. There's no dress code, for example. The management is quite responsive and respects diversity, so for instance, a gay colleague of mine has adopted a child and is taking parental leave with the full support of the team. I don't think he would feel as comfortable doing that in a more traditional company.

So, OK, the basic salary is a bit low. Every year we have performance evaluations and you can petition for more pay, but overall, the benefits really make up for a lot.

🎧 31 Part A, exercise 4

I was lucky to find a job as a team leader, coming here to Germany from Spain. I wasn't planning on having a family, so when I found out that I was pregnant at 27, just after I got my permanent contract, it, how do you say, caught me on the wrong foot. I told my boss right away that I was determined to keep the position and would arrange childcare and that I would be coming back full time after my six months' parental leave. Everyone was supportive, and HR confirmed that I would have the right to return to the same job.

But when I came back, I found it difficult to reconnect with my team. I would work with great concentration from 9 to 5, pick up the baby from day care and then work at home for a few more hours in the evening. During the day I tried not to waste any time with unnecessary chit-chat, but soon I started feeling out of the loop. There was one person in particular who I knew was talking about me behind my back. But before I could do anything about it, my baby fell ill, and I had to

leave work early a few times, and then I stayed at home and teleworked for a week.

When I got back, the atmosphere was really bad. My boss called me into his office and asked me whether I had noticed that something had changed, and of course I said yes. So he told me that someone on my team had questioned whether I was the right person for the job. The person in question had supposedly said that I wasn't pulling my weight. My boss expressed his concern about my recent absence from the office and said they needed a more hands-on team leader. He gave me six weeks to prove that I could in fact lead the team. If that was not possible, he said, he would have me transferred to another department. The company would offer me a similar job consistent with my employment contract. He also warned me that if there was no position available that would suit my abilities, there was a slight possibility that my contract could be terminated the next time the company was downsized. He also explained that he was filing this as a formal reprimand, and asked me whether I would be able to take action in the coming weeks.

I was stunned. Suddenly I realized that my team had in fact chosen not to share information with me. So here I was, being bullied, and instead of supporting me, or even warning me informally, my boss was putting me on probation. I was the main breadwinner – my partner was working part-time, it was all a bit complicated – so I really couldn't afford to lose this job. I knew I had to sort this out informally and personally before even considering any formal action. I needed to get my team and my boss behind me again. So the first thing I did was to schedule a meeting with the team and my boss.

🎧 32 Part B, Exercise 3

Doris: So, Hugh, overall you've done a great job for your first year.

Hugh: Well, thank you. I've thoroughly enjoyed being part of the team, and I'm actually quite pleased with how things are going, especially the changes in induction procedure and our new counselling services; those have worked out quite well.

Doris: Right. There is one unresolved issue we need to discuss. When you started here, you had some really good ideas about introducing an anti-bullying policy.

Hugh: Oh, yeah, well that was rather disappointing. I didn't get too far with that.

Doris: Well, you wanted to explore the situation in the company first. I'm particularly impressed by the way you knew there was an issue. And the bullying case we had last month has clearly proved you right.

Hugh: Yeah, but the survey I conducted didn't go as well as I hoped it would. We hardly got any responses.

Doris: OK, when you say 'hardly any', how many are we talking about, roughly?

Hugh: It wasn't more than about 20 or so. I sent the questionnaire to all of the staff, but I frankly don't think they really knew what to do with it.

Doris: So what you're saying is that they weren't ready to deal with the topic in that form? Do you know why?

Hugh: Well, yes. I don't think they were very familiar with the concept of bullying, and they didn't understand why they were getting a questionnaire in English all of a sudden. I think I should have provided the survey in German as well. That was an error of judgement.

Doris: OK … uhm … how do you see the overall situation? Do you want to pursue this topic?

Hugh: Oh definitely. I mean, as you say, the case last month clearly shows that the company would benefit from an anti-bullying policy, especially with social media becoming such a key element of working life. I think we'll be seeing more online bullying, so we should aim for a 'smart use policy' for social networks to help staff protect themselves. You know, at this point I'd like to rethink the issue and redesign the questionnaire completely, and then actually use our social media sites to get more staff response.

Doris: OK, so slow down for a moment. From what I'm hearing, there seem to be two main problems. One is the content side, so the focus of the study and the design of the questionnaire and the larger process you were talking about. And the other is the channel side, so how to handle communications to get the best staff response. Is that correct?

Hugh: Yes, exactly.

Doris: Well, on the content side, can the rest of the department help you?

Hugh: Absolutely. It would be great to have a sparring partner or two here in HR to test the questionnaire.

Doris: OK. But we don't have experience in the channels you're thinking of, do we?

Hugh: Not really. That's why I was thinking that I need to collaborate with other departments. I should probably approach Corporate Communications. They're the channel specialists.

Doris: Very good! Well then, so coming back to your assessment, you might want to think through how you work with others in the organization. For example, when you started this project, you developed it alone, didn't you?

Hugh. Yes. I didn't want to take up anyone's time.

Doris: But now you see you could have approached other people and departments instead, right?

Hugh: Yes, definitely. I should have asked for some initial feedback.

Doris: Right.

Hugh: Well, I can be a bit of a lone wolf sometimes …

Doris: Oh, I don't really see you as a lone wolf. You're very approachable, and your people skills are absolutely first-rate. And working across departments in a large organization such as ours is a challenge even for people who have been here for much longer. So it seems to me that you have plenty of potential for development here, and I would say you will definitely do well to develop your team-building skills.

Hugh: I hadn't really thought about it like that. Interesting.

Doris: Well, good. So this is something to bear in mind for your development plan. OK, so why don't we take a look at the next point. Let's see …

Business file 3

🔊 33 Exercise 2

Thank you for sending me your suggestions to incentivize our employees in view of the bonus cuts. Let me give you a brief summary and you can follow what I say on your handout.

First of all, to replace the bonus payments *this* year, it has been suggested that we should include non-cash rewards like special vouchers and awards. A second suggestion was to offer things like training as a reward for jobs well done. Finally, it has been proposed that we should reintroduce stock options. Let me just briefly clarify how those work, and forgive me if I'm repeating what you already know. So, with stock options, the employee is given the opportunity to buy a limited amount of stock at a fixed low price, which translates to a discount later when the price has risen. Selling the stock then provides the employee with capital gains. A stock option is not a payment; it's simply an opportunity to invest at better conditions and to earn capital gains. Since our share price is expected to increase again after this crisis, stock options might be an attractive offer.

Moving on to next year, management has promised to return to paying an annual bonus. As we will probably have lower earnings than before the crisis though, there will be a smaller bonus pool to distribute. We'll therefore need to make very sure we distribute the money fairly.

So, the suggestions. Some of you have suggested redefining the pool of those eligible for the bonus plan. I've done some research, and have found that 39 per cent of the companies in our benchmark class pay an annual bonus only to those employees above a certain baseline. The groups commonly excluded are sales and temporary employees, trainees as well as senior management. A second suggestion was to increase oversight of payout guidelines and limit the size of the bonus. Currently, our only guideline is to have bonuses follow the performance assessment and to range from 80 to 120 per cent, but we do know the average bonus payment is about 112 per cent. This does seem to call for better oversight. On the other hand, others have suggested that we should really leave bonus-setting decisions entirely to the managers, to protect their ability to rate individual performance. Note that giving managers this 'freedom' to decide is being done in only 5 per cent of all companies that pay bonuses. A fourth suggestion was to eliminate non-performance related bonuses, for example those related to the length of service, and to replace them with long-term incentives that pay out after two to three years. Finally, several people have suggested that we should try to downsize by outsourcing non-essential positions.

So, I think that's it. Thank you for your attention. As soon as you are ready, I would like to open the discussion!

Unit 7

🔊 34 Part A, Exercise 1

Pat: It's interesting that you said you and your father have both been responsible for buying power tools but in such different contexts. So let me ask you, do you work for an SME?

Udo: An SME?

Pat: A small or medium enterprise.

Udo: Aha. Yes, that's right and it's family owned, which is quite typical for the German *Mittelstand*. We provide environmental testing services, so we require all kinds of tools, mostly for sampling. My father is retired now, but he used to work for Weglein, a company that manufactures parts used in industrial drills. And after work, for extra income, he would go home and machine-tool parts for other companies, as the owner of a one-man workshop. At Weglein, he was the person responsible for purchasing in his area of work, so he could actually outsource work to himself.

🔊 35 Part A, Exercise 2

Udo: At Weglein, he was the person responsible for purchasing in his area of work, so he could actually outsource work to himself.

Pat: That probably wouldn't make it through compliance these days, would it?

Udo: I know it sounds terrible, but he was a responsible buyer, highly conscientious and entirely trustworthy. That meant that for his workshop he would only purchase the tools he trusted most. If he wanted an absolutely reliable, perfectly calibrated pneumatic drill, it had to be a Hilti, not the Makita selling for hundreds of euros less … or I guess it was deutschmarks in those days. He would always buy the brand known for the patent.

Pat: But purchasing has evolved quite a bit since ISO standards were introduced, hasn't it? Buying and selling individual products and services like that would be absolutely impossible these days.

Udo: Definitely. I can only buy from the suppliers officially listed by my company.

Pat: And just to give you my perspective, becoming a listed supplier is quite a process. We had to go through compliance certification before we could even begin to market our B2B line. And our sales reps sometimes complain how they have to convince corporate decision-makers who don't understand the technology. It can be extremely frustrating. We might have a recently developed tool perfect for a specific job, but if we can't sell the whole series, it's just not worth the time and effort.

Udo: I can imagine. In some ways compliance is actually detrimental, isn't it? I mean, you might have to settle for a solution that is not entirely satisfactory.

Pat: Well, every system has its deficiencies, I guess. So how did your father source the tools he needed for his workshop?

Udo: He had good contacts to an authorized Hilti dealer from work, so he would get sizeable discounts.

Pat: OK. Well, we're thinking of taking much of our marketing online now to reach SMEs. Do you buy supplies online these days?

Udo: I do tons of research online, but buying? Not really, to be honest. There are the online catalogues you can go through, and additional channels that didn't use to exist, like discounters and resellers. But I prefer to work with a dealer. We have to plan our overall budget anyway, you know, so it makes more sense to meet up and get the big picture of what we need.

Pat: To negotiate better deals?

Udo: And also to have someone you can approach for after-sales service under warranty if anything should go wrong. The service you get from a trusted dealer is simply unbeatable. I remember one time years ago when we were testing a building site for contamination, we needed machine-drilled concrete core samples. So our supplier came round and brought us a brand new model to help us out. He let us test it on site. It was an excellent pitch; we bought it on the spot. He did good business with us. And you won't get that kind of great service tailored to your needs from an online discounter just interested in making one sale! Personal marketing from someone who really understands your business needs is priceless!

Pat: But you pay more, don't you?

Udo: Sure, but B2B is very different from B2C. At home my family and I shop online all the time to save money.

Pat: OK. But wouldn't you say there are more options now to save money in B2B, too?

Udo: The market is more diversified. But we have to meet more and more exacting industrial standards. There is more risk involved if we cut corners. I'd say that quality is more important than price, at least for us.

Pat: Do you notice differences in the quality of the actual products you buy?

Udo: Well, some brands seem to be moving down-market. You sometimes notice that handles and switches are flimsier than they used to be. But in tools I think brand loyalty is huge. You can show people test results, but no matter what, people will still buy their favourite brand. Challengers entering this market have their work cut out for them.

Pat: Hmm. How important are PR and advertising to you?

Udo: Not very. I'd say user stories relating to my area and reviews shared in online forums are my key sources. Professional networks are extremely useful. And I do like going to trade fairs like this to keep up with the latest developments.

🔊 36 Part B, Exercise 5

Vera: So, Father, we have a problem on our hands. Not only does it say here that we have to respond within 10 days, which now only leaves us three, but Robert is out of town, in Ghana, until next week.

Father Steven: Well, Vera, we're on exceedingly dodgy ground if 'Advent purple' now really belongs to a chocolate company. How utterly ridiculous!

Vera: This could just be a scare tactic, you know. How can they claim infringement? Our chocolates don't look anything like theirs. And I don't quite know what's at stake here. What are 'equitable remedies'?

Father Steven: I haven't the foggiest idea. Whatever they are, they'll probably make us absolutely miserable! Well, Vera, if this purple is their trademark, they're in the right and there's not much we can do about it. We could try and contest it and take them to court, but who is

going to pay for that? I really think our hands are tied. I frankly wouldn't have a big problem with, say, changing the colour to red. So, could we change the colour on these advent calendars?

Vera: Well, the calendar itself is paper and is printed in purple, so we'd have to design and produce new ones. We can't reuse anything. Oh, couldn't we just stand our ground and ignore this cease-and-desist order completely and sell off as many calendars as we can? It would be a shame to lose the income from the calendars. We need to pay the cocoa farmers after all.

Father Steven: Just ignore it? Mmm … I'm afraid Catchoo would see right through that. No, I think we need to go at this whole thing from a different angle.

Vera: Oh?

Father Steven: Why don't we demonstrate our general willingness to change the design? Maybe then we could get away with asking them to let us sell off our purple stock. We could say that we were acting in good faith.

Vera: I'd feel a lot better if Robert were handling this.

Father Steven: So would I. When will he be back?

Vera: In a week. Should we just play for time and acknowledge receiving this letter?

Father Steven: Maybe that would be best.

Vera: Well, let me try again to get hold of Robert. He wasn't answering his phone – probably in back-to-back meetings – but perhaps I'll try texting him instead.

Unit 8

🔊 37 Part A, Exercise 2

Bernd: Let me say that we are shocked and deeply saddened by the appalling news that factories supplying us have been found to use child labour. Compliance with international labour laws and standards is a critical element of our factory audit programme. The findings of the latest report have brought to our attention that, without our knowledge, one of our suppliers has been subcontracting to sweatshops that not only fall short on 'social compliance' but also fail to meet our well-known safety standards, which surpass those of the industry. I'd like to make perfectly clear that we do not condone subjecting any garment worker, let alone children, to the dangerous and illegal conditions that the report has brought to light. We pledge to get to the bottom of this. In the next few days I'll be meeting with national and international stakeholders to work towards a legally-binding accord on continuous workplace monitoring and human resources management. I'll be happy to take your questions now. Yes?

Reporter 1: How do you explain the notice on the wall saying that the factories were high risk? If A&G knew about it, why didn't anybody follow up?

Berndt: OK, so you're implying that we were monitoring the factory, but as I said earlier, we were not even aware of its existence until today.

Reporter 1: But wasn't there an A&G official who posted the notice on the factory wall? There have been allegations on Facebook and Twitter.

Berndt: I'm afraid I can't discuss that until we know more. What we know for sure is there was no official report filed at Headquarters. We'll provide the details as soon as we get the full story.

Reporter 1: So you admit not knowing about this factory. Do you expect your customers to buy products that may have been produced in a dangerous sweatshop?

Berndt: If you're asking whether we expect our customers to accept practices that we condemn, then the answer is clearly 'no'. We most definitely do not endorse employing children. We don't deny losing oversight of this vendor, nor do we want to justify doing so. That's why we need industry-wide agreement on this to uncover abuse and ensure transparency at all levels of the production process. Yes, the gentleman over there.

Reporter 2: You say that you are seeking an industry-wide agreement on transparency. Which high street apparel brands are currently making their compliance statistics available to the public?

Berndt: I'm afraid I don't know off the top of my head, but let me get back to you on that. I'll know more next week.

Reporter 2: So, I'm inferring from your statement that, on the one hand, you plan to continue working with this unethical vendor while, on the other hand, you say that you uphold ethical standards. How do you reconcile working at both ends of the ethical spectrum?

Berndt: OK, I think there are several questions there. Let's take them one at a time. First of all, it would be too early to label our vendor 'particularly unethical' for using this subcontractor. That would be jumping to conclusions. We are in the middle of our investigations, and I'll have a much better overall picture after we meet. Secondly …

🔊 38 Part B, Exercise 1

Classical compliance, and by this I mean adhering to standards, regulations, and other requirements, is an approach that provides a solution of sorts. It can provide certain assurances, but the overall effort does not seem to be aligned with the industry. The whole approach would appear to be a bit short-sighted. I would say, for all practical purposes, the only real outcome is illegal subcontracting, with all its adverse social and environmental impacts.

🔊 39 Part B, Exercise 3

In the garment industry, a surprising number of companies simply do not know who is manufacturing their product. I'd say that this is what makes supply chain visibility by and large the most important KPI for a company in this industry. On the whole, increasing supply chain visibility promises to add substantial value to a company.

What my company does is to develop metrics for KPI reporting, to enable our clients to document and demonstrate their continuous improvement.

For example, we recently provided Alpia, the outdoor clothing and equipment company, with a reporting system that feeds into their website and presents their current supply chain information in an interactive map. It shows the factory locations and links them to the demographics of the people working there. Users can trace their purchase back through the supply chain to its origin, see where it was produced and who produced it. What Alpia is doing here is showing the places of production with a sense of pride, not treating them as something that should be hidden away. If you think back to all the many scandals in the garment industry, all the lies and cover-ups, it really seems to me that on the whole showing pride rather than fear would be a much better incentive to suppliers to engage in good reporting. Overall, I think that old-style compliance tends to fail since it often appears to force vendors to sweep things under the carpet and to lie to get an order. By and large, it just breeds contempt and prejudice. So, for all practical purposes, that system would seem to be broken.

But social corporate responsibility is about value creation. Supply chain transparency means a company has to make its business model work long-term, or it will fail very publically. So a market leader who embraces a transparent and sustainable business model will have positive knock-on effects for the entire industry. By and large, I think we should be seeing many more such efforts. In the end, it will be up to the consumer – and perhaps to the fashion victim – to hold companies accountable for the way they do business.

Business file 4

🔊 40 **Exercise 2**

Reporter: It is certainly ironic that undeclared horsemeat has been discovered in the organic paella that your seafood has helped to make so popular.

Monica: It's terrible. We are dedicated to producing top quality organic seafood at a reasonable price. Over the past five years we've worked very hard with Sonnenschein to make sure all of our processes comply with the very strict regulations. We are proud of how far we have come, and very happy with how well we have worked together, so this comes as a great shock. We're also frankly extremely disappointed. It almost looks as if Sonnenschein are cutting corners with other suppliers. I mean, I certainly hope that is not true.

Reporter: How do you feel about the horsemeat issue?

Monica: Well, the whole thing is absurd. Traditional paella from Valencia doesn't contain beef, or even beef stock, so how did horsemeat sold as beef get into the product?

Reporter: So what are you going to do next?

Monica: I am sorry, but I really can't comment on that right now.

Reporter: Are you angry?

Monica: Uhm … I can say this much. We feel that compliance is a two-way street. We are committed to holding up our end of the deal, and expect our customer to do the same.

Notes

Bildquellenverzeichnis

Cover/oben: shutterstock/Pressmaster; **S. 6/links:** shutterstock/Belinka; **S. 6/Mitte:** shutterstock/Nadir Keklik; **S. 6/rechts:** shutterstock/stockyimages; **S. 8/9/Hintergrund:** Shutterstock / Mario Tarello; **S. 8/Unit 2:** shutterstock/Kinga; **S. 8/Unit 4:** shutterstock/g-stockstudio; **S. 8/Unit 5:** shutterstock/ESB Professional; **S. 8/Unit 8:** shutterstock/Rajesh Narayanan; **S. 9/Unit 1:** shutterstock/Potstock; **S. 9/Unit 3:** shutterstock/wavebreakmedia; **S. 9/Unit 6:** shutterstock/Jeanette Dietl; **S. 9/Unit 7:** shutterstock/ita_esper; **S. 10:** shutterstock/wavebreakmedia; **S. 11:** shutterstock/wavebreakmedia; **S. 12/1. von links:** shutterstock/stockyimages; **S. 12/1. von rechts:** shutterstock/Belinka; **S. 12/2. von links:** shutterstock/Potstock; **S. 12/2. von rechts:** shutterstock/wavebreakmedia; **S. 12/Mitte:** shutterstock/ESB Professional; **S. 14:** Endress+Hauser AG; **S. 15:** Endress + Hauser GmbH + Co. KG; **S. 21:** shutterstock/Monkey Business Images; **S. 22/links oben:** shutterstock/My Good Images; **S. 22/rechts oben:** shutterstock/muratart; **S. 22/unten:** shutterstock/Kinga; **S. 24/Foto/Grafik:** SBB Cargo AG; **S. 30/A:** shutterstock/goodluz; **S. 30/B:** shutterstock/Boguslaw Mazur; **S. 30/C:** shutterstock/Scanrail1; **S. 30/D:** shutterstock/Konstantin Chagin; **S. 33:** shutterstock/wavebreakmedia; **S. 34/oben:** shutterstock/kurhan; **S. 34/unten:** shutterstock/wavebreakmedia; **S. 36/links:** shutterstock/sirtravelalot; **S. 36/rechts:** shutterstock/risteski goce; **S. 37/oben:** Vollmar Wissen + Kommunikation/beo GmbH, Stutthart; **S. 42:** shutterstock/AlexLMX; **S. 43/1. von links:** shutterstock/sirtravelalot; **S. 43/1. von rechts:** shutterstock/wavebreakmedia; **S. 43/2. von links:** shutterstock/Rajesh Narayanan; **S. 43/2. von rechts:** shutterstock/kurhan; **S. 44:** shutterstock/g-stockstudio; **S. 45:** shutterstock/ESB Professional; **S. 47:** Fotostudio Lichtmalerei, Christian Moser; **S. 52:** shutterstock/Mario Tarello; **S. 55:** shutterstock/Nadir Keklik; **S. 57:** shutterstock/ESB Professional; **S. 58/Grafik:** MorphoSys AG, Dr. Simon Moroney; **S. 59:** MorphoSys AG, Dr. Simon Moroney | Andreas Pohlmann; **S. 64/1:** shutterstock/stockyimages; **S. 64/2:** shutterstock/Jeanette Dietl; **S. 64/3:** shutterstock/RobinE; **S. 64/4:** shutterstock/mimagephotography; **S. 66:** shutterstock/ruigsantos; **S. 67:** shutterstock/Jeanette Dietl; **S. 68/Foto:** STEIN12 MANAGER SICHTEN/Michael Reusse; **S. 69/Grafiken oben:** STEIN12 MANAGER SICHTEN; **S. 74:** shutterstock/espies; **S. 76:** shutterstock/ita_esper; **S. 77:** shutterstock/Rawpixel.com; **S. 81:** shutterstock/Alexander Prokopenko; **S. 86/Logo in 1.:** shutterstock/nuvrenia; **S. 86/unten:** shutterstock/bleakstar; **S. 89/oben:** shutterstock/Rajesh Narayanan; **S. 90/Hintergrund oben:** shutterstock/Hintau Aliaksei; **S. 96/Verkehrszeichen:** shutterstock/foxy cat; **S. 97/oben:** shutterstock/wavebreakmedia

Textquellenverzeichnis

S. 15: Jens Kröger, Endress + Hauser GmbH + Co. KG; **S. 22** oben: Hau L. Lee, Stanford University; **S. 24/25:** "Jan-Erik Galdiks, SBB Cargo AG"; **S. 36** oben: Zitat von Andrew Carnegie; US-amerikanischer Industrieller und Philanthrop; (1835-1919; **S. 47** oben: Dr. Gill Woodman, Ludwig-Maximilians-Universität München; **S. 59/59:** MorphoSys AG, Dr. Simon Moroney; **S. 81:** "Scott, Cameron. "Nutella exemplifies how not to use social media"". https //www.adweek.com/digital/nutella-exemplifies-how-not-to-use-social-media/ [21.05.2013] Copyrighted 2013. Beringer Capital. 269693:0618DD"; **S. 37:** Gabriele Vollmar, Vollmar Wissen + Kommunikation; **S. 68:** Franz-Josef Nuß, STEIN12 MANAGER SICHTEN; **S. 90/91:** Reprinted by permission of Harvard Business Review. "How the Voice of the People Is Driving Corporate Social Responsibility", Jen Boynton, https://hbr.org/2013/07/how-the-voice-of-the-people-is, July 17 2013 © 2013 by the Harvard Business School Publishing Corporation;all rights reserved

Coursebook

Track				Time
1		Copyright		00:51
Welcome!				
2		ex. 1	1	01:02
3			2	00:52
4			3	00:52
Unit 1				
5	A	ex. 2		02:18
6		ex. 4		02:39
7	B	ex. 1		04:05
Unit 2				
8	A	ex. 4		02:55
9	B	ex. 2		02:35
10		ex. 5		01:53
Business file 1				
11		ex. 2		01:35
Unit 3				
12	A	ex. 2		04:13
13	B	ex. 2		06:20
Unit 4				
14	A	ex. 3		02:22
15		ex. 4		06:47
16	B	ex. 2		03:56
17		ex. 5		00:33
Business file 2				
18		ex. 2	1	01:21
19			2	00:59
20			3	01:00
21			4	01:03
22			5	01:00
Unit 5				
23	A	ex. 3		01:03
24		ex. 5		04:40
25	B	ex. 2		04:09
26	C	ex. 4		01:04
Unit 6				
27	A	ex. 2	1	01:03
28			2	01:15
29			3	01:00
30			4	01:14
31	A	ex. 4		02:55
32	B	ex. 3		04:20
Business file 3				
33		ex. 2		03:27
Unit 7				
34	A	ex. 1		01:09
35		ex. 2		04:37
36	B	ex. 5		02:25
Unit 8				
37	A	ex. 2		03:18
38	B	ex. 1		00:40
39		ex. 3		02:38
Business file 4				
40		ex. 2		01:19
Total running time				**93:48**

Workbook

Track			Time
41	Copyright		00:51
Unit 1			
42	ex. 7		01:12
Unit 2			
43	ex. 10		02:16
Unit 3			
44	ex. 3		02:07
Unit 4			
45	ex. 4	1	00:48
46		2	00:44
47		3	00:40
Unit 5			
48	ex. 7		02:34
Unit 6			
49	ex. 7	1	00:58
50		2	00:33
51		3	00:33
52		4	00:41
53		5	00:30
54		6	01:03
Unit 7			
55	ex. 4		02:31
Unit 8			
56	ex. 6		00:40
Total running time			**18:53**

Studio:
Clarity Studio Berlin

Aufnahmeleitung:
Christian Schmitz

Tontechnik:
Pascal Thinius

Regie:
Christian Schmitz
Janan Barksdale
Anna Batrla

Sprecher/innen:
Denis Abrahams
Tania Carlin
Yvette Coetzee
Mala Ghedia
Marianne Graffam
Martin Klemrath
Kevin McAleer
Jeffrey Mittleman
Oleksandra Odnorog
Lucía Palacios

Helena Prince
Christian Schmitz
Dharmander Singh
Nikolina Skenderija
Kenneth Spiteri
Andrzej Szpakowski